If You Must Stay

GARY MacPHEE

Copyright © 2023 by Gary MacPhee

All rights reserved, including the right of reproduction in whole or in part in any form without prior permission of the publisher, except as provided by USA copyright law.

All Scripture quotations, unless otherwise indicated, are taken from The Holy Bible, New International Version®, NIV®. Copyright © 1973, 1978, 1984, 2011 by Biblica, Inc.® Used by permission. All rights reserved worldwide.

Scripture quotations marked (NLT) are taken from the *Holy Bible*, New Living Translation, copyright ©1996, 2004, 2015 by Tyndale House Foundation. Used by permission of Tyndale House Publishers, Carol Stream, Illinois 60188. All rights reserved.

Gary MacPhee
7307 Quiet Pond Place
Colorado Springs, CO 80923
www.garymacphee.com
info@garymacphee.com

Publishing Services provided by BelieversBookServices.com
Editorial team: Marcus Costantino and Vickie Deppe
Cover image Credit: NicoElNino. iStockphoto ID:1286478172.

ISBN-13: 979-8-9886559-0-9

First Printing, 2023

Printed in The United States of America

DEDICATION

To Judylynn, the one who knows me and loves me like the very envoy of God and has been by my side since the beginning of our spiritual journeys. This book and the path to greater faith that it represents could never have happened without you taking every step with me. Early on in this journey that took us so far away from home and anything we ever knew, after I had preached in a church, the pastors and elders gathered around to pray for us. As they did, one of them—a stranger to us—spoke out, "For this is what the Lord says, 'They will say to you, man of God, bring the seer, because she will have the Word of the Lord in her mouth." I can testify today that you have never failed to speak the truth, the life, and the love of God to me and everyone in your life. I could not have known that the young teenager I fell in love with would be such a woman of wisdom, grace, beauty, and strength, that would be such a steadying and centering partner in life—truly the nucleus of our marriage and the atomic mass of our family as I've been a spinning electron—and the constant confirming witness of the work of God in our lives and in our mission.

> A wife of noble character who can find?
> She is worth far more than rubies.
> Her husband has full confidence in her
> and lacks nothing of value.
> She brings him good, not harm,
> all the days of her life... Many women do noble things,
> but you surpass them all.
> Charm is deceptive, and beauty is fleeting;
> but a woman who fears the Lord is to be praised.
>
> Prov 31:10-12, 29-30

TABLE OF CONTENTS

PART I - A NEW HEART vii

Foreword ix

Introduction xi

Prologue xix

Chapter 1 If You Must Stay 1

Chapter 2 The Principles of Positioning 19

Chapter 3 The Missionary Heart 43

PART II - GOD'S HEART FOR THE WORLD 59

Chapter 4 Initiation 61

Chapter 5 Relationship 77

Chapter 6 Identification 97

Chapter 7 Restoration 125

Chapter 8 Intercession 147

Chapter 9 Reconciliation 165

Chapter 10 Intermediation 189

Chapter 11 Redemption 209

PART III - YOUR HEART 231

Chapter 12 Inference 233

Chapter 13 Revelation 247

End Notes 261

PART I

A NEW HEART

FOREWORD

If You Must Stay inspires readers through moving stories and great insights resulting from the well-seasoned, God-authored life of Gary MacPhee. When meeting Gary more than 20 years ago, he'd launched into a dynamic journey of unique missionary service, and I resonated with his passion and urgent desire for every person to "discover where they fit in God's plan to reach the world." This book, marinated in experiential daily learning over 20 years, reveals a personal and comprehensive understanding of God's heart for every person.

God has uniquely designed each of us to experience full engagement—daily—in his plan to live as a heart on fire and a life on purpose! With a high view of scripture, Gary supports each chapter with biblical foundations that undergird his own life mission and explains how it can be the same for you.

Sharing personal and dynamic stories of God at work across the world, Gary's communication style is riveting and relatable. He conveys God's revelation that the practical application of his own gifts and talents from the Holy Spirit could become a way he could go to "the ends of the earth," supporting the ongoing proclamation of God's love. Seeing a world yearning for restoration, Gary affirms that to be a part of God's plan, we must maintain a fervent commitment to the local church as God's worldwide first line of action.

If You Must Stay is a bold challenge to every member of the Church to "find your unique fit in God's restorative plan for the world and every person in it – from the Eastern hemisphere to the east side of your town."

What a timely and fresh reminder of God's plan for every believer to discover and embrace God's heart and global restoration plan—to the ends of the earth!

Dwight Robertson
Founding President & CEO
Forge
Championing Jesus' Mission of More Kingdom Laborers

INTRODUCTION

"Perhaps all books must be lived before they are written. That is certainly true of books like this one. I make no claim to be living out the full implications of this book. But I have begun the pilgrimage."[1] Like Ron Sider, who penned that nearly 50 years ago, this is indeed a pilgrimage for me, and in this book, you will find along the way both a confession from me and a challenge to you. In my spiritual journey, I somehow missed it. How could I have missed it? What is *IT* exactly?

It is simply this. In choosing to follow Jesus, I never caught how I fit in God's plan to reach the world. In fact, I hardly knew He had such a plan. And I definitely did not share his heart that beats to reach every man and woman. So, the question this book will leave you asking is just that: "How do I fit in God's plan to reach the world?"

I never understood the implications that knowing the answer to that question might have on my life, my marriage, my family, my career, my ultimate future. I believe my first glimpse into the kingdom of God came through a not-so-uncommon, but narrowly focused lens of the Fall and redemption story, as Gabe Lyons masterfully sums it up in his book, *The Next Christians*. Nothing was wrong with this story, but it is woefully incomplete. It's not until that "half-story" is bookended by creation and restoration—which Gabe calls the "Full Story"[2] —that those implications for my life and yours all begin to make sense.

God indeed has a plan that He is orchestrating from the beginning to the end of the Scriptures (from creation to restoration), and though He is sovereign in all creation, He chooses to work through you and me to reach the world. This baffles me. Why would the God of the universe, who could speak the world and the heavens into being—who exists outside of space and time himself—*choose* to involve himself so intimately in the affairs of men that He would choose to work through such limited, finite, and often selfish beings as you and me?

In the following pages, we will find answers to those questions, and the bigger question I began with: where do you fit in all of it? I am certainly not the first person to ask such questions. Searching for the meaning of life is a continual quest in the human condition. But for the Christian, it must always bring us back to God's design, the intent of the Creator for his creation, and our willing participation in that design. The *Westminster Shorter Catechism* from 1674—along with its counterpart, the *Westminster Larger Catechism*—are arguably the most significant works to come out of the English Reformation. They answer the question, "What is the chief end of man?" with "To glorify God and to enjoy him forever." But how do we do that? What does that look like? And can it really be so simple?

As much as this is an historical question down through the ages, many contemporary authors are refreshing the dialogue in our generation, bringing similar ideas and questions to this conversation too.

Rich Stearns, in *The Hole in Our Gospel* asks, "What does God expect of us?" and, "How are we to live?"[3]

Rick Warren, in *The Purpose Driven Life,* asks, "What on earth am I here for?"[4]

Dwight Robertson, in *You Are God's PLAN A* (and there is no Plan B), asks, "Where was it along the way that we lost track of Jesus' plan?"[5]

David Platte in *Radical,* asks "[Am] I going to embrace Jesus even though He said radical things that drove the crowds away?"[6] and "Where have we gone wrong?"[7] and "Is He [Jesus] worth it? Do I really believe He is worth abandoning everything for?"[8]

Gabe Lyons, in *The Next Christians,* asks, "What does mission look like in America in the 21st century? What does it mean to be a Christian in a world that is disenchanted with our movement?"[9]

Ron Sider, in *Rich Christians in an Age of Hunger,* asks, "Can overfed, comfortably clothed, and luxuriously housed persons [truly] understand poverty?"[10] and reminds us, "Am I my brother's keeper?"[11]

Eugene Cho, in *Overrated*, asks, "Is it possible that we all love compassion and justice... *until there's a personal cost* to living compassionately, loving mercy, and seeking justice?"[12]

Charlie Marquis, in *Mudrunner*, asks, "Is God's kingdom cause truly worth any cost to my life?"[13]

Glenn Packiam, in *Lucky*, asks, "So what, then, is the kingdom of God?" and "How do we live in the tension of the "now, but not yet"? What should we do? What can we do?"[14]

All these authors have journeyed on something of a pilgrimage, and their lives and writing have influenced my life in profound ways as God called me into my own pilgrimage. You will find me quoting them—and many others—throughout the book. These questions have often challenged the very core of my world view; but I come back time and time again to the simple question posed over 100 years ago by Charles Sheldon, in his classic Christian novel, *In His Steps*: "What would Jesus do?"[15]

Once we have grappled with the arguments for and against the existence of God, as well as the proofs that Jesus uniquely came into the world as the full representation of God to live, die, and be raised to life again, we must then answer this question before we continue on our personal journey. *In his Steps* is a wonderful story of a humble pastor who is challenged by an unemployed, recently widowed, homeless man who is looking for compassion and understanding. The pastor struggles with his initial response, finally admitting his own selfishness, and then gains this conviction that he passes along to his congregation—to not do anything without first asking, "What would Jesus do?" The characters that embrace this challenge then find their lives—and the lives of those they touch—profoundly impacted.

I have grown convinced over the years, as I have grown in this journey from an architect to a missionary evangelist, that no one really needs to know much about me or what I do. What you need, dear friend, is to know Jesus, and what He does. And what He's done.

When preachers say, "I think…" I almost immediately tune out. You don't need to know what I think—we all need to know what God thinks! Now I do believe that it helps to speak from something within my own experience (again, all books must be lived before they are written), but that experience only serves as a testimony to who God is and how He works in us. The fruit of my life as I journey along with God becomes the only thing I have worth offering to you.

Journeying through my story—and the biblical foundations that have underpinned the pilgrimage—will lead to this powerful understanding: In his call to you to live and work as his partner to reach the world, God will not ask you to do anything that He has not already done himself, demonstrating and showing the way for us to follow in his steps. This is not my proposition. It is the truth of the Scriptural record! His nature, his character, his spirit is unchanging. From the beginning to the end of the biblical story, God is doing something extraordinary. And through the millennia, He deposits all of himself into his people who have heard his invitation and choose again to follow in his steps and do the same.

Jesus left the throne room of Heaven and clothed himself in the limitations of humanity—the God-man as it were—to reach humankind and fulfill the plan set in motion at creation. He did not stay in Heaven and simply send a book to Earth. He became the "Living Word!" And after his earthly work was accomplished—the redemption of humanity—He commissioned us with, "Therefore go and make disciples of all nations…" (Mt 28:19) to effectively do the same as we bring a message of forgiveness, reconciliation, restoration, and redemption.

If You Must Stay is a call to the Church—every believer—recognizing that Jesus said, "Go…" At the same time, we have a scriptural model in the local church that shows how many are indeed called to *stay*. But in the staying, do we know that God has a purpose for those in that place that still fits uniquely into his plan to reach the world? We must. That's as missional as the one who is called to go. But when was the last time you felt like you were living your mission when you walked into church? This is the promise you get

Introduction

as part of the Body of Christ—his Church. The early Church must've been missional by its very nature. It was never there, and suddenly it was! Crossing barriers of culture, religion, race, ethnicity, gender, economics, and language, it was—and still is—the culmination of the story of God's work in the world, and you get to be a part of it!

You will hear a lot of talk of mission, missions, service, and "reaching the world" from me as we go forward. I wholeheartedly affirm David Platte's thoughts, because they have been exactly mine too: "In all this missions talk, you may begin to think, *well, surely you're not suggesting that we're all supposed to move overseas.* That is certainly not what I'm suggesting (though I'm not completely ruling it out!). But this is precisely the problem. We have created the idea that if you have a heart for the world and you are passionate about global mission, then you move overseas. But if you have a heart for the United States and you are not passionate about global mission, then you stay here and support those who go. Meanwhile, flying right in the face of this idea is Scripture's claim that regardless of where we live—here or overseas—our hearts should be consumed with making the glory of God known in all nations. From cover to cover the Bible teaches that all the Church—not just select individuals, but all the Church—is created to reflect the glory of God to all the world. Because every single man, woman, and child in the Church is intended to impact nations for the glory of Christ, and there is a God-designed way for us to live our lives here, and do church here, for the sake of people around the world who don't know Christ."[16]

In the first half of my spiritual journey, most of my decision-making was based first in responsible, calculated, strategic planning, and only afterward would I give a nod to God by implicitly asking, "What do you think about that, Lord?" At that time, I would not have thought that's what I was doing, but hindsight gives great perspective, doesn't it? I was actively pursuing a plan for my life that was a combination of working hard to use the gifts and talents God had given me, serving in and through my local church, and seeking the Lord's blessing in it all for me and my family. But all the blessing we were living in was a consumption model of bourgeois materialistic gain and ever-expanding capacity. It seemed like it was working too—for me, my family, and my church. But this ever-increasing capacity became an ever-increasing burden, until the American dream version of my Christianity became a nightmare. Amid success on almost every front of life, I became more aware than ever —like David Platte's subtitle for his book *Radical*, "Taking back your faith from the American Dream"—that something had to change. But how?

The first step was learning just how entangled my faith and the American Dream had become. I was unaware that I had very little real-life experience that caused faith—an ultimate dependence and hope in God—to grow. The Bible reminds us that "faith is confidence in what we hope for and assurance about what we do not see" (Heb 11:1), but I had been achieving most of what I hoped for and making "seen things" into a testimony of God's faithfulness to me. I was an architect, both fully employed at a major public research university and nearly full-time employed in my own private consulting business.

At some point, a dozen years or so into my career, I began to experience the futility—or perhaps the vanity—of it all. My faith-based worldview did not match up well with the institution I was publicly serving every day, and in my private consulting work, I was serving many private clients who spent whatever they could on themselves and their personal dreams—and I was making it happen! I began to wistfully define architecture as the chief of godless professions filled with self-absorbed egomaniacs making monuments to their own creativity, and I was one of them! But what was I to do? This was my career. I had dedicated myself to the grueling education in it, the equally daunting licensing process, and now the practice of it. The rest of my life was laid out before me, and I saw no way out. Here I stood, trapped, "amid an American Dream dominated by self-achievement, self-esteem, and self-sufficiency, by individualism, materialism, and universalism."[17]

The undoing of all of that is the beginning of the story. I heard it said once that Moses spent 40 years in Pharaoh's house, then 40 years in the wilderness to unlearn everything from Pharaoh's house (the ways of the world), and *then* he was ready for 40 years of ministry. I certainly am thankful that it didn't take *that* long for the lessons to begin in my life! Once the process began of discovering how I was to fit in God's plan to reach the world, things moved along; but the speed at which God moved to get me to a place of faith not just tied to external proofs but that could move mountains was alarming and totally unexpected.

PROLOGUE

Thanksgiving Day

The pain is nothing short of blinding. My leg is propped up in a freshly made, Emergency Room plaster cast. I can barely cope with the increased pain when I lower it for even a moment. I cry to the Lord, like a persecuted psalmist envious of those around him seemingly prospering. Torturing myself, I ask, "Why did it happen? How could this have happened? How and why could *YOU* let this happen, Lord?!" The series of questions that tortured me most went something like this: Is this God? Is this the Devil? Is this an attack? Is this a test? Do I submit? Do I resist? And in the end, I got no answer. Well, no clear answer anyway, but I thought of Jesus referring to sparrows being sold for a penny, then saying, "But not a single sparrow can fall to the ground without your Father knowing it" (Mt 10:29, NLT). Surely, I did not fall to the ground without him knowing. I suddenly realized deep in my spirit that "I can't know. I'll never know. But I know the One Who Knows." And this has become my mainstay for the many years that have followed. "Who among you fears the Lord and obeys the word of his servant? Let the one who walks in the dark, who has no light, trust in the name of Lord and rely on their God" (Is 50:10).

Just *days* earlier—after a 2-year journey of soul-searching—my wife and I had made the commitment to God and to an international missions ministry. It was the greatest faith-step we had ever taken, turning our lives upside down and inside out, moving our family away from all our friends and extended family. But here in this moment, I heard another still small voice speaking to my spirit that went like this, "Gary, you think you know what faith is all about in trusting me and serving me, but you really know nothing of the sort. As you embark on the unknown journey ahead, you need to learn greater and deeper faith—and quickly."

And suddenly—think of the heavenly host of angels appearing in the sky over the shepherds on Christmas night—in the middle of my tortured thoughts and prayerful angst with God, a picture came into my mind of a menu board, the sort of thing you'd see above the registers at a fast-food restaurant. It was red and bright and glossy…not exactly a "vision" of biblical proportions (like angels breaking through between heaven and earth) but an image that felt like a vision from the Lord, nonetheless. As I looked, I saw that it said "Fast Faith" with a menu list of choices. It was as if God were saying, "Gary, you need more faith for what I'm calling you into, and I need to give it to you fast. There are several ways I can do this. None of them are very good (to clarify, that's how I heard it, but what it meant was none of them *feel* very good), but any of them can be effective." The "menu" choices were these: I could have my house burned down, we could lose a child, or I could fall from a ladder and shatter my leg. Now if I had actually *had* a choice, I would've chosen the one that only directly impacted me more than my entire family, but that is beside the point. The point is, God was serving it up, and I was his guest.

We began our day in the cold and wintry weather of a Buffalo, New York Thanksgiving Day. Our family minivan was parked in our narrow sloping driveway and my 10-year-old son was brushing off the layers of crystalized snow that had fallen overnight. I had the van warming up, readying ourselves to head to my parents' home for dinner. When I had gone out to the car to start it, I noticed a problem high up on the house. An ice dam in an upper gutter had developed overnight. I went to work quickly, pulling out my extension ladder to run up and smash it out quickly with a hammer. I had just gotten to the top and begun my work when my son asked me if I could move the ladder a bit so he could get around the front of the car to brush it off. I scooted down, shoved it over a foot or two and scooted back up. But the second time, I did not pay close enough attention to how I had footed the ladder on the icy driveway. I no sooner got to the top when the bottom of the ladder slid quickly away from the house, bringing me crashing to the ground straight down along the house wall. In what could have only been 2 seconds, with nothing to grab or break my fall, I landed flat-footed, mostly on my right leg on the concrete driveway, shattering my tibia from the ankle up to the knee.

I spent months in a cast—the first several weeks still in excruciating pain whenever I lowered my leg from an elevated position. The orthopedic surgeon said that there were so many vertical shatter lines that he didn't know where to begin screwing things together, so his professional treatment was to leave it alone and let new bone grow in all the fractures—taking nearly 5 months. In that much time, I lost half the muscle mass of the right leg. The ligaments and cartilage of the ankle were damaged, and inherent weaknesses in the knee were amplified. An entire year of concerted physical therapy did not restore the leg to anything better than 70% strength and flexibility. It's only gotten worse over the years. Limping is a way of life, and daily pain and stiffness have been a part of my life ever since, just as the orthopedic surgeon predicted.

The days and weeks that followed during my recovery period were full of "quality time with God." Like the ones in my opening paragraphs, I had many questions for the Lord—and some answers from him too, actually. Many days of quiet and solitude made me introspective and prayerful, and I began keeping a journal I titled "My Life of Faith." Some of the lessons God taught me through this period are included in the rest of this book. The biggest lesson to take away is that God was teaching me about *learning* to live by faith. You see, though I thought I understood walking with God and living in faith, I really didn't.

My life of faith that began when I was 16 was still mostly a story of an American kid—a reasonably secure and marginally affluent, well-educated, career-oriented, white male—making the most of opportunity, talent, and hard work. How does faith grow in that environment? It would be arrogant to compare myself to the apostle Paul, but when I read his discourse in 2 Corinthians 12, I experience a tremendous resonance in my spirit—and a powerful conviction from the Holy Spirit. He speaks of having been privileged in so many ways and given "surpassingly great" revelations, but before you might accuse Paul of being too high-minded, he then goes on to explain,

> Therefore, in order to keep me from becoming conceited, I was given a thorn in my flesh, a messenger of Satan, to torment me. Three times I pleaded with the Lord to take it away from me. But He said to me, "My grace is sufficient for you, for my power is made perfect in weakness." Therefore, I will boast all the more gladly about my weaknesses, so that Christ's power may rest on me. That is why, for Christ's sake, I delight in weaknesses, in insults, in hardships, in persecutions, in difficulties. For when I am weak, then I am strong. (2 Cor 12:7-10)

And there's the crux of the whole story. Synonyms for conceit would include pride, self-importance, arrogance, vanity, and a host of other things that all set themselves up against the knowledge of God or the need to have faith in him instead of trusting in our boastful, prideful selves. How does a young man like me in my position socially and economically ever learn weakness? The hardship that came into my life that day—and has remained with me ever since—was the beginning of real faith growing in my life. And that faith has sustained me through serving God in missions, through sacrifice, darkness, weakness, and dependence. And that has made all the difference.

CHAPTER 1

IF YOU MUST STAY

Thanksgiving Day, 2 years earlier...

"If you must stay here, if you must, stay only if you're called. Well, if you must...go find those—the streets and the towns are full of them. Somebody said yesterday of this little town, "But we don't have the homeless, and I don't see the poor." Why should it not be that this town be famous like it was just over a century ago for hospitality for those who are wounded? Why not? If you must stay here, become famous for looking after the wounded and the poor, the strangers and the aliens; for they were—right from the beginning—the privilege of God's people. Always included with his special people were the aliens, the strangers and the guests, always to be able to share in [His blessing]. But be equipped, for if you must stay here, then you will begin to see them and to find them. And if you do go elsewhere, where there are the poor that have never heard anything, it will kill you."[1]

And so it began, as I, an architect from Buffalo, NY, in a state of exhaustion after the long road trip with my family, watched a video-recorded message at Asbury Seminary in Wilmore, Kentucky, from the couch of my friends' little college apartment. The town of Wilmore was famous for its reputation of reaching, rescuing, and serving the wounded, the lost, the alien and stranger from among the members of both the Union and Confederate armies during America's Civil War. Phil and Marsha Matanick were so excited to introduce us to this missionary and her message, that they could not wait to push everything aside and sit us down to hear her. Jackie Pullinger, a British woman who had spent her life reaching gang members, opium addicts, and prostitutes in Hong Kong's despicable "Walled City" was speaking in the chapel service. (Her biography *Chasing the Dragon* tells the whole story.) Who could have known that Jackie Pullinger was God's very oracle for me that day?

For days afterwards, her words came back to me. I couldn't escape them, and I sensed it was God himself asking me, "Gary, *why must you stay?*" It was as if God was speaking directly and only to me, though a little while later I learned that my wife was feeling the same way! When Jackie said, "If you must stay here, if you must, stay only if you're called," she was speaking to an assembly of seminarians, presumably most of whom believed they were preparing for fulltime ministry work. She was giving a challenge to them not to look only for the status quo sort of ministry opportunities, but to "look to the fields that were white with harvest." This was supposed to be their *kairos* moment—a propitious moment of decision and action for *them*! She couldn't have known that an architect and his wife from Buffalo, New York were going to hear her and be totally unprepared for the life-changing series of events that would follow. But I'm getting ahead of myself.

I had a long list of answers to the question—very valid reasons why I must stay. My permanent appointment at the State University of New York at Buffalo managing its architectural design team for campus planning and development was atop the list. "Permanent appointment" was a classification a bit like tenure at the university, but for the professional class of non-academic employees. People don't ever leave those jobs—they die in them! Or they leave at the end of their career with a very healthy retirement account, and probably an early retirement at that. Surely after God had blessed me so abundantly with the outrageous favor and miraculous, divine orchestration of events to obtain the position, He himself was aware of this overwhelming reason I must stay.

Close behind on my list was my consulting business. Working at a large public research institution allowed me the privilege of developing my own private architectural consulting practice in my spare time, without ever creating a conflict of interest. The flow of clients and work seemed endless, without any advertising or effort on my own to broadcast the news of my new business. My clients were private homeowners, small businesses, semi-custom home builders, churches, and local public government. The work expanded often to consume the wee hours of the mornings during my work week—and as demanding as it was, I could see how I could bless my family so much more with just these extra 25 hours a week or so. How could I deny that this was an incredible blessing from God?

My church ministry life was up there on the list too. My wife and I spent three or four nights a week and most of Sunday in church or in homes serving our local church and its families. Over the years since we were teenagers, we had served together in almost every form of church ministry: teaching children's Sunday School, leading worship, participating in the choir, leading small groups, teaching Bible studies, performing in amateur Christian theater, and assisting in leading the youth group. By this time in our lives, most of our closest friends were the pastors, elders, and deacons with whom we co-labored. We began attending leadership conferences at Elim Bible Institute (a nearby Bible school) with them, and training under each of them in their areas of ministry expertise. Partnering with the associate pastor for worship, I was the platform worship leader for half the services of our thriving 1500-member church. Mentored by the small group pastor, I developed Bible studies to teach weekly. We regularly heard them say, "You must be called to the ministry." I would only half-jokingly respond, "Get behind me Satan!" And during those busy years, my wife would sometimes ask me, "Are you sure we're where God wants us to be?" and I would say to her on more than one occasion, "If I hear something different, you'll be the first one to know!" I was convinced my friends just saw me—an architect and volunteer minister—using my gifts and talents, working hard to serve alongside them in their ministries, like Samuel, looking at Jesse's oldest son and just judging in the natural— "Surely this must be the Lord's anointed!"

Let's not forget our "This Old House" special—a derelict old depression-era home we bought and were remodeling into the gem of the village on the north edge of Buffalo. This made the list too as a significant reason that we were called to stay. God had miraculously opened the door for us to turn our first home—a duplex—into a rental income property, and then buy this dilapidated eyesore of the neighborhood. But we had vision! We can still remember my mother walking through it already defeated and almost below her breath murmuring, "You must *love* work." Well, for the better part of eight years we worked, gutting and remodeling that thing from foundations to roof—all while we lived in it! Almost every Saturday and the couple of nights a week I wasn't in church, I was working on house renovation projects. And as Jackie Pullinger came into our lives, we were only a bit more than halfway done. Nearly every disposable dollar I could earn from my two jobs went into "her." Today I call the house a mistress that never loved me and I never loved her, and she robbed me of nearly a decade of my life. Vanity, vanity, all is vanity. But here again I am getting ahead of myself.

Our children's education was paramount on the list as well. Our church had created a private school, and we were heavily invested in its success, giving and volunteering, serving in ways that most parents were expected to in those early days. Our family was relatively well-known, and our oldest son Drew was already on top of the Headmaster's List as he entered third grade. Then, at about the same time as that Wilmore trip, we took our youth group to an Acquire the Fire convention, and I bought a little book off the table by Ron Luce entitled *Inspire the Fire*. The message of the book was about how and why we were failing to pass the torch of faith to the next generation, and his obvious yet revelatory idea that sums up the whole book was "lack of relationship." A big idea in the book is this: 10 years or so into raising our children, they don't necessarily see their parents' passion for loving and serving God—especially since by the time they are teens, we spend barely 60 minutes a day (if that!) with them. By that time in their lives, they see parents stressed out with the demands of career ladder-climbing, retirement planning, saving for college, failing health, and even church work 4 nights a week. Hmmm, sound familiar? From that point, I heard another call right alongside the "Why must you stay?" question. Bring your children home. The following year we began homeschooling and didn't stop till our last one finished high school. It had been a growing dream of my wife's, especially since she had studied early childhood education in college. But up until then there was no room for such a thing in my well-planned, over-achieving, performance-driven, people-pleasing, never-say-die life that I was already projecting on my kids.

So, there it was. My answer to the question, "Why must you stay?" On and on it went, a seemingly endless list of me and my stuff. And it left me feeling empty and despairing. How can this be, God? I have experienced your blessing at every turn and have sought you on every major decision of my life since I gave my heart to you at 16. You have blessed me with a beautiful wife of noble character, full of wisdom and discernment, who has sought you since she was only 14! As that young dating couple, we believed early on you had us together to rescue us from our brokenness and our dysfunctional families, put our feet upon a solid rock, and write a new history for us and our future family. And together we've built a life of faithfulness, service, and hard work! Nothing. Nothing but silence came back from my rant. No justification, no acceptance, no rationalization could bring me peace after that conversation with God. There was suddenly an overwhelming sense of selfishness and superficiality to my entire Christian life, and we could hardly bear it. My wife and I began to tell our friends and family, "We can't stay." They would naturally ask us, "Where will you go?" and to that we'd blankly say, "We have no idea."

A New Kind of Search

…with an old kind of strategy. Judylynn sensed early on that God was saying, "Position yourselves to hear from me." For my wife and I to hear God clearly, we knew we had to return to some basics. This new search to understand how and where God was leading us took us back to prayer and worship around our piano in our living room. We began here as teenagers, newly introduced to the Lord and one another... that was the end of the '70's, the beginning of the '80's, when a new thing was brewing that today we might look back on with a bit of nostalgia. Following the Jesus movement, worship became something for relationship's sake—not just a time of singing songs—for the sake of drawing nearer to the heart of God, to discover more of him and understand what He is up to in the world and in our lives—with worship and prayer flowing seamlessly together for hours at a time! But by now, our busy lives left little time for that practice at home, and in my role as a worship leader on the platform of a large church, worship had become a responsibility more than a privilege, a *part* of my spiritual life rather than the very *essence* of it...weekly preparation and a task to complete on Sundays.

As we began to pray and worship more often at home, we began to get a glimpse of something different. To be honest, I would have preferred not to have to go there. It meant change. Now I'm not one to fear change any more than the next guy, but I am one who loves to plan and who loves *a* plan—and we were "working the plan" to use the language of network-marketing. I was a design professional after all: a creative, problem-solving architect. Something "different" almost certainly meant leaving the plan we were executing for our lives—the one we knew God led us into, the one that established order from the chaos of our former lives, provided for our family, and ended with ensuring peace and tranquility, promoting the general welfare, and securing blessings of liberty to ourselves and our posterity. Since when did my calling in the Lord sound an awful lot like the preamble to the United States Constitution?! But this is where we find ourselves today in churches all across the Western world. Not knowing any better, I somehow was handed—and readily consumed—the Western, American Dream-version of Christianity...and it was working for me. And therein lies the heart of the problem: it was working...for me. How was that connecting at all with the heart of God?

So, we had to ask ourselves, if this isn't it—if we can't stay and this is not the plan—then what else do you have for us, Lord? We thought we knew a few absolutes...as a 16-year-old teenager, new to following Jesus, I discovered quickly that I loved to study the Bible, theology, history, and culture. I was raised since childhood in a Lutheran church that taught me a lot of Scripture—and suddenly it meant something to me! I began to invest hours each week in deeper study of the Bible, getting to know the God whom I had always professed to know, but never really did. I loved that study time! And I knew for the first time in my life, I loved God. At the same time, I was already groomed to pursue the study of architecture in college. From childhood I had loved to draw, create, design, and beautify whatever I could touch...I attended a vocational technical high school, and "majored" in the building design and related technologies program. So, I came to a crossroads way back then. I clearly remember walking along the streets of my neighborhood that bordered the University at Buffalo campus, where I eventually went to college, asking God how to reconcile these two conflicting passions—should I go to seminary and pursue the ministry, or should I continue on the path seemingly set out for me (by the unique design of my life) and become an architect? Without much fanfare, I chose architecture. Looking back now, it feels like I just stuck to the plan.

But God allowed me to build a life with that plan—a good life, one that was full of spiritual growth and fruitfulness; a sweet and lovely and supportive wife; children, a heritage from the Lord; a career, business, houses, and growing prosperity and influence. And when time had come to its fullness, so to speak, when it seemed like everything we touched turned to gold, God arrested me and challenged every assumption I had built my life upon.

So, as I'm beginning to pursue God because He's now told me I can't stay, I had to ask him, "So what have the last 15 years been all about? What was the point of all this if I am now to leave it all behind?" Thank God for a friend, Cindy Short, the wife of one of our pastors back in those days, who gently encouraged me as she prayed with us. God works in different ways in different seasons, she said. And it was suddenly a revelation to me! God might have more than this for our future, but the next season depends on the completion of the season before. To God this was a natural outcome. To me, it was like the shock of the shears pruning away the best branches on the plant to ready it for next spring. I still couldn't see it and didn't yet understand. But He had been leading us this way, knowing it was supposed to lead us to where we found ourselves right now, like the natural unfolding of the seasons, the natural growth of healthy, fruitful plants.

So where is it that He was leading us, you ask? We didn't know yet...but we knew we had a bunch of options! Like the classic engineering analysis within a problem-solving exercise, option one is always "do nothing." Stay where we are, continue climbing the ladder at the university, building my consulting business, buying and remodeling houses and rental properties, raising a family, and serving the local church. But we knew more than anything else, this was no real option for us anymore, because "we can't stay." And the painful reality was that it was self-serving at its core. I wasn't making enough extra money to give to ministry efforts beyond our normal tithe and small extra missions pledge, and I certainly had no extra time to give in answer to this call that required some sort of "going." Jackie's message had refocused us on Jesus' words in the Great Commission, "*Go* into all the world..." It was as if to say that the only justification that's possible to *not* go, is to know unequivocally that you are called to stay (more on that later, as we are all called to be part of a local church). And we just knew we could no longer stay.

If the first one was immediately rejected, the second seemed immediately obvious. If this new thing somehow means that indeed—as our pastor-friends had been telling us all along—we must be called to the ministry, then I guess I need to go to seminary and get another degree in ministry, theology, or whatever, because who wants an architect in ministry? Little did we know. As I mentioned, my wife and I had begun a relationship with Elim Fellowship and Elim Bible Institute, a local Bible school in the area, attending leadership training and conferences there, and it seemed a logical end to pursue more formal education there. One of our pastors had done exactly that, uprooting his family in the middle of his career years and pursuing his pastoral ministry education—he's the one whose wife talked about the seasons, as if she knew something about this.

Another immediately obvious possibility was to accept the invitation of my closest friend and mentor in ministry who at the time was leading a church across the border in Canada and had invited me to join him as his associate pastor and minister of worship. Patrick Prior ("Pastor Pat") was the one who had raised me up and trained me to do that in the first place, and now here he is asking me to partner with him. Our wives were the closest of friends, our children were growing up playing in each other's homes, and we were already partnered in so many areas of life. It seemed right, too.

Then there's the dream of every architect—to live in a home he has designed himself. It's a pride thing I'm sure (I can say that now), but it was my dream, too; and certainly this was the direction we were heading. One of my builders who used me exclusively had been holding land on which he could build my home. With all this "I can't stay" talk, it hadn't occurred to me yet that I might not be able to follow God into this next season and still pursue this dream—I mean the house was already designed!

In this same season, I had applied for and was short-listed among the top three candidates for a new position at Cornell University (which we jokingly referred to as the *other* major public research institution in the State of New York) as the Director of Architectural Services. This was a seemingly custom-made position for me as a young 30-something to grow into from my work at the University at Buffalo. Less than a three-hour drive from Buffalo, it was also only a stone's throw from Elim Bible Institute and one of its largest churches, Zion Fellowship, where we already had friends. Too many puzzle pieces seemed to fit here to ignore.

And finally, missions to the poor. This was the one option that spoke most directly to the challenge that came through Jackie's message but was also the most foreign (pardon the pun) concept—almost entirely outside any realm of our Christian experience. Much of Jackie's message was built upon her heart's burden, her calling, and her experience in service to the poor, and it was unmistakable that she was implicitly demanding that her audience consider a life that would do the same. She didn't hold back when she said, *"And if you do go elsewhere, where there are the poor that have never heard anything, it will kill you."* But amazingly, she continued to testify that the difficulties and hardship and the sacrifice were all outweighed by the joy of doing the will of her Father. "And who wants that old life, anyway?" she said.

We had come home from Asbury and found ourselves saying, "We can't stay." We knew we needed to seek God about all these options, believing one of them must be where He's leading; but it was also the busiest and most successful career year of my life! A year later, we were no closer to knowing the will of God than before. We found ourselves hosting the annual missions conference in our church that November. I was leading worship, and Dr. Dave Martinke, one of our elders and the then-director of Operation Serve (an outreach ministry to those living within the garbage dump villages of Mexico City and later Cairo) gave the closing message of the weekend. He quoted a mentor of his, who said,

> There are two great tragedies in the world. One is the tragedy of the wasted soul, and the other is the tragedy of the wasted life. The wasted soul is happening all across the world—those dying without ever hearing of the love of Christ. But the wasted life is happening right here among us, within these four walls. It's those of us who know Christ and are saved with the assurance of heaven as our future home but have not connected with the real plan of God for our lives.

It was as if I found myself right back in the chapel at Asbury Seminary and God was speaking only to me! I knew God had spoken to me a year ago and yet here I was a whole year later no closer to understanding what He was saying. Well, that night I did some business with God. I prayed and confessed and repented and resolved to not leave until I knew something more—and He met me again. I had a vision of a mud hut, like the typical African images we might all be carrying from years of National Geographic as children. I left that night wondering if maybe God was telling me, it's all about overseas missions among the poor.

So here we found ourselves praying about six possible open doors. I latched onto to Rev 3:8, "I know your deeds. See, I have placed before you an open door that no one can shut." For good or bad, whether this was good exegesis or not, I said to God, "if that's true, then I'm going to start taking steps to go through every one of these doors and trust you to shut the ones that are not right for us. Obviously, I can't do them all, but any one of them is something I *could* do and probably do well...so I need you to keep me from making the wrong choice." And one by one He shut every door, except the one that scared me half to death.

"EMI, send me."

> *Then I heard the voice of the Lord saying, "Whom shall I send? And who will go for us?" And I said, "Here am I. Send me!"*
> *Isaiah 6:8*

So how did EMI come into the picture and how did that become the mission to the poor that we would do? Engineering Ministries International was an obscure little mission outreach of engineers and architects based out of Colorado. For this little miracle piece of the story, I need to go back to the beginning. I mentioned that I was new to following the Lord at age 16. It was September of my junior year of high school, and a crisis in my life brought me to the Lord in repentance. The very next day on the bus (I took a city bus across town to get to school in the heart of downtown Buffalo's redlight district) I met a guy reading his Bible. He looked a few years older than me—college age at least (I learned later that he was in law school)—so I struck up a conversation with him. Before we were done, Dwight Saunders had gotten my name and phone number and for the next six weeks he called to invite me to a youth group that he helped lead in a local Baptist church. I finally relented and agreed to go with him, and I never looked back. I was hooked. It was a community of other young people that served God wholeheartedly, were ardently pursuing Him, and actively growing in discipleship, evangelism, and ministry to others. That man and his younger brother-in-law (Neil Boron—now a Christian radio talk show host on stations across New York State) became significant mentors to me in those early years of my Christian walk.

Many years passed and by the time I was in my late 20's, my mentor and friend from that day on the bus had since left his law practice (*he couldn't stay!*) and was himself off to school once again getting another degree (in ministry this time), planning to become a pastor. Today he is a missionary evangelist for the sake of Ugandan children with disabilities (definitely more on that later!). He had received a packet of ministry announcements and opportunities, and from that he sent me a little postcard about this mission organization called EMI. It described this group as mobilizing short-term volunteer trips made up of architects and engineers to serve in missions, helping to design facilities that missionaries needed to fulfill their mandate to serve the poor and reach the world with the Gospel. Sounds compelling, huh? Sounds perfect for me, right? Nope. I received it from him, but my reaction was ambivalent, at best. I was a busy young 20-something, raising kids, remodeling homes, working two jobs, and serving in the church four days a week. Volunteer missions work was never going to happen. But out of respect for who had given it to me, I couldn't throw it away. So, I filed it away, never to be thought of again…until a few years later when Jackie Pullinger's challenge became the calling of God in our hearts, and then the missions conference at home made me think that maybe serving the poor was a part of God's plan for us. I knew exactly where I had filed that thing away and went and dug it out.

I called the office of EMI and spoke directly with its founder and Executive Director, Michael Orsillo, who was recruiting volunteers for a project to Indonesia to design an orphanage. He invited me to come with him. That same year we were planning to lead our youth group to serve an orphanage in Belarus, and I began to imagine how these two things could be linked somehow in God's timing. Amazing how God works, huh? Nope. In the end it all came to nothing: the trip with our youth had to be cancelled because the doors started to close in Belarus, and without that piece making the obvious connection, my overloaded life quickly squelched the excitement I had felt about the two mission outreach opportunities being paired together. That fall and winter seemed to provide no more clarity as to where we would go, and I forgot about EMI.

But EMI had not forgotten about me. The next spring, I received a cold call from Glen Woodruff, the only other architect in EMI, and the operational director of projects—I was on the "hot list" of potential volunteers that had expressed interest in the past, and this new man from EMI was trying to find an architect to join a team to Trinidad. My wife and I listened to the message left on an answering machine on Friday afternoon, just before we each left on weekend youth retreats, she with the girls and me with the boys. We agreed we would each be praying during the weekend, and we could talk when we got home Sunday evening. We couldn't help but hear God knocking once again, repeating his invitation. Six weeks later I had obtained my first passport, joined my first mission trip, and was overseas for the first time, as an architect to serve the poor.

To say I came home changed is an understatement. The trip represented so many "firsts" for me that I could hardly contain the excitement. I shared for hours with my wife as we sat on our couch, and I poured through video that I had taken on a little 8 mm camera a friend had lent me. I was reeling from seeing and experiencing how the poor of the world live for the very first time and couldn't escape the tremendous burden I now felt to become a part of the answer to their needs. I could never again return to my "normal life," insulated from the needs of the world. The "world" now was people with names and faces.

My wife, the wise and prayerful woman that she is, had mobilized our kids to make different cards every day that I was going to be gone and packed them in my bags for me—every day I had three new cards to open from them, and read about how they were praying for me, wondering what my life was like, or what Trinidad was like. When I returned home, my wife shared with me that God had led her to pray a jealous prayer, something like this: "Lord, I know what you're going to do in my husband's life through this trip, and I need you to do the same in me right here as I'm praying for him." She testifies today that God met her in a powerful way and gave her the same heart and burden to serve the poor, and God gave her the grace to release me to serve—not just then, but the many years that were to come that we couldn't yet imagine. Our family mission statement—as Judylynn heard it in her heart and wrote on a chalkboard in our home—became "Lord, make us the answer to other people's prayers today."

> "Lord, make us the answer to other people's prayers today."

Meanwhile, one by one, the other doors closed, some very abruptly, others slowly over the course of the next several months. Eventually, only one was left open: the one for which we felt least prepared. Like Isaiah's call and response, when God calls out, "Whom shall I send? And who will go for us?" And I said, "Here am I. Send me!" (Is 6:8), we found ourselves answering God's call, somewhat tongue-in-cheek, "EMI, send me."

We went to a small conference that EMI held later that year. We participated with them, led worship, listened to missionary speakers, and met with leadership. EMI had only a small handful of full-time staff back then. For their conference theme, EMI chose Isaiah 58:10-12:

> ...if you spend yourselves in behalf of the hungry
> and satisfy the needs of the oppressed,
> then your light will rise in the darkness,
> and your night will become like the noonday.
> The Lord will guide you always;
> He will satisfy your needs in a sun-scorched land

and will strengthen your frame…
You will be called Repairer of Broken Walls,
Restorer of Streets with Dwellings.

Today, I'd say that those verses are interwoven into the very strands of my DNA. Back then, it was the promise of God, come to make the calling of God possible. A promise to equip us, no matter how incapable we felt. And we truly felt incapable. I was literally asking God, "Do you really want me to serve the poor through EMI? Does EMI really need me? How can I really do this?" I had very little experience or understanding of such things and didn't really realize at that moment how much I was disqualifying myself from answering this call. Over the years, I have learned that "How?" is a faithless question. What we really must do is "Start with *Why*."[2] Enter Luis Bush, EMI's keynote speaker for the conference.

Luis Bush is the well-known and respected Christian missionary strategist who coined the term "The 10/40 Window" in 1990 to refer to regions of the Eastern Hemisphere and the European and African regions of the Western Hemisphere, bounded by 10- and 40-degrees north latitude. This "window" gave us a view to both the highest levels of socio-economic challenges and the greatest resistance to the Gospel message. In the middle of his keynote talk, Luis said, "The poor of the world are crying out, 'send us your Christian design professionals!'" Once again, I could not deny this *kairos* moment, as his words bore into my heart with the answer I was looking for. That's *why* I can't stay!

After the conference, we had some time to meet with the staff of EMI and in one brief meeting with its founder and executive director, he said something that was like the Holy Spirit himself whispering in our ears, "Here at EMI, we're not looking for architects and engineers; we're looking for people who are called to minister, who *happen* to be architects and engineers."

With these confirmations we felt we'd received through our time there, we came home, prayed with our team of leaders in our church, and asked them to seek God with us because we were at a point of decision-making. Pastor Dan Hamlin was our senior associate (soon to become our lead pastor) who was very personally mentoring me along with a small group of others as a small group leader and Bible teacher. His wife Nancy was our school's principal. We were quite well connected to them and trusted them implicitly.

It had been a few weeks since we presented the idea for our pastors and elders to prayerfully seek God with us. We were all at the wedding of a fellow church member. As we were dancing together, my wife and I came close to Dan and Nancy and talked for a bit about it. Nancy asked, "What if we all don't feel this is what God is saying?" I quickly and unequivocally replied, "Then we won't go!" We knew we couldn't launch without the help of our friends and co-laborers to confirm we weren't crazy! Just days after that it was time to prepare for our church's annual missions weekend. Pastor Dan called me as he was preparing the missions booklet for the

> ### Confirmation of our Calling
>
> *Early in the process of our growing conviction that, "We can't stay," we came by the school one day and spoke with Nancy about the decision to homeschool our kids and pull them out of the school that we were so heavily invested in. Nancy encouraged us to speak to the many different families we knew—and who knew us because of our relatively high profile in the church—to let them know how God was very personally speaking to us about this, and not out of any dissatisfaction with the school. In that context, we shared with her the bigger picture of why and how it fit into the rest of the sense we had that "we can't stay," and we were seeking God for what He had for us. Suddenly, Nancy became animated, and excitedly drew us into her office. As we waited, she went to her desk and reached into a drawer where she pulled out a self-addressed stamped envelope that she had mailed to herself many months earlier. It was still unopened. In it was a note she wrote, impressed by God in her personal prayer time that God was calling the MacPhee's into full-time ministry, and when the time is right, they will need some confirmation of this drastic step!*

services. "So, are we putting you into the booklet as new missionaries we are sending out?" he asked. "Well, does that mean you all agree that we *should* be sent out?" I answered. "I guess it does!" he replied.

We immediately made a commitment to EMI. It was mid-November. We could hardly imagine all that it would take to extract ourselves from the lives we had built in order to make the transition to volunteer, faith-supported missionary workers, but we thought we had a handle on it. The list of what needed to happen was long: raise support, finish house renovations, sell properties, close or hand off my consulting business, resign from the University at Buffalo, pack and sell stuff, and put an axe to the root of everything that held us there. But a couple of weeks later my world was about to change again, forever.

It was Thanksgiving Day, two years later. Two years to the day since we heard a new call from God through Jackie Pullinger.

C.S. Lewis, my dear, departed mentor since I was 16, said in *The Problem of Pain*, "God whispers to us in our pleasures, speaks in our conscience, but shouts in our pains: it is his megaphone to rouse a deaf world."[3] God roused me—He got my attention. God was so determined to teach me to live a different way—a way that would divert me off the fast-lane of my performance-driven, over-achieving, myopic, self-focused, domesticated life that was careening only toward a crash and burn—that He put me flat on my back with my foot in the air so that I would cease all my activity, seek Him wholeheartedly, and silence the high pitched whir of a life constantly in over-drive so that I would hear his voice and learn to follow Him. The accident that changed my life forever allowed me to embrace my weakness, so that God's power would be made perfect in me. The process of finding how I fit in God's plan to reach the world had begun.

CHAPTER 2

THE PRINCIPLES OF POSITIONING

His Purposes...and Promise

The immediate future presented some clear and present challenges to the new plan—namely, to begin the process of raising support and extricating ourselves from the American Dream to become missionary workers. I was completely unable to work—not my day job at UB, my night job consulting, or my day-and-night job of house renovations. It seemed like a major setback to seeing the new plan come to be. But here is the amazing fruit of it—I now had *time* that I never had before. Hours and hours of free time, albeit from the couch, flat on my back. I had built up huge amounts of sick days in more than a dozen years at the University, so my paycheck kept coming unencumbered by my injured condition. I could not, however, fulfill any current consulting contracts, so that created an immediate financial shortfall. I had grown dependent on that extra income for our family budget and renovations to our home. It was a bit disconcerting to add to our debt each month that I wasn't working my consulting business.

I began the "Life of Faith" journal that I mentioned, chronicling the events of that time and the lessons God was teaching me through those events. I began writing letters of all kinds to all kinds of people in my life—past pastors and friends, old school mates, coworkers, family, and neighbors. In my personal devotional times, I prayed hard for a creative plan of attack to share the vision for missions that God had given us. I could not remember ever "connecting" with any visiting missionary at our home church over the years—certainly not like our profound connection with Jackie Pullinger that had propelled us into this faith journey. And that certainly contributed to me missing the real heart of God all those years. So, my earnest prayer request became, "Lord, show me how to connect with people the way she did with us! Help me inspire others to seek you with us and to draw people into a new vision for mission and service—together." I had not yet synthesized it down to the burning question I pose to you today, "How do you fit in God's plan to reach the world?" but that was it in its most embryonic form. It was about six more weeks before I was finally able to go back to church and when I did, God birthed two new things in me that have grown to maturity over the years and have been the answer to that prayer.

The first was this. As I sat in my seat on the end of a pew, my crutches leaning against my chest in worship, I could easily observe *someone else* leading worship—the role that I normally filled—and the congregation having no problem with that! In that moment of self-introspection (self-pity, more likely), I immediately heard the voice of God speaking in my head and heart, "Gary, I am calling you to a little-known work, in the middle of nowhere, where no one is going to see or know, and no one will applaud or thank you. Are you alright with that?" Faced with the very real prospect of anonymity in mission service, and understanding the humility of it and my need for total surrender, I could not say no. I thought back to Jackie Pullinger saying—with or without the incredible fruit of lives redeemed and rescued—they would continue to do the work they do, because it is her delight to do the will of her Father. I said, "Yes, Lord."

Flashing quickly backward and forward in my mind, I was painfully aware of the people-pleasing, over-achieving, approval-addict that I was. From childhood these things developed, and as I worked very hard to employ the gifts that God had brought into my life along the way, I was usually propelled into success in most areas of my life. In that quiet moment, it became clear that God was going to be my only reward as I followed him into this unknown territory. Nothing I had done before was even relevant. And no amount of hard work that I could do would earn me more money, approval, confidence, or security anymore. Instantly He became my audience of one. He was standing at the shores of the sea of my life and beckoning me to follow him.

If I were one of the disciples He had called at the Sea of Galilee, I would've had a barrage of questions for him: What about my livelihood? My family? My retirement? Do you have a job description? A list of benefits? A mutually beneficial contract for each of us to sign? Will I be alright? Will I be safe? Are there any guarantees? Perhaps the disciples that "left their nets and followed him" had the same kinds of questions. But we're left with no answers of those kinds in the scriptural record. Jesus did say elsewhere that, "Whoever finds his life will lose it, and whoever loses his life for my sake will find it" (Mt 10:39). "Jesus clearly acknowledged that following him involves risking the safety, security, and satisfaction we have found in this world. But in the end, Jesus said following him leads to a radical reward that this world can never offer."[1]

After serving God for over a quarter of a century in missions work now, I can hear Jesus' answer to the disciples: "No, I have none of that. But you will see the dead raised, the blind see, the lame walk, and the kingdom of Heaven come to earth! Fair trade?" And it has been! Dear friend, I traded up! I walked away from my plan for my life and walked into an abiding relationship with Jesus like I had never known before, and that intimacy is the greatest gift I have to offer anyone[2] as He sends me into all the world to do whatever He has ordained for me. Like the disciples, it has been filled with sacrifice, risk, and the unknown (with some danger), but it is a trade I would make again in a heartbeat!

The second "new thing" that God birthed in me came within weeks through a visiting speaker at our church, the then-president of Elim Bible Institute, Paul Johansson. The message he brought to our church that day has never left me, and I knew that it was to be part of the core message that the rest of my life would be about. It has become part and parcel of my life and has grown over these many years into the complete outline of this book. "Brother Jo,"—as my old friend and mentor Patrick Prior introduced him—probably doesn't remember me; but just as with Jackie Pullinger, I will be thankful for him for the rest of my life.

He focused on Ezekiel 22:30, "I looked for someone among them who would build up the wall and stand before me in the gap on behalf of the land so I would not have to destroy it, but I found no one." He spoke about how God positions each one of us for unique service and outreach, and the basic ideas of intercession *for* the world, communication *to* the world, and identification *with* the world. That was it! I knew in that moment the approach I needed to take in sharing the vision God had given us, and God etched a title across the page of my mind: "God's Principles of Positioning." This was not meant just for me and my family, but for everyone—especially those that God would have me reach with this new vision for partnership to reach the world. I developed this message and began preaching in churches across Western New York; Ontario, Canada; and Pennsylvania; everywhere Elim, our church, and the pastors we had sent out had taken us. And that is the substance of this chapter.

Beyond the summary of this chapter, however, God brought me back to Ezekiel 22:30 over and over from that day on, until my preoccupation became a passion. The Lord began to reveal more to me about that verse, until it became the most fascinating verse in the Bible to me. Why? It seems to provide for us a summary of what God *has* done, *is* doing, and *continues* to do in and through us, his Church, all in just one verse! So much so that it forms the basis for me of all the purpose-related work that I might do or that we all might be called to do in the world today. You might think this is a reach, and I understand that. I think so too!

I can remember while working in Nigeria many years ago, having a conversation with Chad Gamble (now EMI's Regional Director of Asia), at the time a new up-and-coming leader at EMI with whom I was co-leading a team to train him. He recalled a preacher saying, "All of the Bible can be summed up in this one idea..." to which he quickly said, "Really?! It's a pretty big book. I think God has a lot of things to say!" I have laughed at that very idea for many years—thinking that we could sum up all the Bible in one verse seems almost ridiculous, but as we venture into the rest of this book, you will see how virtually all of the scriptural story from beginning to end can indeed be fit into this one verse! I am excited for you to see it with me, and to think about this throughout the rest of this book, and indeed, perhaps for the rest of your life!

> "I looked for someone among them who would build up the wall and stand before me in the gap on behalf of the land so I would not have to destroy it, but I found no one." Ez 22:30

It's a verse that many readers would be very familiar with, especially in the context of pulling out the phrase "Standing in the Gap." I have seen this phrase used many times over the years for many different purposes, including missions conferences, service opportunities, local community outreaches, prayer meetings, and book titles.

But for the sake of your introduction to it in the context of this book, and its dissection in the pages to come, let's look at the verse first from the 35,000-foot point of view. In the most general sense, God is looking for someone who would be uniquely *positioned* to do his work (that's just how Brother Jo phrased it), to fulfill a particular calling, to "step up" as it were. We will get into much more detail about the meanings of various phrases in the verse in later chapters, but for now, let's just focus on the idea of being positioned "in between," which is the meaning of the original portion translated from Hebrew as *in the gap*. Even as the verse tells us that God is looking for someone who is uniquely positioned, we must make no mistake at the outset here that God is sovereign, and He chooses to use his people—the Church—to accomplish his purposes in the world. The mystery of it all is that He leaves us with free will to choose—or *not* to choose—to be willing participants in his sovereign plan.

Positioning—that incredible dance of God's sovereignty with our free will—begins with God's purposes, not our preferences. Oh, our preferences have a lot to do with whether we ever hear the call of God to be sure, but this process doesn't begin there. Scripture reminds us that in all things God works together with those who love him to bring about what is good (Rom 8:28). That is why I love to call it a dance. God invites us to "dance" with him, completely engaged in a uniquely positioned pairing with him, as He would lead. The sort of dance designed for a couple is hardly possible for one alone, and I would argue, not very effective or fulfilling. But it has all been designed from the beginning by God to be done together with him for those who love him. Isn't that a beautiful picture of us cooperating with God to bring about something wonderful and beautiful?

At is most fundamental, being positioned is God at work in the world and in the Church. It's not at all about us striving for a position, or to position ourselves most advantageously for the next big thing. From the Garden to today, that's been mankind's downfall, and that's the message we get all around us; Hollywood, the world of sports, business structures, politics, and even friendships and familial relationships are all proclaiming or reinforcing the typical "position is everything" philosophy. The best position is considered one of power and influence—and the people in those positions typically make the decisions. Because of this, there is a general striving with humanity for position. But this is not that. "God is seeking to position his people in places where He himself has beforehand arranged for them to be prepared so that at a certain time—at a certain signal—they shall rise and do what He calls them to do."[3] The Bible teaches, "He made known to us the mystery of his will according to his good pleasure. In him we were chosen...according to the plan of him who works out everything in conformity with the purpose of his will" (Eph 1:9-11). It all begins with a promise! It begins with his purposes. "For it is God who works in you to will and to act according to his good purpose" (Phil 1:13).

Positioning of this sort is rarely readily apparent or even understandable. There are often many years of development going on in our lives to bring us to God's unique position which He has designed for us. And these years are usually characterized by a shaping and molding process in our lives—a carving or chipping away, like a sculptor at work on a piece of granite to reveal the ultimate creation beneath that was in his mind from the beginning. It's a cutting away of the excess.

Bob Sorge—another pastor friend and prolific author from within the Elim family—calls this "The Pruning Process" in a chapter of the same name in his marvelous, vulnerable retelling of his own story (with the advent of a significant physical injury to his voice) in his seminal book, *In his Face*. "Jesus' foremost concern is not your personal happiness or comfort. His primary concern is that you be fruitful."[4] The whole chapter is a brilliant explanation of what Jesus is getting at when He likens us to branches on the vine and being pruned in the Gospel of John, chapter 15. The process is painful. It can be brutal. It can look ugly. It doesn't just happen right away, but it is the calculating, loving and often-misunderstood hand of God at work in our lives.

I for one, as a gardener myself, love to see fruitful plants thriving in my garden. But the advance work that must be done to bring them to that place requires my forethought, a constant review of my design, and my intervention in the natural course of things for each plant. The best and most thriving plant will soon be out of control and threatening itself and the others around it if it is not carefully pruned and guided along its growth process. Now that doesn't seem to make sense, does it? But that's how it works. A thriving plant must be cut back! It must be in order to ensure its continued and increasing fruitfulness.

And the analogy becomes even more acute for gardeners in my home state of Colorado. Our climate in Colorado Springs is described as a high, arid desert. Not exactly what comes to mind when you think of Colorado, right? Instead of miles and miles of the undulating Rockies, green forests, rushing crystal rivers, and purple mountains' majesty, we have long dry winters when every living thing turns brown (except for pine trees that seem unbelievably to be able to thrive growing out of rock!). The biggest cities of Colorado are lined up against the "front range," the eastern side of the Rocky Mountain range, and the state divides into two distinctly different halves. The western half is what everyone thinks of populated by vacation ski towns; the eastern half is where everyone lives! And that half is full of challenges like draught, long dry winters, fire danger, short summers, and hail. All of this creates challenges for the gardener, so we gardeners must be extremely proactive! For half of the year, my garden is dormant, and we don't enjoy looking at it. But I am busy during that time with the hidden preparations and work of cultivating, pruning, and deep watering (on days when it's warm enough to pull out the hose). And after the barren winter, the magic that happens from May to October is exhilarating! It blesses us and every visitor who might come and sit for a while.

As I struggled with the questions that swirled in my head after I shattered my leg, I felt the acute bleakness of this winter-like pruning season. I regularly came back to a frustration that it just didn't seem to be the right "next thing" to come along in my life after I had just committed myself to the unique service that God had apparently been positioning me for all along. But as I continued to pray and journal, I understood that God was taking me from "faith to faith" in a new and deeper way; I found the most amazing peace—a place of rest like none other. So there, amid my turmoil and pain, I could anticipate a future season of greater fruitfulness, on the other side of a grey and barren winter.

We don't want to admit that this process is indeed a scriptural pattern that we see over and over. But we must. From beginning to the end of the biblical story, those who God prepares in advance for a unique position often seem to walk through hell and back before their ultimate positioning is revealed. And if it's not actually physically painful, it's emotionally daunting to the body, spirit, soul, and mind. The years of waiting for the fulfillment of God's plan and purposes are often as painful as the actual events that occur within them. Abraham is remembered as the Father of Faith because he believed God, and it was credited to him as righteousness. But God's plan was taking so long—and he was getting so old! —he found himself in his "winter of discontent;" something must've gone terribly wrong. Joseph had his vision from God as a teenager, then found himself nearly killed, sold into slavery, falsely accused, and thrown into prison before the final chapter revealed God's positioning plan in his life. Surely something went wrong! David was anointed as the future king of Israel but endured all those years of Saul's resentment and distrust, living on the run as he was hunted down. Again, this can't be right, can it?

As I said in my introduction, Moses spent 40 years in Pharaoh's house, then 40 years in the wilderness to unlearn everything from Pharaoh's house, and *then* he was ready for 40 years of ministry! This actually *IS* right. What is God up to when He prunes? He is cutting away so that something new—something *more*—can fill that space. Even Jesus spent 30 years on earth before He was positioned for his earthly ministry—just three short years! What was happening in all those years? The Bible is mostly silent, but we can easily imagine that He was living the human experience, to be sure. And what is common to that experience? He experienced love, joy, pain, sorrow, sickness, success, failure, exhilaration, exhaustion, doubt, temptation, and faith. The list is endless. But it all leads to maturing, until "in the fullness of time," God's plan can be fulfilled. Jesus was uniquely positioned "in between" heaven and earth, to accomplish all the work that becomes the rest of this book. And even Jesus, "Son though He was, He learned obedience from what He suffered and, once made perfect, He became the source of eternal salvation for all who obey him" (Heb 5:8-9).

When I consider the gravity of Charles Sheldon's question, "What would Jesus do?" I cannot help but come back to the verse that inspired his title: "To this you were called, because Christ suffered for you, leaving you an example that you should follow *in his steps*" (1 Pt 2:21, emphasis mine). For all those years leading up to the trip to Kentucky and Asbury Seminary, I was unaware of just how I was to "follow in his steps." But the proactive work of God was developing me up to that time such that I was perfectly positioned to hear his voice, answer his call, and fulfill his purposes that He had designed for me all along.

Our Posture

If indeed this partnership with God is like a dance, and He has extended his hand to us in invitation like a young man at a school dance looking for a partner to join him, then it follows that He is waiting for us to respond to that invitation. The young lady has only herself to blame if she misses the invitation—whatever the reason—and goes home disappointed. This is what happens across the world every day with God's invitation to his people.

God has been working according to his purposes and promise to create for us the perfect positioning opportunity in our lives, but He then stands with his arms opened toward us and waits for us to respond. Our response will be determined by one primary thing—our *posture*. So, if God indeed does the positioning, it follows that we respond in a *particular* posture. Another word for posture is attitude. It encompasses so much, from our outlook on God and on life (our worldview) to our understanding of ourselves and others, and our awareness of the needs of the world (wherein we find our purpose). Our posture determines if we are going to recognize the opportunity when it comes our way. Are we even going to see it? And if we see it, will we understand it?

After the ladder accident, I spent months in a cast and hobbled around on two full-length crutches. My posture was always bent over and looking down. It was the wintertime in Buffalo, NY... need I say more? It was not only difficult, but dangerous to move about or try to go out in the snow and ice that defined our everyday lives for months. I was unable to fully engage with anything or anyone because my posture was so poor, crippled by my injury. I can remember trying to go into a drugstore through a single sliding door, the threshold a pool of icy slush. Taking way too long to do so, I could feel the tension and impatience in the line of people that had developed behind me, but I couldn't look up or focus on them for fear of falling in the slippery wet surface of the entrance. You could have been one step ahead of me offering assistance as I was navigating my way, but I wouldn't have known it. My condition kept me narrowly focused on only my immediate need at hand. This can often be how it is with God's quiet leading—or even his unknown pruning—in our lives. He is working, readying things, inviting us, but we are "looking down," completely unaware of the bigger picture at that moment. We are self-focused and self-absorbed. We are blind to what's happening all around us.

Worse than just being unaware, is being stiff or inflexible when God's invitation comes. Again, the real-life lesson that has personified this for me has been living with an orthopedic leg injury that has hobbled me for the entire rest of my life. Daily I must work out my leg by climbing on an elevated treadmill or elliptical machine, and I am often so stiff and inflexible at the start that it takes 20 minutes before the joints are fluid enough to allow a reasonably normal range of motion, with or without pain. And every day I live with pain that comes and goes, and sometimes the leg almost entirely gives out without warning. Sometimes I even wonder if lopping off the entire lower leg and replacing it with a prosthetic might not be a better way to go! But all of it has led me to embrace God more, like the apostle Paul with his thorn in the flesh, because I'm that much more aware of my desperate need for God and how I must rely only on him—"for when I am weak, then I am strong" (2 Cor 12:10).

Are you stiff or inflexible when it comes to responding to God's invitation? Surely, I was. Anyone caught up in the American Dream version of Christian faith can't help but be. I had my plan, and I was working on it. The plan was comprised of all the reasons why I must stay. At that point in my spiritual journey, there was little room for the Master Potter to do anything more to mold this little lump of clay. Oh, I would say that I was learning and growing in life and godliness, but it was still such a rigid, self-made, self-focused journey that I was never going to allow God to interrupt with a new invitation to dance with him. And, oh how disappointing that must be to God!

The last thing that influences our posture is our perspective. God has the ultimate perspective. From outside space and time, He knows the end from the beginning. We do not. We cannot. If God's perspective is like the bird's eye view, then ours is the worm's! We cannot help but become narrowly focused on what's right in front of us unless we allow God to invade our lives with his boundless perspective. Our limited perspective is usually just that: limited! And as such it is often wrong, too. I once flew over the Sahara Desert in a window seat during the day—both of which were highly unusual. I observed the Sahara for hours seeing nothing for hundreds of miles, then suddenly there were signs of life—human and otherwise. They were barely visible as everything seemed to be swallowed up in the vastness of the desert. But it gives me another picture for perspective's sake. A tree, no matter how giant it might be in that context, is barely visible from the bird's eye view at 35,000 feet. But from the ground rising above the horizon, it would be all anyone would see, drawn to it for its sheer difference as it stands high above the horizon line of the sandy plain.

After our first child was born, we had an alarming event one night at home that illustrates the negative impact of our wrong perspectives perfectly. My wife had labored for over 24 hours to bring our son into the world. Nearing the end of a long day, the baby was showing signs of critical distress. He was posterior and pinching his umbilical cord. When the doctor finally arrived at the hospital late in the evening, he made the decision quickly to take him by C-section. My wife was whisked away, I was left to wait outside the emergency surgical suite, and our dreams were quite quickly becoming a nightmare.

All was well in the end, with Mom and baby both recovering from the stress of it all, but as we returned home, Judylynn was in rough shape. I tried to help with everything as much as I could to relieve her of the extra burdens that were so challenging in the early days right after. So, I would do most of the back and forth in the

The Principles of Positioning

night, bringing our son Drew from his bassinet to my wife in our bed so that she could nurse him, and then I would change his diaper, swaddle and cuddle him and return him to his crib. I would do this at least twice during the night.

One night, I was holding him on my chest in our bed after his feeding and my wife drifted back to sleep. Shortly afterwards, I got up and did the whole routine with him and then came back to bed. I was awakened sometime later by my wife's frantic voice as she was down on the floor looking around, "Gary, where's the baby?!" The last thing she knew, he was in bed with us, so she thought he'd either been smothered or fallen from the bed to the floor! Now I'm blurry-eyed, barely aware of her reality, and knowing that I had put him back to bed, I shouted, "He's not in his crib?!" You can see where this is going. Downhill, fast. While she's in her own thoughts of panic, I'm thinking someone broke in and stole our baby! We each had different perspectives on the facts. And as each of us were gripped by fear that propelled us instantly into fight or flight mode, our precious little boy was snugly tucked into bed sleeping quietly and peacefully. Oh, to have the bird's eye view perspective right at that moment. My wife just looked at me and said, "He's in his crib?"

Now this is just a silly little innocuous story, but what of the bigger events in our stories? We are almost forever bent to only see the thing that's right in front of us—limited, finite, blinded. Will we see that God is behind them, inviting us into his presence through them, that we might know him better and more fully understand the "dance" to which He is inviting us? Our lives are like a tapestry that the Master Weaver is creating, always pulling strings to create the perfect and beautiful thing called our lives. If we never seek God's perspective, we will never behold that work of art, instead seeing only the back: a jumble of strings dangling, cut, or knotted—the mess, the pain, the futility, and frustration of it all. All too often we are bent toward misunderstanding what God is up to, especially as it pertains to painful things, the stuff of life that truly builds character and draws us into closer relationship with and dependency on our Lord. I already quoted C.S. Lewis in *The*

Problem of Pain: "God whispers to us in our pleasures, speaks in our conscience, but shouts in our pain: It is his megaphone to rouse a deaf world." But he goes on with this powerful thought echoing the apostle Paul, "We are most keenly aware of God's character in our suffering. It is when our self-sufficiency is peeled away that we see how weak we really are."[5]

What of Joseph's slavery and imprisonment (wherein he got to explore his gifts of discernment and leadership)? What of Moses' exile from Pharaoh's palace to live in humble rural simplicity for 40 years? What about Paul's thorn in the flesh? What of my own shattered leg? God is positioning us to hear his voice and respond to his invitation. And ultimately—if we want to truly follow in his steps—it's going to require everything we have in our response. It requires embracing weakness and surrendering our self-directed reasons for why we must stay.

> Do nothing out of selfish ambition or vain conceit. Rather, in humility value others above yourselves, not looking to your own interests but each of you to the interests of the others. In your relationships with one another, have *the same mindset* as Christ Jesus: Who, being in very nature God, did not consider equality with God something to be used to his own advantage; rather, He made himself nothing by taking the very nature of a servant, being made in human likeness. And being found in appearance as a man, He humbled himself by becoming obedient to death— even death on a cross! (Phil 2:3-8, emphasis mine).

"The same mindset" refers directly to our posture or attitude. If even Jesus "learned obedience through what He suffered" (Heb 5:8), then we must not resent, despise, or otherwise misunderstand the dealings of God in our lives. As He is positioning us, we must be on the lookout for his purposes, his perspective, and his promise! When we think of all this in light of the big question we're asking here ("How do I fit in your plan to reach the world, Lord?"), then whatever we give up, endure, or humble ourselves to will only more fully reveal what He's positioning us for and what his ultimate purposes are.

Perseverance

If positioning is only recognized by having the right posture, and the right posture always requires surrender, then it follows that we must live lives of obedience and perseverance. Perseverance can best be understood as persistence in doing something despite difficulties, obstacles, delays or discouragement. Does this sound like our stories? How about the stories we've mentioned or the countless other heroes of faith throughout the Scriptures? We will not have the plan of God worked out in our lives without it. We will never answer the question of how we fit into that plan without it. We must have a certain indefatigable determination to prioritize all our lives around only one thing: our relationship to the one who has called us. Not the current circumstances, not our past achievements, not our well-crafted plans, systems, or principles. Our only posture is to persevere in our singular focus on him, the One Who Knows. Eyes up, hands out, feet ready to go—wherever He may lead.

So much of who God wants us to become—in fulfillment of his grand design, his master plan for each of us (Ps 139)—is developed in the waiting. This is where the "pruning process" matures us. It's where the final result of God's design begins to unfold. In the crucible of life, we are cast. And it takes time. Time, and our perseverance to not jump ship in our impatience. Over the years of ministry through EMI, we created a workshop-based program called "God's Workmanship" (Eph 2:10), to help people understand who God has created them to be and then help them discover how they might engage their "fit" in God's plan to reach the world. Many of the teachers and authors around me have done similar things. Why do we all do this? It is because during our lives—in the long periods of waiting, following, and trusting God—we are forged by the fire of God's love and purposes. But the pieces of our lives are so often enigmatic—still waiting to be fit together—that many people never see the final puzzle that God has created.

I created a graphic for workshops that I teach that begins with the acronym that Rick Warren popularized in *The Purpose Driven Life*: SHAPE. SHAPE stands for Spiritual gifts, Heart, Abilities, Personality, and Experience [in life].[6] From that beginning point, my graphic funnels through a directional arrow that directs purpose and power to the main mission of life (mine, and yours).

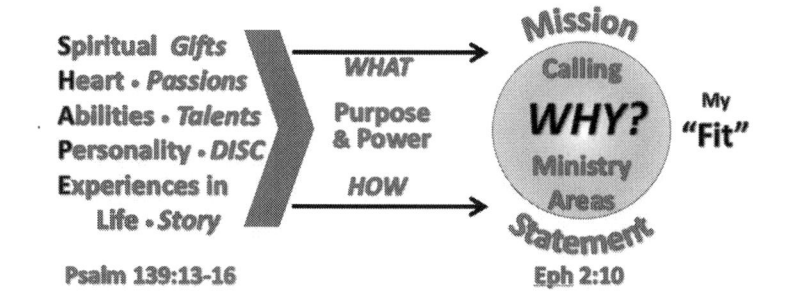

Spiritual *Gifts*   **WHAT**   **Mission**   My
Heart • *Passions*   **Calling**   "Fit"
Abilities • *Talents*   **Purpose**   **WHY?**
Personality • *DISC*   **& Power**   **Ministry**
Experiences in   **HOW**   **Areas**
Life • *Story*   **Statement**

Psalm 139:13-16   Eph 2:10

A second graphic (developed by me, EMI's 4th CEO John Dallmann, and the intern director at the time, Carl Tompson) portrays a Venn Diagram of your life. (Leave it to engineers and architects to use a Venn Diagram to describe spiritual things). The three spheres are your life and story, the things of God, and the needs of the world. Where they intersect is your "Sweet Spot"—what I call the answer to the question, "How do I fit in God's plan to reach the world?"

My friend Dwight Robertson (founder of Forge and author of *You Are God's Plan A*), has a very similar program to do the very same thing and he's called his "The Life Arrow." Dwight also addresses these same ideas in his *Plan A* chapter called "Being You-nique."[7] Rick Warren's last two main chapters of *The Purpose Driven Life* are "Shaped for Service" and "Made for Mission."[8] Why are we all so preoccupied with this? We all are doing this because it is often so difficult to *find the right fit*, the unique fit that is God-designed just for you! And it's difficult to posture ourselves—after we've received the promise, and especially after we've seen pieces of the puzzle of our lives beginning to come together—in a place of waiting, trusting, obeying, and persevering. Especially if we do not yet understand the big picture.

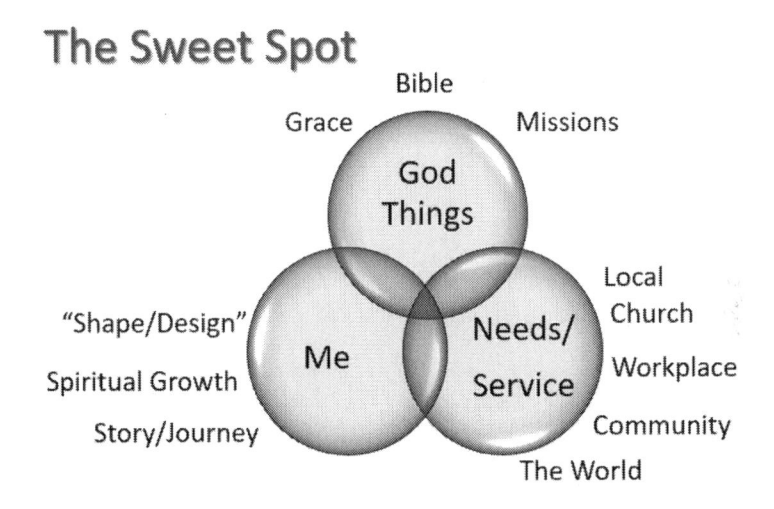

The Sweet Spot

Bible
Grace — Missions
God Things

"Shape/Design"
Spiritual Growth
Story/Journey
Me

Needs/ Service
Local Church
Workplace
Community
The World

Abraham had trouble with waiting. He thought he knew the big picture, but his human timeline and his perspective on the promise of God caused him great frustration. The pieces of the puzzle just weren't coming together as he thought they should. But try to understand and imagine being Abraham in the era in which he lived. In chapter 11 of Genesis, we have the story of the tower of Babel, followed by the long years of family lineage leading up to Abram. We see that he took his family and headed from Ur to Canaan but stopped and settled in Harran. This land was later part of the Assyrian Empire and might possibly be in present-day Turkey. Abram lived there until he was 75 years old, when in chapter 12 of Genesis he hears the command of the Lord to go to the "land that I will show you" (Canaan).

So, who else was hearing the voice of the living God at that time? We have no idea! Perhaps Job, whose story of faithfully following God through an overwhelmingly dark trial is worth recounting;

or the Canaanite king and priest of God Most High, Melchizedek (Gn 14:18), whom Abram meets on his journey. Job most people remember, since there's a whole book devoted to his ordeal. But Melchizedek might be easily forgotten except for lovers of the Old Testament. "...Melchizedek stood as a figurehead or type of God's *general* revelation to mankind, and Abraham correspondingly represented God's covenant-based, canon-recorded *special* revelation to mankind."[9] In any event, we can assume hardly anyone is hearing God! But Abram does the outrageous: believes he's heard God— specifically a command from God requiring action—and obeys him.

> The Lord had said to Abram, "Go from your country, your people and your father's household to the land I will show you.
> "I will make you into a great nation,
>   and I will bless you;
> I will make your name great,
>   and you will be a blessing.
> I will bless those who bless you,
>   and whoever curses you I will curse;
> and all peoples on earth
>   will be blessed through you.
> So Abram went, as the Lord had told him; and Lot went with him. Abram was seventy-five years old when he set out from Harran. He took his wife Sarai, his nephew Lot, all the possessions they had accumulated and the people they had acquired in Harran, and they set out for the land of Canaan, and they arrived there. (Gn 12:1-5)

Abraham is our Father of Faith, and an exemplary model to emulate. After he received God's promise of offspring as numerous as the stars in the sky (Gn 15:5), he "believed the Lord, and it was credited to him as righteousness." God even covenants with him, in a way like no other. Amazing. Truly, this is great faith. But for now, we must focus on Abraham's perseverance, or lack thereof. Abram's crisis of faith is recorded for all posterity in Genesis 16. After living in Canaan for 10 years, Abram and Sarai concoct a plan to fulfill the Lord's inchoate purposes on their own. We have them to thank for the middle east conflict of Arabs and Jews in the millennia that follow!

Waiting can be downright tragic for Christians. We've just got to *do* something! "Be still and know that I am God (Ps 46:10)"? Seriously? I don't think so! Let's get going and fulfill the plan that we've received from the Lord! Paul recounts the very real tragedy of this in his letter to the Galatian church:

> For it is written that Abraham had two sons, one by the slave woman and the other by the free woman. His son by the slave woman was born according to the flesh, but his son by the free woman was born as the result of a divine promise. (Gal 4:22-23)

In desperation, he tried to finish in the flesh what God had begun in the Spirit. God's not speaking right now? Perhaps we can fill in the blanks ourselves! No! Wait for the promise! Don't birth an Ishmael when God has promised you Isaac!

Desperation, which comes from fear—which is not of God—only leads to works in the flesh. How many times—because God's positioning process is taking too long or is forcing us to wait—have we devised a plan when God has promised us something? It's possible to mimic the Spirit—we've seen it all too often. But left to our own devices, we cannot do anything but create counterfeit substitutes that will never fully achieve God's purposes, nor will they reveal the glory of God to a world in desperate need of Him.

> Who among you fears the Lord
>   and obeys the word of his servant?
> *Let the one who walks in the dark,*
>   *who has no light,*

> *trust in the name of the* LORD
> *and rely on their God.*
> But now, all you who light fires
> and provide yourselves with flaming torches,
> go, walk in the light of your fires
> and of the torches you have set ablaze.
> This is what you shall receive from my hand:
> You will lie down in torment. (Is 50:10-11, emphasis mine)

This is the terrible truth of the fruit of trying to make our own way. If we insist on lighting our own torches and determining our path in any other way than total reliance on God's leading and guiding, we will receive torment as a reward. Better to learn how to embrace a journey in the dark: it is in those places that we truly learn to trust him, rely on him, and see a faith grow in us that can move mountains.

I'd be remiss if I didn't share all the second-guessing and doubts we had in the process of waiting and watching God move on our behalf as we responded to his leading and obediently embraced the things we needed to do. This was hard—the process of putting an ax to the root of everything that held us in the grip of our American Dream version of Christianity. It was not all sunshine and roses and miraculous answers to prayer. It was constantly challenging, not only because of our own doubts, but also as a result of the probing, thoughtful questions from our family and friends. On any given day, my wife would be strong in faith while I was asking myself if what we were doing wasn't just a little too crazy? She was, after all, the one who for years had asked me if I was sure we were where God wanted us to be while we were "working the plan" for our lives. Then, there were other days where she would vacillate, and I would have great resolve knowing confidently that we absolutely must *not* stay. I am so thankful for her partnership in the adventure. Without total and complete trust in God and in each other, it would have been impossible. Truly, "two are better than one, because they have a good return for their labor: If either of them falls down, one can help the other up" (Eccl 4:9-10).

When we began traveling around the New York area preaching in churches and sharing our call to missions, we began to receive confirmation and encouragement, and an answer to the very prayer I voiced asking God to help me connect with people and inspire them toward this same kind of journey. One of the first letters we received came unexpectedly from someone whom we hadn't even met yet—

> *[Yours] has been a message like none other in my life. "Submission, Obedience, Perseverance" has become my daily theme. It's just as you said in your message; it's positioning and posturing and circumstances that you see along the way that just get you so excited about God and what He's doing that you can hardly contain yourself. But without your message on positioning, I probably would still be saying, "God, okay, if I'm really hearing your word, where's the answer? How long am I going to have to wait, what should my next move be?" And although I'm still waiting today, I'm waiting with a different perspective. I know that for me to become God's agent, God not only has to position me, but others as well so as to permit my entrance into this service for Him...perhaps it takes his perfect timing, so perfect that I mature and grow in his ways in the meantime...it hits home how much obedience it takes to get up and sell your home and uproot your life and follow God's calling. And I will take comfort in knowing you have done that, because I too will be required to [do that] in order that I might follow God's calling.*

Pondering... Position, Posture, and Perseverance

The story of Esther as it's recounted in the book of the Bible named for her is perhaps a beautiful place for us to ponder how all this works in God's master plan for positioning, posturing, and persevering. What do we know about Esther? Not much, except that she was apparently a beautiful Hebrew girl, *and* she had a faithful uncle. Through circumstances that might otherwise seem just lucky, God positions Esther in the most advantageous and influential place for the sake of the rescue plan He had in mind for his people. But despite this position, it still takes her Uncle Mordecai to speak "truth to power" and admonish her to embrace right posture and perspective. "And who knows but that you have come to your royal position for such a time as this?" (Est 4:14b). In that moment, she understood the magnitude of the *position* she was in; and in a *posture* of understanding, submission, and obedience, she embraced the work of God in her life and *persevered* to the end! "Then Esther sent this reply to Mordecai: "Go, gather together all the Jews who are in Susa, and fast for me. Do not eat or drink for three days, night or day. I and my attendants will fast as you do. When this is done, I will go to the king, even though it is against the law. *And if I perish, I perish*" (Est 4:15-16, emphasis mine).

We know the end of the story: God prepared the heart of the king in advance to receive her and permit her an audience with him, at which point she could "present her case." In the end, the miraculous rescue of God's people is celebrated down through the ages, and the purpose for which God created her was fulfilled!

Before I leave the story of Esther, I want to bring out one more point. It's the second half of verse 14 that most people remember—the part that I quoted. It speaks of destiny, purpose, and power as we move into the things God "has prepared in advance for us to do." But the first half leading up to that is a sobering admonishment to all of us. "For if you remain silent at this time, relief and deliverance for the Jews will arise from another place, but you and your father's family will perish" (Est 4:14a). As I mulled that over, even sitting in the pew answering God's question, "Are you alright with this call I'm giving you to a humble little-known work that's going to cost you?" I realized this poignant truth: God's not desperate for Gary MacPhee. Amazing, huh? But true.

EMI had even used the word "desperate" in conversations with me. EMI only had one architect, Glen Woodruff. The growing challenge was only made more difficult by our branding—EMI was *Engineering* Ministries International. They were desperate for another architect to join them. Though EMI began its ministry life with small scale civil engineering projects (water and wastewater systems, small foot bridges, etc.) for missionaries, by this point most of its projects were driven by larger architectural programs such as hospitals, schools and orphanages—large scale land-use and master planned projects combining multiple engineering disciplines—and EMI's few project leaders were often a little out of their depth. But still, as I was attending EMI's conference with destiny-related questions on the table before God, I knew God himself was not desperate.

    I needed to face the fact that it was out of God's love for me and his perfect design that He was inviting me into partnership, not the other way around. And if I did not see all the positioning and respond with the right posture and then willingly persevere in the call, I would miss the incredible plan that God had laid out for me to fit into! The truth of the full verse is that God will complete his purposes with or without me, but then what would my life have been for? I would miss out on being propelled by God into the storyline of my own life as He had sovereignly designed. He was inviting me to dance with him. Do I understand? Am I watching for it? Will I respond? Will I join the dance? I began to see my life in the timeline of human history as a blip—with eternity past to the left and eternity future to the right, and there's my life in the middle—nothing but a blip on the radar of eternity. But it became so powerful to me, so urgent, that I felt like I had to answer for what I was going to do with my blip! Is it going to be about amassing wealth, houses, cars, and a comfortable retirement? Or is it going to be something that counts for eternity?

    I am reminded now of my first ever mission trip as a volunteer with EMI. It was one of the steps we committed to taking toward investigating those six open doors we mentioned, and though it was only to a small island country off the Atlantic coast of South America on the edge of the Caribbean, it may as well have been halfway around the world (little did I know what my future would hold!). My family was with me in the airport to see me off at the gate. This was customary and allowed in the days before 9-11 and heightened airport security. When the time came to board the plane, I began to gather my wife and children to say a personal goodbye to each one. Four-year-old Hillary was nearly oblivious in her simple trust, dancing and singing around the gate area. "Are you going somewhere Daddy?" All the weeks of talking, planning and praying were unconnected to this moment. Ten-year-old Drew was almost aloof, caught up in the excitement, wandering to the terminal windows, fascinated by the sheer size and closeness of the huge aircraft. I had to call him over to focus on saying good-bye. But seven-year-old Zachary had quietly tucked himself into Judylynn's side. Hiding his face, he had begun to cry, understanding the reality and feeling the weight of our two-week separation. He had never before lived through anything like that.

As I sat down in my seat in the plane, I looked back toward the window where my family was and thought of how each one of my children paralleled different postures that we often take in our walk with God. Like Hillary, we sometimes ignorantly but happily meander through life unaware of God's real purposes. Other times, like Drew, we understand God's purposes, but in enthusiasm and confidence we become rather self-absorbed, blinded by what's right in front of us. Then there are those moments, where we, like Zac, combine the understanding of God's purposes with a tender, trusting, and obedient heart—and it crushes us. At that moment, as my children demonstrated my own behaviors for me, tears welled up in my eyes and I prayed, "Lord, make me like Zac."

CHAPTER 3

THE MISSIONARY HEART

Jackie Pullinger:

[For] about 30 seconds I really enjoyed knowing I had eternal life. I was in a little Bible study class, and this was many years ago, and it was one of those ones where you fill in the blanks. I always think you have to be very stupid not to get 100% in those. And anyway, we filled in the blanks, and it said, you know "For God so loved the blank that He gave his blank that blank believes in blank, blank should receive blank," so I filled in the blanks, and I knew I had eternal life. And then we got to pray. And this was a girls' group. And they all shut their eyes and I opened mine, and I looked at them and they were all thanking the Lord for eternal life, and I looked at them and they were smiling, and I thought "Oh God, they mean it. Oh, well, I just filled in the blanks and well, I suppose I have eternal life too" so I said, "well thank you very much Lord, that's wonderful" and almost immediately this came into my mind, if that is true, that I have eternal life, then the opposite is also true, that means there are people I know who don't. My friends finished their prayer meeting then, they got onto eating, which we Christians always seem to be doing together, and they were frying something called risotto, and I was very intense, you know, I was very young, and I had just received eternal life, and I thought to myself, "Risotto, how can you eat risotto when people are perishing?!" So I ran out to find some lost, so they could enjoy the risotto, and it is about as quick as that. Always for me. [1]

I don't know why, but something was missing in my own personal conversion. After receiving the gift of salvation and eternal hope, I was not immediately gripped with the condition of the lost, and I am ashamed of that fact today.

I can only speak to my own experience in the church, and the lack of understanding that should've exposed me and connected me to God's missional heart that continually reaches out to people, carries a burden for them, makes the ultimate sacrifice, and then ultimately provides the only "fix." Today I realize that it was all there, but I was rather quickly inculcated in a discipleship model that was largely "separatist" in nature.[2] I was introduced to evangelism as a worthy component of my Christian walk, but it was as if by way of introduction it was something I had to learn to do, like most spiritual disciplines of a godly person...not automatically drawn into it by the Spirit of God taking up residence in me. My spiritual life became exactly that—*my* spiritual life. *My* "walk with God." *My* daily disciplines. Looking back, I can easily see now why my reasons "why I must stay" formed a long list of me and my stuff.

Donald Miller, in *Blue Like Jazz*, said, "The most difficult lie I have ever contended with is this: life is a story about me."[3] Referencing an original C. S. Lewis poem, he continues,

> I talk about love, forgiveness, social justice; I rage against American materialism in the name of altruism, but have I even controlled my own heart? The overwhelming majority of the time I spend thinking about myself, pleasing myself, reassuring myself, and when I am done there is nothing to spare for the needy. [Eight] billion people live in this world, and I can only muster thoughts for one. Me.[4]

Whatever your feelings are about him and his contextualizing of the Gospel for a post-modern world, I believe he speaks for most of humanity. He certainly read my mind! I read the apostle Paul's admonition to the church at Philippi and feel like I fall so far short of this ideal that I wonder how can it ever be done?

Do nothing out of selfish ambition or vain conceit. Rather, in humility value others above yourselves, not looking to your own interests but each of you to the interests of the others.

In your relationships with one another, have the same mindset as Christ Jesus:

> Who, being in very nature God,
> > did not consider equality with God something to
> > be used to his own advantage;
> rather, He made himself nothing
> > by taking the very nature of a servant,
> > being made in human likeness.
> And being found in appearance as a man,
> > He humbled himself
> > by becoming obedient to death—
> > even death on a cross! (Phil 2:3-11).

I come away *wanting* to believe that I can think of others as better than myself (as it reads in the New Living Translation), *wanting* to "have the same attitude that was in Christ Jesus," (NLT) but it flies in the face of a heart that's full of its own arrogance and pride. In my heart of hearts, I know I'm always thinking of myself first, nurturing myself above all else, and believing that—at the very least—I'm as good as the next guy. This comes from many different places in my life, not the least being the over-achieving, people-pleasing root that was established in me by my family when I was very young. But beyond that is simply the prideful selfishness that defines the original sin carried by all of us. So what are we to do about this? How are we to get past this life—including our spiritual life, our walk with God—being more than just the possessions and achievements we fill it with? How do we get to the place where we are not looking for everything and everyone to serve *us*, but where *we* become the servant of all?

A couple years into full-time work with EMI, I was leaving to lead a team to Kenya. That day, I read a daily devotional by Oswald Chambers in *My Utmost for His Highest* titled "Missionary Predestinations." Because of the timing of my departure, it came alive to me in a new way. I was living this very devotional lesson. In it, he said,

> I am created for God. He made me. This realization of the election of God is the most joyful realization on earth, and we have to learn to rely on the tremendous creative purpose of God. The first thing God will do with us is to "force through the channels of a single heart" the interests of the whole world. The love of God, the very nature of God, is introduced into us, and the nature of the Almighty God is focused in John 3:16—"God so loved the world..."[5]

"Force through the channels of a single heart the interests of the whole world?!" How can this be possible? It's not. At least not without a complete overhaul of the human heart. But there's the answer to my deeply held unspoken question. When this happens—and it finally happened to me—it crushes us. There's nothing left of me, but the broken and humble vessel that God has already proclaimed his delight in working in and through. Crushed as I am, my life can be poured out as a gift, an offering to the world for the sake of God's purposes. And finally, we arrive at the place where God can work out in us, through his spirit living in and through us, the very heart of Jesus. And in this way, in our relationships with one another, we *can* have the same mindset as Christ Jesus. Since the day I prayed, "Lord, make me like Zac" on my first missionary venture (meaning, give me a tender heart that's aware of your bigger purposes in the world and will break at the weight of it all), God had been developing the answer in my life—that new heart. A Missionary Heart.

The stiffness and inflexibility that I described earlier as part of our posture problem in seeing the positioning plan of God for our lives, hearing his voice, and trusting him more deeply might best be compared to the biblical reference to a "hardened heart." But how can you say that you ask? I am a believer, and my heart has been touched by God and I love him. Please hear me. We see the disciples not understanding Jesus' miracles because "their hearts were hardened" (Mk 6:52). "Hardness of heart" is not a willful, stubborn refusal to believe God. The disciples were not denying the miracle of the multiplied loaves. But even though they had watched it happen, and even though they wanted desperately to believe like Jesus did, they could not. Their hearts were hard. Hardness of heart is a sickness that afflicts the hearts of sincere followers of Jesus Christ."[6] The Message version of the Bible says, "None of this penetrated their hearts." This helps me see how I was afflicted this way before my heart was quite obviously overwhelmed with the heart of God. "A hard heart is a heart that does not [*fully*] perceive or understand at a spiritual level. It describes a dulled spiritual perceptivity—spiritual blindness."[7]

> Chambers also says, "The first thing that happens after we recognize our election by God in Christ Jesus is the destruction of our preconceived ideas, our narrow-minded thinking, and all of our other allegiances—we are turned solely into servants of God's own purpose."[8]

Ah, now that sounds like we're going somewhere! Finally, the American Dream version of our Christianity can be dispelled, replaced by the call of God—the very heart of God for a lost, hurting world. And instead of living for ourselves—to the fulfillment of our hopes and dreams, "our preconceived ideas, our narrow-minded thinking, and all our other allegiances"—we are loosed, freed, and propelled into our mission and his purposes.

> The whole human race was created to glorify God and to enjoy him forever. Sin has switched the human race onto another track, but it has not altered God's purpose in the

tiniest degree. And when we are born again, we are brought into the realization of God's great purpose for the human race, namely, that He created us for Himself.⁹

My life has been permanently altered, switched back to the track that God intended for all his creation. And even there we have the reference to our very purpose—the chief end of man as it's asked and answered in the Westminster Catechism—to glorify God and enjoy him forever. It will never be possible to actually do both of those things if our lives are full of—and our hearts are hardened by—the superficial allegiances and homogenized pursuits of our Western way of life.

We have to maintain our soul open to the fact of God's creative purpose, and not muddle it with our own intentions. If we do, God will have to crush our intentions on one side no matter how much it may hurt. The purpose for which a missionary is created is that he may be God's servant, one in whom God is glorified. When once we realize that through the salvation of Jesus Christ, we are made perfectly fit for [the purpose of] God, we shall understand why Jesus Christ is so ruthless in his demands. He demands absolute rectitude from his servants because He has put into them the very nature of God. Beware lest you forget God's purpose for your life.¹⁰

And so it is with every missionary partner with whom I have worked closely over the last two and a half decades. The development of a missionary heart within us always begins with an unmistakable *initiation* by God—through a very personal invitation to closer *relationship* with himself—to grow in them a new heart that causes an overarching prioritization of their relationship with God and answer to his invitation over everything else, including their home, career, families, culture and comforts (Mt 10:37). That new heart and new set of priorities almost immediately leads to

The Missionary Heart

an overwhelming *identification* with others and their needs. It's a connection, an undeniable understanding or empathy. It is as if the "eyes of their hearts have been opened" (Eph 1:19) and they see need like never before. They see not only the crushing needs of billions of people for physical provision of all kinds—food, shelter, clothing, education, health care, and more—but they see their desperate need for the loving Savior who alone can bring *restoration* to the brokenness of their lives. Their thoughts and passions begin to align with God's as they are drawn into *intercession* for a world they might, as yet, hardly understand, but are drawn into by the Father's heart for his children everywhere. They see a Father like the one in Jesus' parable of the lost son: a father waiting on the porch and looking for him to return home...a father seeing his son from a long way off and running to meet him, wanting nothing but to offer *reconciliation.* Inevitably, this passionate, life-altering obsession leads the missionary into demonstrative, sacrificial *intermediation* on behalf of the people they are called to, and ultimately, the sacrificial giving of their lives opens the door to the message of *redemption* by a loving God who sacrificed his only son for them.

So there you have it. In terms of a testimonial of every missionary I know—myself included now—we have become a "living epistle"(2 Cor 3:3) of God's very word and call from Ezekiel 22:30. Do you see it? As we dive into Ezekiel 22:30 as our source for exploring God's calling for all of us, my prayer for you is Paul's prayer for the Ephesian church:

> I keep asking that the God of our Lord Jesus Christ, the glorious Father, may give you the Spirit of wisdom and revelation, so that you may know him better. I pray that the eyes of your heart may be enlightened in order that you may know the hope to which He has called you, the riches of his glorious inheritance in his holy people, and his incomparably great power for us who believe. (Eph 1:17-19).

As we will see together, nothing happens that doesn't begin with God and then grow out of our intimate relationship with him. He is the one who can open our eyes, soften our hearts, and lead us in the darkness that is the adventure into greater faith, riches, and power. When we see ourselves beginning to live in this new place of revelation—created to be God's servant, one in whom God is glorified—whatever we had to give up is so far in the rear-view mirror that we no longer want it or need it. The new thing that God is showing us is laid out before us, and there's nothing left for us to do but walk into it with Him.

> See, I am doing a new thing!
>   Now it springs up; do you not perceive it?
> I am making a way in the wilderness
>   and streams in the wasteland. (Is 43:19)

> For we are God's handiwork, created in Christ Jesus to do good works, which God prepared in advance for us to do. (Eph 2:10)

So, if indeed He is looking for us to do any work at all with or for him, then we must first consider that He is the author of it. He is the great creative influence at work in the earth and in our lives, having put his imprint on us. And in every way, God has demonstrated for us—modeled for us—the work that He invites us to do in partnership with Him. Everything He calls us to do has already been done or established by God through his never-changing nature, his ever-present work among his people, and ultimately through the work of his son, Jesus Christ. "So, in Christ all will be made alive. But each in his own turn: Christ, the first fruits; then, when He comes, those who belong to him" (I Cor 15:22,23). As Christ has done the work and established the newness of God's redemptive plan, so we all are to experience and participate in it with him.

Ephesians 5:1 says, "Be imitators of God, therefore, as dearly loved children, and live a life of love, just as Christ loved us and gave himself up for us as a fragrant offering and sacrifice to God." Our purpose, our calling, is found in uniting ourselves to Jesus, so that we might know *how* to "imitate" God. Imagine that! Imagine a world full of Christ-followers who actually followed him? 1 Peter 2:21 says, "To this you were called, because Christ suffered for you, leaving you an example, that you should follow in his steps."

The implications of those verses are clear but often not embraced. For there to be new life, there must first be a death of the old. As Christ conquered sin and death through his own death, being made alive once more as the "first fruit," so we who belong to him must somehow die to the old life and live a new life in him. And for those of us who hear his voice and are called, we must know that following in his steps must cause us to embrace hardship or suffering of some kind in order that we might share in his life. In Philippians 3:10, Paul says, "I want to know Christ—yes, to know the power of his resurrection and participation in his sufferings, becoming like him in his death, and so, somehow, attaining to the resurrection from the dead."

You might not think of this as a corollary at the beginning of God's mission to use people to work out his missional plan of redemption, but it is. This is where Abraham found himself as God entered into covenant with him to reach the world through him. God comes to Abraham with a list of promises (referred to as "the promise" or "the promises" by other writers of the books of the Bible) that almost seem too good to be true. God promises to bless him, to make him into a great nation, to make his name great, to bless all who would bless him and curse those who would curse him. But before anyone can think this is "just another example of a petty tribal god whetting the selfishness of an exclusive little clique of followers with promises of exclusive blessing,"[11] God goes on and expands the promises, immediately revealing his bigger purposes—so that "all peoples on the earth will be blessed through you."

But for God's purposes to be fulfilled, He called Abraham to leave the life he had behind. "The Lord said to Abram, "Go from your country, your people and your father's household to the land I will show you" (Gn 12:1). In complete trust and obedience, he did as God said. What he found was the land of Canaan, occupied already by numerous peoples. Regardless of those apparent obstacles, as he arrived in the new land—the land God promised to show him—"God appeared to Abram and said, 'I will give this land to your children'" (Gn 12:7). I can only imagine that Abraham was building a secure future as his wealth and family increased in the old place, but God required him to leave. This must've challenged him and everyone within his family and clan, not knowing what they would find. God was both literally and figuratively placing Abraham and his people in the middle of God's will—among the peoples and the nations—so that his redemptive plan could begin.

To be a part of God's work, to be a partner to Him, I could see that I must walk through this "initiation" of sorts. Until I (along with my wife and children) first embraced the call to leave everything and everyone we had ever known, followed immediately by my life-changing accident, I, as an American Christian, can't say I ever really suffered through anything. As a teenager—before I committed my life to following Jesus—I read the biography of Corrie Ten Boom, *The Hiding Place*, and other historical and biographical stories of believers behind the iron curtain, but never sensed a burden or a conviction that my life was somehow much more selfish than selfless. I came away from those readings simply more thankful that I have the life I have and would never have to suffer like that. Even today, on the other side of this 25-plus year journey, I might read a quote like this from Brother Yun's *The Heavenly Man* and still not understand:

> Thank God He protected and preserved me through these trials. I knew that God was using the wrath of evil men to accomplish his purposes in me, to break down my self-centeredness and my stubbornness. He taught me how to wait on him, how to patiently endure hardship, and how to love the family of God in a more real way.[12]

The Missionary Heart

Wow! Brother Yun, an evangelist of the church in China, was tortured to near-death in prison and he writes this about his captors and prison guards?! I say things that sound like that about bad traffic! Embracing hardship is incongruous with the American Dream, and that is certainly part of our problem. To answer the question posed to me—and that I'm posing to you—"Why must you stay?" we are required to go back to Jesus' original command to those present at the moment He gives the Great Commission. Both Matthew and Mark end their Gospel accounts with the words of Jesus as quite an imperative command that would take them into all the world:

> Therefore *go and make disciples of all nations*, baptizing them in the name of the Father and of the Son and of the Holy Spirit, and teaching them to obey everything I have commanded you. And surely, I am with you always, to the very end of the age." (Mt 28:19-20, emphasis mine)

> He said to them, "*Go into all the world and preach the gospel to all creation.* Whoever believes and is baptized will be saved, but whoever does not believe will be condemned. And these signs will accompany those who believe: In my name they will drive out demons; they will speak in new tongues; they will pick up snakes with their hands; and when they drink deadly poison, it will not hurt them at all; they will place their hands on sick people, and they will get well."

> After the Lord Jesus had spoken to them, He was taken up into heaven and He sat at the right hand of God. *Then the disciples went out and preached everywhere*, and the Lord worked with them and confirmed his word by the signs that accompanied it." (Mk 16:15-20, emphasis mine)

The meaning from the original Greek text implies a continual state of going—as you go, while you are going, at the same time as you go. This ought to be our first clue that every believer must embrace the Great Commission in their everyday lives. Sadly, our own selfishness and "preconceived ideas, our narrow-minded thinking, and all of our other allegiances" tend to extinguish the flames of a growing missionary heart in God's people. We cannot escape Jesus' command to "Go and make disciples *of all nations.*" That requires going to *all the world,* just as the account in the gospel of Mark says! And precisely because that's hard—it requires hard sacrifices to be made—the average missionary speaker will give a challenge and an invitation to an audience and ask, "Who feels called to go?" More often than not, a very small number of people respond to that question with the conviction that they are called to go. Instead, Jackie Pullinger opened her message from the very moment she began with a reverse call, recognizing that Jesus' command to go was a universal one to the Church. Instead, she gives us permission to stay, only if you're called to stay. But how many people have actually asked and answered *that* question? As it came to me, "Why must you stay?" my answers were foregone conclusions and summary judgments, not the result of thoughtful study, analysis, or spiritual conclusions from spiritual beginnings. Pretty simply, my staying was just because that's how things were, always had been, and always would be.

But every time in Scripture that we see God looking for people to partner with him, God then leads them out of where they were, out of the way things always had been, and into something new, often through seasons of preparation, darkness, and molding of new character. Then they are ready to live out the purpose for which God had called them—to "go into all the world." The heroes of the faith all have stories like this: Abraham, Joseph, Moses, Esther, David, Jesus. As we go into all the world, committed to the imperative of making disciples, we will find God there in those unknown and dark places where we might have no other light but Him. Like Corrie Ten Boom's sister Betsie had encouraged her from within Ravensbrook—the Nazi women's death camp to which they were sent—"There is no pit so deep, that God's love is not deeper still." Today, if you would embrace this journey through the study of

Ezekiel 22:30 and the testimony of the Church worldwide in service to the poor, the lost, the broken, and the stranger, you just might find God in a way that you have never before, and you might also find your name added to the list.

And because each of us begins a new journey the moment we commit to following Jesus, Scripture provides a key to understanding how it gets worked out in us. We become new creations (2 Cor 5:17), and there is a new future for us to walk into, and that's where God begins the "destruction of our preconceived ideas, our narrow-minded thinking, and all of our other allegiances and we are turned solely into servants of God's own purpose."[13] Therein lies the reason Ephesians 2:10 follows verses 8 and 9! "For it is by grace you have been saved, through faith—and this is not from yourselves, it is the gift of God— not by works, so that no one can boast. For we are God's handiwork, created in Christ Jesus to do good works, which God prepared in advance for us to do" (Eph 2:8-10). We are filled with the Spirit of God at the moment of this decision—the day we committed to follow Christ. And it's a continuing thought that this act of receiving the gift of God—that has been begun in us by the Spirit of God—now has a missional future. No work has been done by any of us to this point to get us here—it's all God's work, his provision, his gift, his solution to the brokenness of humanity.

Now we can be introduced to all that God has designed us for! That gets us excited, doesn't it? To think, according to his good plan and purpose (Eph 1:11), He's been working to position us in places to do these good works that He's already prepared for us to do. This is where you will begin to see your unique fit in God's plan to reach the world! We are not about inventing something, as if we must find new things that meet our sense of purpose. No, it's just the other way around…we find our sense of purpose as we invest ourselves in these works of God that He's called us into partnership to do with him!

But before any of this can happen, we must come face to face with dying to the old life that He may give us new life—his new life, so that He can live through us to accomplish all this work! "And He died for all, that those who live should no longer live for themselves, but for him who died for them and was raised again" (Rom 14:7). "For Christ's love compels us, because we are convinced that one died for all, and therefore all died. And He died for all, that those who live should no longer live for themselves but for him who died for them and was raised again" (2 Cor 5:14-15). "I have been crucified with Christ and I no longer live, but Christ lives in me. The life I now live in the body, I live by faith in the Son of God, who loved me and gave himself for me" (Gal 2:20). This is truly where the "destruction of all our...other allegiances" happens.

Once we understand this basic idea and embrace the real sacrifices that God might require of us, we can begin to understand how we step into real partnership with God. Amazingly, as I found it laid out in Ezekiel 22:30, this outline follows the process of how a missionary heart develops and grows. It breaks down Ezekiel 22:30 into short phrases that summarize the work of God and his invitation to us to join him in his work. These steps will serve as the titles of the remaining chapters of this book.

"I looked for someone among them who would build up the wall and stand before me in the gap on behalf of the land so I would not have to destroy it, but I found no one." Ezekiel 22:30

Initiation—	"I looked..."
Relationship—	"...for someone..."
Identification—	"...among them..."
Restoration—	"...who would build up the wall..."
Intercession—	"...and stand before me..."
Reconciliation—	"...in the gap..."
Intermediation—	"...on behalf of the land..."
Redemption—	"...so I would not have to destroy it..."
Inference —	"...but I found no one."
Revelation —	Will you be found?

Chapter by chapter, we will learn how God has established the precedent, so to speak, and how we can—following in his steps—do the same. And whether we are called to go or called to stay, we can begin to see how we can follow him in all that He is leading us to do. Indeed, it's not just that we *can*, but that we *must!*

PART II

GOD'S HEART FOR THE WORLD

CHAPTER 4

INITIATION

"I looked..."

*"**I looked** for someone among them who would build up the wall and stand before me in the gap on behalf of the land so I would not have to destroy it, but I found no one."*
Ezekiel 22:30

"I looked" is laden with *initiation*. As Ezekiel speaks the word of the Lord, he establishes that it is God who is instigating this invitation and call. Flash back to "In the beginning," perhaps the greatest primer to the initiating nature of our God; the Bible reader knows that God is the divine creator who initiated everything (Gn 1:1). Literally, He started everything, created everything. Apart from this reality, we are left to determine our own purpose or fate in the human order of things. Answering the questions in my introduction (Why am I here? How do I live? What must I do?...) becomes increasingly difficult, dependent on our own thoughts and ideas, deciphering the meaning of life from the perspective of a single-celled organism's (or even inert amino acids!) evolution over millions of years quite accidentally.

John's Gospel reinforces the theme that begins the Old Testament, establishing Jesus as one with God, and that all creative initiating work was done through him (Jn 1:1-3). Verses 4 and 5 provide even more clarity to the answers to our fundamental questions searching for the meaning of life in a blinding cultural darkness: "In him was life, and that life was the light of all mankind. The light shines in the darkness, and the darkness has not overcome it."

When we consider again the verses in Isaiah 50 about journeying in the dark, this can bring us great confidence that though we may not know, we know the One Who Knows! Immediately after the creation event, God is described as moving in the darkness (Gn 1:2). He is the one who provides light in the darkness. We follow him, because He leads the way, and lights the way! Without God's initiation giving us a place to begin, we would be left to sift through the thousands of diverse and contradictory ideas of men and women down through the ages who wrestled with the questions of Who am I? Why am I here? And What is expected of me?

Instead, we begin with the creative initiation of God, where "God said, 'Let us make mankind in our image, in our likeness.' ... so God created mankind in his own image, in the image of God He created them; male and female He created them" (Gn 1:26-27). In making man, God imbued him with abilities and qualities that were within himself, making us resemble him in critically important ways. He has initiated with his creative nature and draws us in to follow after him. How do we know that we are called to this same activity? Distinguished scholar and best-selling author, Dr. Larry Crabb, in his book *Understanding People*, sums it up well. "We bear the image of God. In certain respects, we resemble Him...The obvious question to ask is, in what way (or ways) are we similar to God? The similarity lies not in our appearance but is deeply etched into the core of our personality. God and man are both *persons*, each possessing the characteristics and qualities that make up a person."[1] Dr. Crabb goes on to extrapolate from Scripture what these elements or characteristics are and summarizes the similarities between God and man as the "capacities of personhood."

"To sum up, God is an *independent* person with the capacity to long, think, choose, and feel. A human being is a *dependent* person with the same four capacities. Our beginning framework for understanding people can now be presented simply. Each of us is: a personal being who longs deeply; a rational being who thinks; a volitional being who chooses; an emotional being who feels. Each of these capacities [build] a comprehensive anthropology that can answer the question, "Who am I?"[2]

This God who created us in his image—what the Bible would reveal as these four capacities—then commissions his first created human beings with a job to do. His first assignments to Adam required initiation, including working, protecting, and *cultivating* the Garden (Gn 2:15). Clearly, this was intended to go far beyond caring for the bushes! It was a broad command related to developing the culture of the earth, as it pertained to being fruitful, multiplying, and taking dominion. It was a commission that did not disappear as a result of the fall, but was then redefined in a long, protracted journey from brokenness to final restoration. And as part of that long journey, over and over we find God not giving up on the creation that bears his image, but continually looking for humanity, always initiating—"I looked for someone..." *to do something with me!* To initiate, to create, to cultivate.

Gabe Lyons addresses this well in *The Next Christians*. In the chapter titled, "Creators, *Not Critics*," he says,

> ...the kinds of goods we create say a lot about their creator and how things ought to be. And the "next Christians" recognize that. They see in God's original job description for mankind that they have a role in partnering with God to fill the earth—creating culture that affirms his values of goodness, truth, and beauty. It shouldn't surprise us that being "creators" is embedded in our original human DNA. We are made in the image of our Creator, and He has called us to exercise our dominion and stewardship by creating and cultivating culture on the earth (Gn 1-2). Though sin corrupts our world, desires, and motivations, we can continue to partner with God as culture creators to restore his intentions for our world.[3]

From the very beginning of Scripture, Christians are introduced to a God who calls his creation "very good." Genesis poetically tells the story of God breathing life into humans and forming them in his own image (the *imago dei*). Knowing God's image exists in every human being explains why all of us—not just Christians—know how to love and be generous, creative, kind, and caring. As people naturally seek to know where they've come from and what they were made to enjoy, the good design of creation explains a lot. For one thing, creation shows us how things ought to be. Our fascination with beauty, hunger for relationships, bent toward goodness and justice, and longing for connection with a transcendent God are all clues about our origins.[4]

We have all of these things in the collective life of mankind because of the creative initiation of God at the very beginning of the creation story.

Scripture repeatedly reminds us that He is still initiating from beginning to the end of the story. Immediately after the Fall when Adam hid himself from God, God went looking. He of course had an already-established pattern of "walking with him." (We'll explore this more in Chapter 5). He initiated. "The Lord God *called to the man*, 'Where are you?'" (Gn 3:9). Much later, speaking through the prophet Hanani, God reminds his people to follow him and rely on him alone: "For the *eyes of the Lord range throughout the earth* to strengthen those whose hearts are fully committed to him" (2 Chr 16:9, emphasis mine). In a warning to the shepherds (the leaders) of Israel, God speaks through Ezekiel again, "For this is what the Sovereign Lord says: *I myself will search* for my sheep and look after them" (Ez 34:11, emphasis mine). And in the New Testament, He promises us that his purposes will be fulfilled in us by his choosing us—looking for us, initiating in us—"You did not choose me, but *I chose you* and appointed you so that you might go and bear fruit—fruit that will last..." (Jn 15:16—emphasis mine).

I never saw it coming—God looking for me. Clearly, He had ordered my steps to the very moment I heard him ask, "Why must you stay?" Perhaps I should say *I* wasn't looking for *Him*, or a new creative work to join him in. But just the same, He might as well have been asking, "Gary, where are you?" He was searching for me, choosing me, and appointing me. But would I respond as one whom God had chosen for this mission? As this new missionary heart was being transplanted into me, I could begin to see the fruitfulness for the sake of the kingdom that lay ahead.

Really, I am quite amazed at this characteristic of our God. We worship and proclaim his sovereignty—the Almighty who rules over heaven and earth—yet He relentlessly pursues us—looks for us—that we may know him, partner with him, and accomplish his will with and for him. "What is mankind that you are mindful of them, human beings that you care for them?" (Ps 8:4). Again, I just don't know why He bothers! Well, of course I do, but I know I wouldn't bother with me if I were him! I would have to say, I could mark specific times He looked for me and I heard his call and responded. It was a bit like the seasons in Moses' life, but instead of 40-year periods, it was 16. I lived my first 16 years in the house of my parents, receiving and inheriting whatever was there, for good or bad. The wealth of understanding of this—now many years later—is the subject for another book! At 16, I heard God calling, "Follow me." I responded and followed him (see sidebar—He Looked for Me). I then proceeded to live into what today I can clearly see was a training ground for 16 more years, at which point, I heard his call again: "Why must you stay?" And like Abraham, it led me to pack up my family and everything I owned and "go to a land that He would show me, to a people who were not my own" (Gn 12:1). And 16 years later, after living in that land, serving overseas alongside many missionaries, I heard him again as He called to me. This time it was a call to write. He put the burden on me to write this book, as clearly as He spoke to the prophets, "Write in a book all the words I have spoken to you" (Jer 30:2).

I confess, early into the missionary service years, I had gotten myself perhaps a little too far to one extreme as I embraced God's divine sovereignty, his ultimate responsibility for everything He's initiating, and Esther 4:14. It was true, God was not "desperate" for Gary MacPhee. He was not on his heavenly throne wringing his hands in wonder or worry over whether or not I would willingly participate and respond to his invitation to "spend myself on behalf of the hungry" (Is 58:10). But I had really moved to such a self-deprecating posture it was as if God would've just as easily spoken into existence the things He was calling me to do, and He really didn't need me at all. I opened with some of this thought in my introduction—Why does God bother using broken, limited, selfish beings at all, when He spoke creation into being? After all, He is the author and creator of all things; He alone initiates; He alone gave order to the universe!

On my first missionary venture to lead a team of volunteers for EMI, we headed deep into the interior of the Brazilian Amazon rainforest. Quite an initiation for me! Absolutely nothing from my previous city-boy life prepared me for it. Our team left Miami at one in the morning on a Monday, flying overnight to Manaus, Brazil, a city of two million people in the center of the country on the Amazon River. From there we took a double-decked, wooden, pirate-like riverboat for another 24 hours down the Amazon to the coastal town of Maues. We slept on hammocks (that we had to buy in Manaus!), swinging shoulder to shoulder with strangers along the rails of the creaking boat. Overnight, at a dozen different little port stops, everything imaginable came on and off that boat—whole families with little children, bagged loads of rice and beans, grain and feed, crated chickens, construction materials, luggage and shipped goods, and a motorcycle! We arrived a day later, sleepless and dog-tired.

Maues is the little village in the Amazon close to where YWAM (Youth with a Mission) had "set up shop." The first morning as we woke up inside our mosquito nets to a cacophony of jungle sounds around 6 a.m., someone said, "This is the best summer camp I've ever been to—where did they come up with all these jungle noises?" It was a landmark learning experience...sort of a baptism by fire and a "jump in with both feet" kind of thing. Piranha and alligators in the river, snakes and monkeys in the trees, tarantulas, and spiders that could blind you for a day were our companions. Ever since that very first leadership responsibility, I have prepped my new volunteers with this perspective-altering advice inspired by that team-member: "in serving with EMI, think of camping in the desert or jungle, and anything better than that will be a surprise."

The vision of impacting the thousands of impoverished villagers in the interior was amazing to us, and I was so privileged to come alongside them to help make it happen. But where did this vision come from? And how was anybody even aware of this need? It was awesome and humbling to know that somehow we had been invited by God to partner with him in this ground-breaking outreach. I took a great team of engineers and architects to survey 100 acres of jungle and develop a masterplan for a Bible Training Center serving the Satéré Indians under the leadership of Mark Barnes, a YWAM veteran, and his Brazilian wife, Iris. Mark's vision was to house and train indigenous new Satéré believers for continued outreach among their own people. Their philosophy was guided by Luke 2:52: "And Jesus grew in wisdom and stature, and in favor with God and man."

They saw that to "follow in his steps," they must *initiate a new work* in the middle of nowhere to help these people—so enslaved by superstition, fear, and poverty—to *develop* into all that God would have for them spiritually, physically, socially, and economically. YWAM's mission is to know God and to make him known—sharing the good news of the Gospel *and* providing hope for a future in this life, too. In addition to our work of surveying and design, we spent every night ministering to the team and the YWAM community, and on Sunday we joined Mark and Iris in a small interior village for their church service and a soccer game afterwards. The "field" was a rough undulating open clearing in the middle of the jungle, and with my leg issues, I wasn't able to play, but the rest of the team did—against Brazilians! Who do you think won?

As we were sharing in devotions together that evening (as all EMI teams do daily), I shared my perspective from Esther 4:14. Namely, that although I know I was doing what I was created for, my life was just an offering to follow God. Just like Esther, He doesn't really need me (or any of us for that matter). His plan would not be thwarted if we failed to respond to his invitation. Mark spoke up with a challenge to me that I will never forget, and it swung the pendulum back to center in my thinking. He said, "That may be true, Gary, but if Esther did not obey God at the moment He put her in a place to accomplish his plan, we might have lost a generation of Jews in the process as they waited for the next person God raised up." Wow. We will never actually know. But what if that was true? We *do* know that God works in our lives over time to prepare us for his positioning. We *do* know that He did that with Esther. We do *not* know if there was anyone else "at the ready" at that moment. From the scriptural record, it sure seems like God—in his divine initiation—put all his eggs in one basket and banked everything on Esther.

I've never thought the same way since. This whole thing—stepping out into the positioned purpose of God, with the posture of the missionary heart, is still a dance. God leads (*He initiates*), we follow, but we do it together, by his Spirit and with our bodies, souls, and minds fully engaged. It can be really tricky too—to stay in step with God, and not lag behind or get too far ahead. It serves as a powerful reminder to me of what God will do through men and women who will put themselves in a place to be used by him to meet the needs of the world with creative initiation...whether I'm in the remotest parts of the Amazon interior or back in the US office of EMI at my desk!

Since "I looked" is so heavily laden with initiation, it's easy to see that his looking for us results in turn in our own "looking," equally laden with initiation. Like Jackie Pullinger's admonishment—go find your poor.[5] When He looks for us He seeks us like the shepherd seeking his sheep. We then must look for sheep in the same way. When He looks for us He is ready to move in—like Revelation 3:20. I invited him in with barely a crack in the door as that 16-year-old kid, and He flung it wide open and came right in and made his home in the very center of my life! Talk about initiation! He *launched* into my life and launched *me* into a new life! When He looks for us He sees us! He's not surprised or repulsed by our sinfulness or brokenness but knows what we need even when we don't. For us to follow in his steps, we must be ready to leave our own life behind in order to take up a life with him.

A bit over a decade before I met him, Roger Blanchard was an insurance salesman in Georgia—and apparently a very good one. I did not know him then. But he took an early retirement and—together with his wife Linda—left it all behind and became a missionary to Honduras, serving people across local villages outside of Tegucigalpa. They evangelize rural mountain villages, train indigenous pastors, care for orphans, and serve the local church. What does he know about doing all that? In his words, absolutely nothing! And yet, there he is, responding in obedience to what God has called him to, and serving God with all his heart, soul, mind, and strength, with whatever gifts and talents he possesses. God has brought increase upon increase to his work there, and when we arrived on the scene, we could see the fruit of it. To hear his stories about the ministry up in the hills, you'd realize right away that we were encountering the Church moving like it did in the first century.

EMI ventured into his mission with him, and that is what built our partnership in the Gospel together. When I first met Roger, I was struck by his absolute ingenuity in his approach to sharing the Gospel message and building partnerships with others for the sake of his missionary vision. First, he saw needs in many different areas— for evangelism, and then pastoral training to equip new believers; shelter for at-risk families and the care of orphans and widows; medical care and education, and more. Though the needs were diverse, his passion was singular—he would find just the right fit for everyone he met. And he would *initiate!* He always had with him a three-ring binder with 8x10 glossy photos and explanations of the needs, and he'd present it like a portfolio of insurance options! But instead of insurance, every potential partner could invest in the kingdom with their time, talent, or treasure—or all three—according to how they connected to the needs! Roger always presented the options, knowing that God through him might initiate *something* in *everyone*, depending on their unique bents or passions. Remember, finding where we fit in God's plan to reach the world has everything to do with each one of us being fearfully and wonderfully made (Ps 139:14), "being You-nique," and putting our SHAPE to best use! Roger would initiate, and let God do the rest!

As is often the case with rapidly growing and over-abundant fruit, some of it was going bad. The Pastoral Training Center that Roger had begun developing was replete with construction nightmares and challenges. The wiring was strung all over (point-of-use water heaters attached to shower heads in the bunkhouse were an everyday electrocution threat!), and the new septic leaching pit didn't work (stay tuned for the play-by-play on that disgusting story!). With development of a nine-acre site already underway and a 60-acre mountain-side site yet to be tamed, Roger was desperate for a clear master plan so he could share his vision with donors and supporters.

Over and over, Roger would express in his humble way how badly he needed our help. He'd never seen nor hosted a team quite like ours. He shared how God had miraculously led them, guided them, and protected them. During Hurricane Mitch, the deadliest hurricane in Central American history, he and his wife plummeted 40 feet off a bridge in their truck—and walked away from the crash! As we learned about the Blanchard's, their ministry, and God's miraculous provision, we grew increasingly inspired to serve them and rescue them from the development challenges they were facing. We looked and saw his need! We initiated all over the campus!

Ryan Nice was a young electrical engineer from Pennsylvania who had joined me a year earlier on a team I led to design a new orphanage campus in Sierra Leone. He wrote after that trip like a changed man, consumed with the desire to know his Lord better, walk with him closer, and to know that he is using his life to the glory of God according to God's perfect plan for his life. He's seeking to know how he fits in God's plan to reach the world! On this trip in Honduras, once the preliminaries were understood for future power needs for the design proposals, there wasn't much more actual design work to be done. So Ryan "looked" around and saw so much need in the existing electrical systems and equipment—downright dangerous conditions—that he morphed into an electrician for the rest of the time there, *initiating* at every turn, ripping apart faulty wiring and those widow-maker point-of-use water heaters attached to the shower heads!

Scott Powell had become a dear friend since joining my team to Haiti a few years earlier. He was still a captain in the army at the time and had no usable skills for that team, but he was absolutely convinced that God was leading him to volunteer. Who was I to stand in the way of God? Since that time, Scott did nothing but *initiate*! He got married, relocated to Denver, left the army, and began working as an environmental engineer. Scott taught himself the basics of developing world civil engineering and water/wastewater design. By this point, he had done three EMI trips and committed to be a part of this team with me again as the lead civil engineer.

It was Scott who discovered that the newly dug septic seepage pit wasn't working. (Warning: the next bit has to do with disgusting civil engineering stuff!) Together he and I pried off the concrete lid—the liquid (and other stuff) was to the top and enough to make you lose your lunch. Hydrostatic pressure was forcing it through the walls just below grade and causing a filthy stench and swampy bog all around it. As we walked around it, our hiking boots oozed into the saturated grassy field. This was a newly dug pit—probably over clay that prevented seeping—and this disgustingly critical condition was brought on by the presence of only 12 extra guests (the EMI team). Roger was expecting many more than that on a medical mission team coming in just two weeks. We needed to act, and fast! A couple suggestions from me, and Scott was busy developing an adapted design to accommodate a new proper leach field that would connect to this seepage pit, effectively making it into a settling septic tank...all while Scott was running a fever and fighting off something himself! The next day we were digging new temporary drainage channels out to a modified leaching field thanks to Scott's quick response—and *initiation*.

I must pause for a moment here to reflect on Scott Powell's story and life, and the impact he made as he followed after God with such faithful initiation. From those early days of getting to know him as a volunteer, friend, and partner in ministry, Scott worked hard to cultivate and re-SHAPE his life for service; he went on to join us at EMI as a full-time staff member and created, established, and formalized our Disaster Response Program. After several years with us, he transitioned to Samaritan's Purse for many more years, and died unexpectedly in service on the field in 2022. Scott's wife, Laura, said that Scott believed

> **The Legacy of an Initiator**
> (Laura Powell's tribute to her husband Scott)
>
> *It is with a heavy heart that I share the news that Scott Powell went home to be with the Lord. Scott had just finished training Samaritan's Purse staff in Uganda, and he was headed to Yemen for a water project. While waiting for the plane to take off, he closed his eyes to take a nap and woke up in the presence of the Lord.*
>
> *While this news is obviously very difficult, I smile every time I think about the fact that Scott left this world doing what he loved most. Scott's favorite thing in the whole world was using his practical skills to demonstrate the love of Christ to people in very tangible ways: rescuing them from their darkest hours following a natural or manmade disaster, getting them drinkable water, equipping them with sustainable practices in Jesus' name in order to improve their lives long term and provide ample opportunities for them to hear the Good News, and training others to do the same work he did. His second favorite thing in the world was taking naps.*
>
> *His philosophy of ministry was "the quality of our work is the platform for our witness," words he first heard from Ken Isaacs of Samaritan's Purse (SP) almost two decades ago, which immediately drew him to want to partner with SP. He wanted to do every project, every task, every interaction, with utmost excellence so that people would see Jesus in him and in his work and ultimately turn to the one who motivated and empowered everything he did.*

that he had lived more life by age 40 than most people live in all their days on this earth, and that if God were to take him home now he would have no regrets. He gave his all, and now he has entered the reward of his labor. I've included some of Laura's tribute to him in the sidebar – The Legacy of an Initiator.

As I think of Scott Powell, I'm grateful to have known him and be one of the witnesses to and recipients of the never-ending, *initiating* grace of God at work in his life. His legacy reminds me of the powerful testimony of those who partner with missionaries to support the work financially and in prayer, because that's where our relationship all began. One of the primary responsibilities faced by new missionary workers is taking the initiation to share the vision with potential partners. I shared how God inspired our message in Chapter 2. We accepted the responsibility to initiate, but the bigger story is the other side of that initiation. Just like Roger Blanchard's partner development, God brought many people alongside us who were excited to learn what God was doing and were tremendously affirming of the faith steps we were taking. Our original initiation turned into more of an interview more times than I can say! These dear friends know where they are called, and as they pursued investing in the kingdom with us, they needed to know all the details. It's almost like they were ready for us before we ever approached them! They knew the "good works that God had prepared in advance for [them] to do" (Eph 2:10). And *they* initiated.

After his early experience with me as a first-time volunteer, before we ever imagined Scott would join EMI in such a significant staff role, he and his wife Laura reached out to us, ready in advance to partner with our family to support us as prayer and financial partners—and even after they joined staff as faith-supported workers themselves they continued to do so! Others have shared with us that they knew God was leading them to partner with us, and they have been some of the most invested and faithful partners in the work with us from then until this very day. Sometimes with very few details their responses were nearly immediate, drawn into partnership by their own missional commitment and the leading from the Spirt of God himself. And beyond the many direct financial donors that build a mission team, others provided for a myriad of other needs in our family—from dentists to hairdressers, borrowed cars and vacation homes, these friends have stepped in to fill unique gaps in our lives. They know where they fit—in at least one of the ways—in God's plan to reach the world!

When God "looks for us," He's already prepared in advance. He comes with the invitation to dance—like so many of our friends were already prepared to do with us. To follow in his steps, we must all be ready to do the same. Like Mark and Iris Barnes, Roger and Linda Blanchard, Scott and Laura Powell, and our many other partners, we step into our places and create new culture in the channels of culture where God has placed us. When God looks for us, truly sees us, and meets us where we are, He doesn't leave us there alone. He's ready to take up residence with us, to fill us, to change us. His ultimate purpose in looking for us? *Relationship.*

He Looked for Me

You may be at a place of spiritual formation in your life where you don't yet see or understand the bigger picture; but nonetheless, God is at work initiating his creative story in you and in your journey. I remember the day that I prayed a prayer of repentance and asked Jesus to be Lord of my life at 16. In a moment of crisis in my life, I prayed. And that was it, so it seemed. Definitely no Jackie Pullinger revelation within 30 seconds of the poor and the lost all around me.

But oh, the next day! God—the one who alone initiates—met me in ways that seemed like a story from the Bible—miraculous, divine, and completely unpredictable and unexplainable, other than He was behind it all. As a junior in high school, I got up and went to school like every other day. I would ride that same city bus every day for over a half hour, from the north side of Buffalo into downtown. That day, for the first and only time, I met a guy on the bus reading his Bible. And you already know the rest of that story!

> *When I got to school, I spent a whole day without swearing. Now that might not seem significant to some of you, but you need to know that I had learned to turn it on and off like a switch when I left my house. I was class salutatorian, consumed with getting the best grades and pleasing my teachers and parents. I did not play all that well with others—or I should say—not many others wanted much of anything to do with me, so one of the few ways I could find to look a little more like everyone else was to talk like them. So that's what I had learned to do. But that day? It was gone.*
>
> *Finally, as an assigned reading for that day, I read—in my public school's literature book—Jonathan Edwards' famous sermon, Sinners in the Hands of an Angry God. How can anyone explain that? That—and the other things—can only be explained by the divine initiation of God to rescue this poor sinner and begin a new work in him. I went home that afternoon and showed the sermon in my textbook to my mother (I don't think I mentioned the swearing deliverance), and she simply and wisely said, "I don't think this was an accident." And dear friend, from that day forward, I can say the initiation of God is never an accident! God sought me, and found me, and never turned away from that work that He began that day. And though I did not understand the bigger picture for many, many years, He was always initiating.*

CHAPTER 5

RELATIONSHIP
"…for someone…"

> *"I looked **for someone** among them who would build up the wall and stand before me in the gap on behalf of the land so I would not have to destroy it, but I found no one."*
> *Ezekiel 22:30*

God is looking for someone who would hear his call, respond in a right posture, and rise up to do what God has positioned him or her to do. God says clearly, "I looked *for someone…*" We might as well say a man or a woman, a partner, someone…*anyone*. A living, breathing human being. Why would He do that? God went looking. Didn't He already know what He'd find!? I've often thought this same question to myself regarding God "looking" for Adam in the garden after Adam's disobedience caused him to hide from God in shame. What was that all about? Certainly He knew where Adam was and what He had done. Certainly He was not taken by surprise. Certainly He already knew the plan of redemption and restoration He would personally fulfill in the unfolding of the future.

We've established in a general sense what God was looking for: relationship with humanity. And not just a transactional working relationship, but a relationship established first in his love and grace (Eph 2:8,9) that leads us into a fulfilling, empowering, working relationship with him (Eph 2:10). God is always at work; He's always been up to something. And though it is often unfathomable and unrecognizable to us, it's actually our privilege to find out what. "It is the glory of God to conceal a matter; *to search out a matter is the glory of kings"* (Prv 25:2, emphasis mine). So God goes looking—at his initiation and invitation, He opens himself to us in relationship, and the Scriptures reveal what happens when we find him; or rather, when we are found by him.

In his uncomfortably honest examination of the American church today, Glenn Packiam says,

> Far too often, rumors about God originate in church. We hear a preacher say something about God with confident certainty, and we take it to be truth. What we don't know is that he heard another preacher say it, and that preacher heard another preacher say it, and so on. We could blame them. But we would do better to blame ourselves for turning down God's *invitation* (emphasis added), for closing our ears and our eyes when He has tried to show himself to us. No technological advancement, no access to information, no invention of convenience has been able to change the strange human impulse to shun God, to cover up and hide, the way the first man and woman did.[1]

In quoting Glenn's *Secondhand Jesus*, I am definitely not trying to place blame anywhere but squarely in my own lap. I am accountable for me and why I "missed it." God is always looking, always initiating, but—as Glenn said—in my blindness, in my over-working, in all my distractions, I missed God's invitation to his divine dance. If you are anything like me, you may have lived the performance struggle of life, continually striving to win favor, approval, and affirmation. Certainly it is a commonly repeated theme among the talented staff and volunteers of EMI, full of top-of-their-class, over-achieving engineers and architects. So much of our performance traps are rooted in a cover-up of some sort, as if the God of all Creation can be fooled or otherwise assuaged by our good deeds. This is often a difficult and knotted up mess to untangle in our lives as we seek to come to an understanding of what it means to be sons and daughters of the Most High God, not because of anything we've done (or not done), but simply because we have his Name imprinted on our hearts and lives, bought by the sacrifice of his only son, and chosen by the Father to be a part of his family!

I have already repeated a couple of times my wonder at this very fact. My friend and prolific author on the subject of true communion with God, Bob Sorge, agrees with me. He—like many others—likes to refer to our intimate relationship with the God who has called us as "walking with God."

> Wow, it's mindboggling to consider that the great God of the universe is so intensely interested in us! When we walk with God, we enter the dimension where God unfolds the secrets of his kingdom...Through Christ, you can explore the glorious riches of knowing God like they did [ancients, like Noah, Abraham, and others]—and even to a greater degree because of the Spirit which has been given to us! God wants to walk *with* us before He works *through* us. So He will wait to act until He finds the right man or woman through whom He can work. To put it bluntly, God works with his friends.[2]

I love how Bob plainly states that God is looking to work with his friends. Doesn't work become much lighter, much more enjoyable, when you are doing it with friends? You don't feel alone when you're with friends. You don't have to bear up under a burden on your own, because the workload is shared. When you read the stories in the Bible of

> *God is looking for those who want to be his friends! Those who will indeed walk with him—those who have settled some things, left some things, obeyed some things, sacrificed some things—all to walk with God. And then miracles happen.*

how God worked in and through the lives of the heroes of faith (the ancients, as Bob calls them), you begin to think, "Well, I know God loves all people, but it sure seems like He likes *some* more than the others!" It only seems that way because He's looking for those who want to be his friends! Those who will indeed walk with him—those who have settled some things, left some things, obeyed some things, sacrificed some things—all to walk with God. And then miracles happen.

Like my recounting of the story of Esther and God's rescue plan worked through her, Bob continues,

> When God has a Noah, He can do a flood. When God has a Joseph, He can give Pharaoh a divine dream. When God has a Moses, He can plan a mighty deliverance for his people. When God has an Elijah, He can send fire from heaven. When God has a Samuel, He can test Saul's heart. When God has a Jesus, He can save the world. Oh, beloved, learn to walk with God![3]

We walk with God because He has looked for us and chosen us—invited us to come hear him, see him, *know* him. And in the choosing, He initiated his divine plan to reach the world. Ann Voskamp, in *Waymaker*, recounts a revelation she had as a young girl thinking about being asked to a dance (an actual dance) by her "Farm Boy" who would later become her husband.

> When you trust that you're chosen by someone good, you can trust that you're always being taken to good places. The chosen are simply the ones approached by an enamored God who can't stop thinking about you. This is worth returning to. This turns and reorients a life. I lit with the epiphany: Where there's chosenness, there isn't aloneness. Feel wanted, and you want for little else. Whatever the dream is, the dream is to feel special. When you feel special the whole world becomes special to you. Chosenness isn't about being better—it's about making everyone know they belong. Know your chosenness—and you choose to make everyone know they're chosen too.

> ...We have not chosen God. He has chosen us. There is no concept of a chosen God, but there is the idea of a chosen people...We do not say that we are a superior people. The "chosen people" means a people approached and chosen by God. The significance of this term is genuine in relation to God rather than in relation to other peoples. It signifies not a quality inherent in the people, but a relationship between the people and God."[4]

God chose us. In responding to him, we choose others. Sounds to me like the beginnings of a missionary heart growing right out of this relationship! Knowing we have been found by God makes us want to welcome everyone else into the same place—to be found, fully known, invited to the dance. At once, united to God in Christ. C. S. Lewis wrote,

> Every Christian is to become a little Christ. The whole purpose of becoming a Christian is simply nothing else.... The Church exists for nothing else but to draw men into Christ, to make them little Christs. If they are not doing that, all the cathedrals, clergy, missions, sermons, even the Bible itself, are simply a waste of time.[5]

He caps it off by saying, "[This] matters more than anything else in the world. Each one of us has got to...[take his or her] place in that dance. There is no other way to happiness for which we were made."[6] Ann Voskamp adds,

> This points the way to a surrendered trust without horizons in him whose holy ways are higher than ours. We want things to be the way we choose—and God wants us to choose to trust his ways. We expect more—and God expects us to trust him more. The ways God chooses for his chosen are ways that beg us to choose trust. It's impossible for us to please God unless we trust God with the impossible

(Heb 11:6). There is no pleasing God without trusting God. Trusting God is no small thing. To God, it is everything. God wants to be chosen too.[7]

It is so critical that we understand this about the relationship that God has initiated with us. Like Dickens wrote at the start of *A Christmas Carol*, "This must be distinctly understood, or nothing wonderful can come of the story I am going to relate." The relationship that has been established by God is by his choice, but He waits for us to respond...to hear his still small voice, to *follow in his steps*, to join him in the dance. No "secondhand Jesus" experience here—every believer has this same opportunity by God's own invitation into relationship! The Lord did not set his affection on you and *choose* you because you were more numerous than other peoples, for you were the fewest of all peoples. But it was because the Lord *loved* you (Deut7: 7-8).

The original Hebrew word used here for the Lord's love is *hesed*. You were chosen because of *hesed*.

> ...[God] can't not choose to be with you. *Hesed* [is often translated] as "lovingkindness," a word literally invented in an attempt to translate the all-encompassing Hebrew word *hesed*... *hesed* is the forever covenantal, always unconditionally, unwaveringly loyal, kind love of inseparable bonding, of divine family, of eternal attachment. That's what *hesed*-love is: *Hesed* is attachment love.
>
> *Hesed* is an entirely singular kind of love that says: you are chosen because God simply and forever chooses to perfectly *hesed*-attach Himself to you. You are not merely endured, you are not hardly tolerated, you are not barely accepted—but *you*—your very being, your actual presence, your whole soul, all of the miracle that is you is wanted—picked, chosen, delighted in, special—simply because your lungs expand to take in his love.[8]

This is relationship for relationship's sake, and an exchange, life for life. We give him our lives, and He promises to give us all of himself, as his Spirit comes to live in us. We walk with him, and his Spirit lives in us! The *hesed* relationship that God himself initiates with us brings new life to us and is *designed* to draw us into faith in him. We trust him implicitly step by step in the dance. And this relationship will carry us to the ends of the earth to accomplish all that He has called us to. "Remain in me, as I also remain in you. No branch can bear fruit by itself; it must remain in the vine. Neither can you bear fruit unless you remain in me. I am the vine; you are the branches. If you remain in me and I in you, you will bear much fruit; apart from me you can do nothing" (Jn 15:4-5).

The impact of God's initiated relationship of *hesed* with us ripples through all the rest of the actions we might take in the ministry work that lays before us in Ezekiel 22:30. "We do nothing out of vain conceit, but in humility consider others better than ourselves" (Philippians 2:3). In *hesed* lovingkindness, as Voskamp writes, we do not "endure, tolerate, or barely accept" those to whom we are called to serve, but to us—like God—they are "wanted, picked, chosen, delighted in, special." This is the heart of a missionary. This is God's heart. And though our names will never be recorded for all eternity, know that you matter to God! Like Esther and all the others, He's built his plans around you. Dwight Robertson reminds us,

> Everyone yearns to personally experience the love of God, tangibly expressed in and through the lives of countless faithful Kingdom laborers. Rather than call a few select people to make a difference, God's strategy is to mobilize a vast army of laborers who go into every place of need in every corner of the world. Significant Kingdom work will be accomplished by nameless, faceless people who do what they can where they are—with God adding the increase to their labor. That's God's Plan A...

All of us—no matter what role we play in the Kingdom—have a meaningful, influential, and critical role to play. No exceptions. You matter to God and His plan. [9]

In his book, *You Are God's Plan A*, Dwight recounts dozens of great stories of everyday people who are connecting with others in the normal course of their lives and finding ways to share the love of God and the Gospel message through the normal everyday life they share. From shared hobbies and interests that bring people together, they "have all found ministry expressions that look like them—based on what they already love to do."[10] This is exactly why I—and Dwight, Rick Warren and many others I know—devote so much of our discipleship time with people to help them discover their "You-nique"ness, their "SHAPE." From my God's Workmanship Workshops, to Dwight's Life Arrow, to Rick Warren's *Purpose Driven Life* curriculum, we all want to see people discover their real "fit" for which God has made them (more in Chapter 2). Dwight continues:

> What if we spent our lunch hours developing relationships and made our homes, apartments, decks, and porches into hospitality centers? What if we stopped spending all of our social time with our Christian friends and began spending intentional time with unbelieving friends? What if we noticed overlooked people and needs, traveled off the beaten paths of our lives, and moved up close to the poor and the marginalized in our communities and beyond? What if instead of pursuing spotlights and stages, we looked around for the mud puddles of human need and waded in them?[11]

Missions—and your mission personally—is always driven by *relationship*. Our intimate relationship with God *births our vision*. Our relationship with friends and co-laborers *confirms that vision*. Our relationship with the world *achieves that vision*. Truly, I have discovered this as a missionary worker, so I say it from the viewpoint of having lived it! Though where you ultimately fit in God's plan to reach the world will have a lot to do with the unique factors of your life, it is not dependent on you being anything other than in relationship—first with God, and then with people all around you.

Gabe Lyons tells a tale that illustrates this very well, but in reverse. Exactly what true relationship-building is *not*. Bill was an evangelism-focused Christian leader in a missions organization, and new to the community. For the Halloween festivities in his neighborhood (which are a real community bonding experience), he decided he would include Gospel tracts with the candy he doled out to happy children.

> *Missions—and your mission personally—is always driven by relationship. Our intimate relationship with God births our vision. Our relationship with friends and co-laborers confirms that vision. Our relationship with the world achieves that vision.*

But the next morning there was a collective groan among the neighborhood moms. Comparing stories…the moms were appalled. As they put the evidence together, they discovered that Bill, the new guy, was the culprit. They were a bit surprised at the energy a neighbor would put into proselytizing their kids on Halloween night. To be fair, [Bill] thought he was doing what was best. Thinking he was building bridges, he had actually accomplished the opposite. His plan to show love to his neighbors had backfired.

…Bill's approach strikes me as ironic. Professionally, his mission was to take the message of Jesus to the world, but personally, he had turned every one of his neighbors against him. His good intentions fell short of any real, substantive progress. He likely ruined his chances of having meaningful interaction [*relationship*] with any new neighbors anytime soon.¹²

He cut off relationship before it ever had a chance. I have observed Dwight Robertson living out his book's message (remember, all books must be lived before they are written!) over gatherings and lunch meetings in restaurants. He lives his mission in a way that suits him, to be sure, but it is most fundamentally a relationship-building life, getting "up close and personal" with people. The care and concern he exhibits in his interactions with every person—from the hostess to the wait staff to the managers—endears himself to them. With repeated visits to the same restaurant, he builds genuine relationships. He learns something about their lives, work, and the challenges they face. He commits to pray for them—and tells them so. On return visits, he checks up on them and allows our business to wait. This is living in relationship that becomes missional by its very nature. Like the early church suddenly established in an antagonistic society (Jerusalem and Judea) or pagan culture (the Mediterranean and middle eastern world), we must recognize that our post-Christian culture of today requires this kind of apostolic witness.

If your growing missionary heart compels you to find those new relationships—to love people where they are, to get "up close to the poor and the marginalized" —beware as your life starts to look more and more missional! Your friends might think it strange. When my wife and I started telling our friends, "We can't stay," they certainly thought we were maybe just a little bit crazy. It just seemed a little too far out there, too far-fetched, maybe even too surprising or "extraordinary." In a seminar at the 1976 Urbana Student Missions Convention, Elisabeth Elliot said,

> ...our use of mythical language tends to glorify missionaries. Missionaries don't "go," they "go forth;" they don't walk, they "tread the burning sands;" they don't "die," they "lay down their lives." Many unfairly place missionaries on pedestals.

But they are ordinary people with ordinary problems. Yes, most missionaries I know are heroes, but only because they are ordinary people with an extraordinary God.[13]

Ordinary people. Laborers. Missionaries at large.

Relationship-building across cultures is perhaps one of the most critical hurdles to get over in any successful service or missionary work. Dr.'s Mark and Doreen Babo are a missionary couple who have been developing outreach projects and hospitals in West Africa for much of their lives. They have hearts for the people of the world suffering with malaria and other medical problems and without access to quality medical care or the means to afford it. Mark is an MD, and Doreen is a DrPH in healthcare administration and an expert in healthcare management, delivery, and its related systems. I wouldn't meet Mark until years later, but as we came to Nigeria to serve them, we were ably hosted and directed by Doreen as she ran their ministry in-country.

Our design team could have done nothing without her incredible expertise speaking into the design process for the new hospital they were planning. Doreen is currently director of Heal Our World, a nonprofit medical missions organization they've established striving to increase access to care for the neediest populations of the world. Doreen has over 30 years of experience and has worked in at least a dozen countries. She is responsible for designing, building, equipping, staffing and managing *three* hospitals in Nigeria, a clinic in Kenya, and an outpatient clinic/diagnostic center in India. She has also consulted on dozens of global projects—one of which we did together in Cairo—related to the design and management of healthcare facilities.

What she created on the ground there in Nigeria could easily be compared to the early church—a community of believers including Americans and Africans partnered together to bring hope to others. They lived, slept, worked, and ate in one building. The EMI team did the same while we were there. We attended church with Doreen—affectionately known by multiple endearing titles like

Doctor, Mama, and Mrs. Babo—and within ten minutes of arriving with our whole team in tow, a message was passed to her asking if her guest would preach that morning. That was me, sitting right next to her. She leaned over and whispered to me, "They want you to preach."

30 minutes later, there I was, preaching from Ezekiel 22:30 to a strange church of several hundred Nigerians and international visitors from which I could sense an overwhelming acceptance, love, and responsiveness. This had nothing to do with me. It was the fruit of Doreen's lifetime of love and service, caring for the health of hundreds and giving her life to that community and people, creating the bridges of trust and relationship that allow the Gospel to go to the ends of the earth.

And speaking of missionaries and heroes, I must once again come back to Jackie Pullinger's testimony to illustrate the power of relationship in ministry—and very possibly, *your* ministry.

> *When you see our lovely Hong Kong team some people ask me "Do you always bring this lot?" No, we usually take different brothers every time. This isn't the best team, they're all the best team. These are not our stars, they're all stars. They're brilliant. We've got hundreds, we've got hundreds who will listen to God. That's why I don't go by myself because they always support me by hearing what God is saying and sharing it. They will listen and they will share. They go out into the streets, and they will work, most of them from six o'clock in the morning until midnight, regularly. Walking up and down the [tenement] stairs visiting families, going to prisons, holding people while they vomit, touching them as they pray, taking them to doctors, wiping up their excrement, shaving them, delousing them, washing them, rejoicing with them, sharing their rice with them—yeah we've got hundreds, it looks like a success story, but it didn't most of the time.*
>
> *Most of the time our story looked like death. Most of the time. Most of the time it didn't look good at all. And if you walk*

this path, neither will you and neither will your people. Not for a long time, because this ministry is very slow to start, and it is very sure to endure. For the poor, you see, learn nothing through books, they learn everything through your life. They can't understand a Bible study on God's faithfulness. They don't know where to fill in the blanks and they don't understand your logic. But they do understand if you're faithful. And that means visiting them when they're late and going on visiting them. Waiting for them, waiting overnight, and when they dare you to stop loving them, because they will, and when they swear at you and when they fight you, and you still love them—and you still love them—and when they cheat you of everything you've got and you forgive them, then they know what Jesus is like. And that's a lesson they'll tell their friends without being able to read. Do you understand what I'm saying? They're always watching. I suppose it's something like Jesus. You see, God could've sent from heaven a book. Excuse me, I'm not being rude about the Bible, but He didn't send from heaven a book to save us, He sent the Living Word; and so we must be a living word, that those who cannot read about him may see him.[14]

Her 40-minute talk and testimonial has so challenged and transformed me, that what I've learned I've integrated into my entire mission. And here are two very personal reflections from my prayer letters on the why and how of *relationship,* how we fit in God's plan to reach the world, and why we do what we do in missions. One was at the very beginning of the transformation of my missionary heart, and the other over 20 years later, at a moment when my heart was growing discouraged.

My own personal initiation into cross-cultural relationship-building came through my very first mission trip experience as a volunteer with EMI… He had been 11 days at sea…his shoulders blistered and bleeding…his hands red and raw from abuse…the scorching sun beating down on him. Every movement is painful. Everything takes more energy than He has. He has to rest now even between thoughts..." I'm going to die. Is anyone out there? God, if you're real, help me..." Orlando passed out.

Orlando is one of thousands of Cuban refugees. His second attempt to leave Cuba was hastily arranged, as rumor spread that he was a marked man. Somehow, his small boat got turned around. Instead of ending up in Miami, he spent 11 days in the wrong direction, heading towards the open pacific. He ran out of fuel and water on the eighth day at sea, and somehow lasted three more days. Raised as an atheist, in a communist country, he knew nothing of a loving Creator.

Orlando was only slightly conscious when men boarded his boat. Their boat, registered in Venezuela, contained sections that were off limits to him. They were men with a secret...and guns. They dropped Orlando on the beach in a country unknown to him, Trinidad. Wandering the streets, he finally found a woman who spoke to him in Spanish. She gave him food and water and put him in touch with Missions International. A pastor and his wife took him in. He began to learn English. He began to learn about Jesus.

From another part of the world and from another kind of life altogether, I arrived in Trinidad with an EMI team, my first overseas volunteer mission, to serve Missions International in the development of a medical clinic. I had come, sensing the call of God to become more involved in international ministry, and asking God for direction. On a private back porch on the pastor's home overlooking densely forested yards that I began to call an "altar" (because I had met God there every day), our two lives came together. I heard his story and was drawn to him. He was engaging and had an infectious smile. I cared about him immediately. We talked in passing over the days, but never alone. Finally, we were on the porch together.

Orlando had just come from drinking at his friend's house. He began to tell me his life's story...drinking, partying, and friends. Because my past was filled with siblings living that way, I could share with him like I might one of my own brothers. I told him that this kind of lifestyle is just an artificial substitute for what we really want and need—God in our lives. He volunteered that he had not yet accepted Christ (so I could gather that he had been invited to). Since he knew so much about the Gospel in his short time in the pastor's home, I asked why he hadn't become a Christian. He said he wanted to be good enough. And there it was. A way to truly connect in relationship with him. I shared my life-struggle of trying to be good enough, to be worthy of love, to earn favor and acceptance. I shared what I knew: sin, isolation from God, the impossibility of ever being good enough, God's love and grace and acceptance of the sinner. He wanted more.

I shared 2 Corinthians 5:17: the old has passed away and the new has come. He began to understand that he did not have to change his life by himself. He asked me to pray for him. I promised that I would never forget to pray for him, but he wanted me to pray for him right then and there. I suggested that he ask the Lord into his heart. He was timid. He said he wasn't ready. So I took his hand and prayed as directly as I could that God through Christ would come into his life. I let him know that he could pray that same prayer on his own at any time. I told him, "I believe God sent me thousands of miles to meet with you right here on this porch. Maybe this is the only reason I am here...to pray with you."

Two men, thousands of miles apart...one calling out to God—not knowing if He is there; the other one knowing God and asking for direction. Events that took place months and years earlier were coordinated by God's positioning work, planning, and initiating so that these two lives would collide on the porch of a mission house on a little island in the Caribbean.

Many years after that first experience in Trinidad, I was heading back to the far reaches of western Kenya, to work in small remote villages beyond the Rift Valley. The night before I left, I received this tragic email from our ministry partner—an American woman who has connected us to the local church there so that we can serve their community rescuing orphans:

> *Please pray for the village of Kabondo, especially for the school children there. I just discovered from pastor Julius that my friend, a dear woman of God, humble, joyful, gracious, passed away unexpectedly recently. She was the children's preschool teacher for many years, and much loved. My heart is broken at her loss. She, like many others, died of complications to HIV/AIDS. Because there are no medical facilities, no doctors, no medicine and no transportation to the nearest hospital 1 ½ hours away, she died. She was not the first, and I know she won't be the last. Many prayers would be appreciated! I know the village must be grieving.*

I grieved. I know you would too. As we get involved in relationship with the world's poor, there's a lot that grips our hearts. And there's a lot of grief. And because of that, we are more resolved than ever that we are called to reach so many who are so unreachable in so many ways! How many times do we go into nearly forgotten places? (Not forgotten by God, of course, only by us.) In fact, it's precisely because God sees where we can't see and knows what we can't know, that He then sends us as his ambassadors and mediators (more on that in the coming chapters).

We were serving native Kenyans of very humble means who have a vision for what God can do through men and women who move by his Spirit. Members of the local church, who themselves have very few resources, have been caring for a growing group of orphans, but the need to create homes for them is great. The church had obtained a small piece of land (very small), in the hopes that we can help develop this with them. I'd be lying to you if I didn't say that it seemed like we were sent to do an impossible task. But I can testify to this—many times now over many years—we serve a God who does outrageous things in the face of insurmountable odds over and over again, when his people will listen and follow him. I am both humbled and hopeful. We know that our job is to respond in faithfulness and obedience, humility and perseverance...easier said than done. "But we have this treasure in jars of clay to show that this all-surpassing power is from God and not from us" (2 Cor 4:7).

I often pose a few questions I picked up from YWAM to my team to debrief them after their often-life-changing experience on the mission field...What did you see? How did it feel? How have you changed? How will you respond? Here's my take on those questions and the very real impact I was feeling:

The formal ministry trip was over. We had held our closing meeting the night before, and then made the trip back to Nairobi in preparation for our evening flight home. Our tour and transport service owner had brought us to a store established over 30 or 40 years ago as a way to provide a living to at-risk women. They had a variety of polished stones, jewelry, pottery, hand-crafted cards, bags and leather goods, all made by the women employees. The team was inside looking for last-minute souvenirs and gifts. I was standing outside waiting for them.

As I stood there, a young, well-dressed, Kenyan woman struck up a conversation and after introducing herself (her name was Caroline) asked me where we were from and what we were doing there. I replied, "We're a team of volunteer engineers and architects from across the US. We've been designing children's homes (an orphanage campus) for a small community out in Western Kenya near Kisumu." She then said something that seemed a bit unusual: "Oh, the children must've loved you." That caught me by surprise. I wanted to put the team in a humble light; but in retrospect, my response now strikes me as a bit strange: "Oh yes, they treat us like we're some kind of heroes."

At that she became startlingly animated and turned more directly toward me and looked me very much in the eye and with a smile almost shouted, "But you ARE heroes! I grew up in a children's home—no parents; my sister with me, and my brother at another home. I wouldn't be here today if it weren't for that. They loved us! And we had visitors just like you, who made it all happen. They would pat our heads as they loved us...and we loved them." She paused to collect herself as she said "I might cry, but I won't because I am strong. They gave us homes and sent us to school—the local kids in the school were jealous of us in the orphanage with no parents! You are heroes *to me*."

I was so taken aback I had to assemble the team outside the store and ask her to repeat her story to them. I don't think anyone on the team except my new team leader in training, Kevin Keiter, with whom I constantly debriefed, could've known just how significant this moment was for me. All week I had struggled with just how incredibly poor this local church community was that was "hosting" us. Kevin and I talked about this almost daily—there was hardly anything they could do for themselves or us except cook us meals twice a day. If it weren't for the American couple who has single-handedly accepted the mantle of support-raising and partner development on behalf of this community and their orphans, this local church could have never even approached EMI. Our team was financing all the in-country costs of several thousands of dollars. It will be this couple's job to raise all the construction cost donations for them, too. Over and over, events that week had challenged me to love in the face of almost feeling taken advantage of—and everything from *When Helping Hurts: How to Alleviate Poverty Without Hurting the Poor and Yourself* by Fikkert and Colbert just screamed at me. Questions within me—and from the team—swirled all week, but the biggest one was, "If church members are currently taking care of these orphans in their own homes, how is creating a western-supported orphanage any better of a solution?"

Near the end of the trip, I had begun to see just how stretched their minimal resources were as they attempted to care for the orphans in their own homes. This was not a sustainable solution to this growing problem of orphans that had been thrust upon them. Apart from outside intervention, it would likely eventually fail. But I still wasn't convinced—so God sent an angel to speak to me audibly! It occurred to me *finally*—but only after hearing this girl's testimony—that the vast majority of all the ministry projects I had ever done for EMI were Western-funded, and dependent upon outside *relationships* and partnership to make them happen. Why was this project any different? Truth be told, it wasn't. It just *felt* different to me, and perhaps that was a propaganda-like message that had forced me too far from center, forgetting that we have indeed been sent by God—*in relationship with him and the world*—as ambassadors to fulfill the Great Commission and the Great Commandment regardless of whether partner investments are equal or commensurate. And if that doesn't include us being "taken advantage of," then it would hardly be worth the calling.

CHAPTER 6

IDENTIFICATION

"...among them..."

*"I looked for someone **among them** who would build up the wall and stand before me in the gap on behalf of the land so I would not have to destroy it, but I found no one."*
Ezekiel 22:30

To be *among them* speaks of that relationship that is established with people, because we are with them. We know them. They know us. *Identification* in its simplest form is knowing, understanding, being like another person. That can almost be intimidating, because if we're not living what we profess it would make our testimony of Christ's message in us worthless. But assuming we *are* living in the transforming power and love of Christ, this relational living "among them" can build a powerful bridge to sharing the Gospel and reaching the world. Whether they are right in our immediate circle of influence—our family, neighbors, coworkers, and community—or we've been sent halfway around the world to live among them, we know them. They know us.

We love and serve the God of gods and Lord of lords who incarnated himself—the most human level of identification—in order to connect with people in relationship. Incarnated!? If we don't pause on that for at least a moment, we'll miss something essential, and of course, miraculous. God's love for humanity drove him to give himself from the very beginning. As the Apostle's Creed summarizes, He was "born of the Virgin Mary, suffered under Pontius Pilate, was crucified, died, and buried; the third day He rose from the dead." He knew all of this would transpire even before He uttered the words, "Let there be light" (Gn 1:3). He offered his *life* as a substitutionary sacrifice for *our sin*. This is the Gospel, and this is the uniqueness of Christ.

What ultimate sacrificial lengths God took to send his Son to reach us, communicate his love to us, reveal the kingdom of heaven to us, and pave the way back to Himself! The Son left the throne room of Heaven, an equal member of the triune godhead, and became a common man. To be among us. "The Word became flesh and made his dwelling among us" (Jn 1:14). Leaving no room for doubt as to how to follow in the Lord's steps, Paul commands the Philippian church, "In your relationships with one another, have the same mindset as Christ Jesus: Who, being in very nature God, did not consider equality with God something to be used to his own advantage; rather, he made himself nothing by taking the very nature of a servant, being made in human likeness. And being found in appearance as a man, He humbled himself by becoming obedient to death—even death on a cross" (Phil 2:5-8).

It is easy to see how relationship drives us to the ends of the earth with a missionary heart. When we serve in a foreign context, we are very literally copying the model Jesus gave us, as we follow in his steps. Leaving everything that is comfortable, familiar—and often blinding and crippling to us spiritually—we venture into the culture of another people group. We embrace the challenges of "clothing" ourselves in a new language, culture, traditions, history, and even worldview, that we might know and be known. We have *become like* those in our new community.

Identification leads immediately to immersion in the lives of those we are sent to reach. In love, we become involved in their lives. The Great Commandment draws us into relationship quite naturally, as it should be. With its coupling with the Great Commission, we have the perfect doorway to present the truth of the Gospel to people in love, grace, truth, and power. Evangelical workers in relief and community development call this "integral mission." And Jesus' whole mission was "relief and development!" Jesus came to bring "relief" from the bondage of sin and darkness, and to "develop" his kingdom and his character in the hearts of humanity!

When we think of sharing the Gospel, we can take identification a step further—we share that common trait of having been trapped in sin with no way out on our own. With the missionary heart growing within us, compassion grows, love grows, the Spirit of God grows in us, and we can reach out to people with that fact in common. And as we go into all the world, we are "living epistles" (2 Cor 3:3). We are sent by the God who has looked for us and put his spirit in us. We go, looking for others. Find your poor, Jackie Pullinger said. It's that same spirit of looking, seeking, finding. Again, in Jackie's words: "He didn't send from heaven a book to save us, He sent a living word, and so we must be a living word, that those who cannot read about him may see him."

When I think about Jesus' example, both as God come in the flesh to identify with us and to build a relationship with humanity *and* how He demonstrated relationship among the people with whom He walked for his three years of ministry, I am challenged, to say the least. More like ashamed. Jesus' approach to people speaks deeply to the idea of identification. And He connected with people—even those who hated him—on a level where relationship was always available. He did not close off those who would eventually close him off, and He did not close off those whom the "righteous" people of the day had already judged. Instead, He went right into the middle of the "mud puddles of human need" and got himself dirty.

But in the process, relationship with Jesus meant a new identification and a changed life. Jesus knew how to reach directly into people's hearts and lives and speak to their deepest need—but He didn't do it from a podium or pulpit, did He? He stayed at Zacchaeus' house (Lk 19:1-10). He sat quietly at the well with the Samaritan woman (Jn 4:4-32). He joined his friends Mary and Martha around the table in their home (Lk 10:38-40). He stood face to face with the woman caught in adultery (Jn 8:1-11) and walked with his disciples along the road to Emmaus (Lk 24:13-28). He identified with people at every turn, over the simplest of human experiences that we all have in common—and it opened the door for them to meet the One who could satisfy all the longing in their hearts.

Jesus redefined what it meant to be a follower of God. For the Jews of the day, rabbinic tradition had joined, if not eclipsed, conformance to the Law as the measure of devotion and piety. Jesus fulfilled the Law and dispensed with the burdens religious leaders had placed on the people, modelling and teaching a new paradigm not just to teachers, Pharisees, Sadducees, and scribes, but also to everyday people: fishermen, tax collectors...even women and children!

> On one occasion an expert in the law stood up to test Jesus. "Teacher," he asked, "what must I do to inherit eternal life?"
>
> "What is written in the Law?" He replied. "How do you read it?"
>
> He answered, "'Love the Lord your God with all your heart and with all your soul and with all your strength and with all your mind'; and, 'Love your neighbor as yourself.'"
>
> "You have answered correctly," Jesus replied. "Do this and you will live."
>
> But he wanted to justify himself, so he asked Jesus, "And who is my neighbor?"
>
> In reply Jesus said: "A man was going down from Jerusalem to Jericho, when he was attacked by robbers. They stripped him of his clothes, beat him and went away, leaving him half dead. A priest happened to be going down the same road, and when he saw the man, he passed by on the other side. So too, a Levite, when he came to the place and saw him, passed by on the other side. But a Samaritan, as he traveled, came where the man was; and when he saw him,

he took pity on him. He went to him and bandaged his wounds, pouring on oil and wine. Then he put the man on his own donkey, brought him to an inn and took care of him. The next day he took out two denarii and gave them to the innkeeper. 'Look after him,' he said, 'and when I return, I will reimburse you for any extra expense you may have.'

"Which of these three do you think was a neighbor to the man who fell into the hands of robbers?"

The expert in the law replied, "The one who had mercy on him."

Jesus told him, "Go and do likewise." (Lk 10:25-37)

Here, after reminding them that loving devotion and relationship with God and people are the hallmarks of those who truly follow God, Jesus again reinforces the idea of identification with people and their need. Who cannot see and understand the tremendous lack of connection, empathy, or identification within the first two people in Jesus' story who ignored the man who had been attacked? Jesus chose a Samaritan for the story precisely because of the dissociative relationship the Jews had with the Samaritans. The Jews did not want any sense of identification with the Samaritans. It would've been beneath them. It would have sullied their reputation. It was shameful.

And this is precisely who Jesus is, was, and what He does. Identifying with the human condition and struggle (sin and brokenness), He came right into it with us (our mud puddle of human need), to show us the "Kingdom of God is *among you*" (Lk 17:21ISV, emphasis mine). Where Jesus is, there is the kingdom of God. And where is Jesus today? Among us. By his Spirit, living in the heart and soul of every believer who calls on his Name and makes room for him in their lives.

The apostle Paul becomes an exemplary model for us in this, willing to personally demonstrate and sacrificially take on the mantle of identification with people *everywhere*! In his answer to challenges that came to him from the church in Corinth, he declares the rights of an apostle, how he freely lays them down, and then how he employs that freedom.

> "Though I am free and belong to no one, I have made myself a slave to everyone, to win as many as possible. To the Jews, I became like a Jew, to win the Jews. To those under the law, I became like one under the law (though I myself am not under the law), so as to win those under the law. To those not having the law I became like one not having the law (though I am not free from God's law but under Christ's law), so as to win those not having the law. To the weak, I have become weak to win the weak. I have become all things to all people so that by all possible means I might save some. I do this for the sake of the gospel, that I may share in its blessings." (1 Cor 9:19-23)

I can hardly imagine the inner fortitude of Paul to keep it all straight! He makes my head spin as he almost appears to be schizophrenic in his resolve to be everything to everyone! But oh, that we would catch a glimpse of the vision and calling of an apostle of God! "Follow my example, as I follow the example of Christ," Paul said in that same letter only paragraphs later (I Cor 11:1). And I truly do thank God for his magnificent follow-up only another chapter later reminding us we are all parts of one body with many members, so it would seem there's room for all of us to find and use our unique SHAPE and find where we fit in God's plan to reach the world!

> Just as a body, though one, has many parts, but all its many parts form one body, so it is with Christ. For we were all baptized by one Spirit so as to form one body—whether Jews or Gentiles, slave or free—and we were all given the

one Spirit to drink. Even so the body is not made up of one part but of many...in fact God has placed the parts in the body, every one of them, just as He wanted them to be. If they were all one part, where would the body be? As it is, there are many parts, but one body. (1 Cor 12:12-14, 18-20)

Today I realize that as a new believer I was rather quickly inculcated in a discipleship model that was largely "separatist" in nature.[1] It took the growing of a missionary heart in me to see it and turn away from it. But for many years it stunted the growth of God's heart for the world in me. This is part of my confession of course. How could I have missed it? But in the realization of this, and the "[forcing] through the channels of [my] single human heart, the interests of the whole world," my eyes were opened to the blinders that were on them.

I would highly recommend reading the full chapter "A Parody of Ourselves" in Gabe Lyons' *The Next Christians*. It gave me words for the problem many years ago, and I have come back to it time and time again. In short, Gabe summarizes how Christians have interacted with current culture. He divides those into two categories: Separatist, which includes Insiders, Culture Warriors, and Evangelizers; and Cultural, which includes Blenders and Philanthropists. I won't get into the specifics of each one in detail here but leave you to do that exploration yourself. You can likely imagine, however, simply from the names he has given to the groups, what they look like, how they sound, and what they do in the world.

I found myself wholly identifying with the Separatist Insider:

Insiders earn their label from the spaces they choose to occupy—or perhaps the spaces they avoid at all costs. Their lives revolve primarily around "Christian" activities and functions involving other believers. [They] spend the majority of their time in Christian communities—"safe" places. Their motivations for retreating and separating from the broader culture can be attributed to the longing for purity, integrity, and holiness in life. But by default, their choice to live outside the typical rhythms of culture makes them seem awkward, disconnected, and judgmental toward others."[2]

For my wife and me—who met as young teens and new believers in a church youth group—this suited us well. We each had come from families riddled with worldly traps and dysfunction, with addictions of all kinds plaguing our parents and siblings. God put us into a new family, set our feet on a sure foundation, and gave us the start of a whole new trajectory for our lives.

Sometimes I can also identify—at least a little bit—with the Evangelizer (like Bill, mentioned in Chapter 5). I am burdened for the lost and consider it important to have sharing Christ a priority in my life, but not to the extreme of an "at any cost" strategy that ignores relationship and real love and concern for people. But here is the problem. If my life before becoming a missionary was largely consumed with my own family and the activities inside the four walls of the church, where was I ever going to build relationships with people with whom I quite frankly did not hold *any* identification?

For most American Separatist Insiders or Evangelizers, our greatest interaction with the world comes through our jobs. For 13 years, I worked within the same office with mostly the same group of guys at the University at Buffalo. It was a relatively small group of engineers, architects, and construction managers—about a dozen of us—and as I grew through the ranks and had a few promotions (God-ordained and miraculous—that's part of why I must stay, remember?), we became peers (though I was at least 10 to 15 years younger than most of them). Over time, I got to hear about their families, their marriages, their hobbies and interests, and occasionally even their struggles or pain. I grew to love those guys, and although I would try to introduce them to Jesus, my faith, and the work He did in my life as part of the occasional conversations that might allow it, I never got very far. Why, I wonder? Well, I did not ever participate with them in anything outside the office.

Several of them often stopped together for a happy hour after work and not once did I ever do that. I couldn't. I didn't know how. I was a young dad (all our kids were born in our twenties) who needed to get home to my family at the end of a workday. My siblings—and my wife's too—struggled with alcoholism or drug addiction. We couldn't go to happy hour, could we?

There is one man from among that group with whom I still have a lifelong friendship, and it is worth noting why. Larry Chlebowy was my first supervisor, took me under his wing, and treated me like a brother. He helped mentor me and when I was promoted and became his peer and fellow manager, he was incredibly gracious. I worked on a project with him at his home, I got to know his wife and sons, and have done outings and shared meals with them. Pretty simple. A connection for life was made through relationship and identification.

Today I am a different person. I know that the apostle Paul somehow managed to become all things to all men and understood how to do it without compromise or a crisis of faith. And certainly Jesus did it, time and time again, eating and drinking with "tax collectors, prostitutes, and sinners." Every time Jesus got up close and personal, lives were changed. Do you remember the end of the stories I just mentioned above? As a result of Jesus identification with them—an interaction made possible by initiation and relationship! —eyes were opened, hearts were healed, lives were built up or changed, and the kingdom of God came to earth through his life and presence.

Zacchaeus:
> All the people saw this and began to mutter, "He has gone to be the guest of a sinner." But Zacchaeus stood up and said to the Lord, "Look, Lord! Here and now I give half of my possessions to the poor, and if I have cheated anybody out of anything, I will pay back four times the amount." Jesus said to him, "Today salvation has come to this house,

because this man, too, is a son of Abraham. For the Son of Man came to seek and to save the lost." (Lk 19:7-10)

The Samaritan woman:
Many of the Samaritans from that town believed in him because of the woman's testimony, "He told me everything I ever did." So when the Samaritans came to him, they urged him to stay with them, and He stayed two days. And because of his words many more became believers.

They said to the woman, "We no longer believe just because of what you said; now we have heard for ourselves, and we know that this man really is the Savior of the world." (Jn 4:39-42)

Mary and Martha:
As Jesus and his disciples were on their way, He came to a village where a woman named Martha opened her home to him. She had a sister called Mary, who sat at the Lord's feet listening to what He said. But Martha was distracted by all the preparations that had to be made. She came to him and asked, "Lord, don't you care that my sister has left me to do the work by myself? Tell her to help me!"

"Martha, Martha," the Lord answered, "you are worried and upset about many things, but few things are needed— or indeed only one. Mary has chosen what is better, and it will not be taken away from her." (Lk 10:38-42)

The woman caught in adultery:
At dawn He appeared again in the temple courts, where all the people gathered around him, and He sat down to teach them. The teachers of the law and the Pharisees brought in a woman caught in adultery. They made her stand before the group and said to Jesus, "Teacher, this woman was

caught in the act of adultery. In the Law Moses commanded us to stone such women. Now what do you say?" They were using this question as a trap, in order to have a basis for accusing him.

But Jesus bent down and started to write on the ground with his finger. When they kept on questioning him, He straightened up and said to them, "Let any one of you who is without sin be the first to throw a stone at her." Again He stooped down and wrote on the ground.

At this, those who heard began to go away one at a time, the older ones first, until only Jesus was left, with the woman still standing there. Jesus straightened up and asked her, "Woman, where are they? Has no one condemned you?"

"No one, sir," she said.

"Then neither do I condemn you," Jesus declared. "Go now and leave your life of sin." (Jn 8:2-11)

Disciples on the road to Emmaus:
He said to them, "How foolish you are, and how slow to believe all that the prophets have spoken! Did not the Messiah have to suffer these things and then enter his glory?" And beginning with Moses and all the Prophets, He explained to them what was said in all the Scriptures concerning himself.

As they approached the village to which they were going, Jesus continued on as if He were going farther. But they urged him strongly, "Stay with us, for it is nearly evening; the day is almost over." So He went in to stay with them.

When He was at the table with them, He took bread, gave thanks, broke it and began to give it to them. Then their eyes were opened, and they recognized him, and He disappeared from their sight. They asked each other, "Were not our hearts burning within us while He talked with us on the road and opened the Scriptures to us?" (Lk 24:25-32)

I have learned—as a direct result of immersing myself in the lives and struggles of people all around the world—that a simple point of identification in their human experience can open the doors of people's hardened or closed hearts. I have also prayed under my breath and asked God for words of knowledge and discernment, that I might truly speak to people, like He did with the woman at the well! And not just overseas, but in line at Starbucks! In so doing, with hearts of compassion and mercy, we acknowledge our shared understanding with those around us and connect with them at some level: we know what it is to feel pain, abandonment, hunger, and hopelessness.

International travel repeatedly offers easy points of sharing Christ with some very simple people-centered, humbly couched comments to establish connection through identification. It's so easy it's become almost predictable! After living and working overseas for a couple weeks at a time, I'll board a plane somewhere to begin my trip home (this also works in reverse, as I head out to any overseas location). If conversation ensues with any fellow passenger nearby, inevitably the question comes up, "What are you doing here?" (Or some variation on this theme.) I always try to understate our mission and respond in a way that speaks to service, teams of people collaborating, and maybe even how challenging it was for me. "I've been here with a team of volunteer engineers and architects from around the world, designing a hospital way out in the bush—a 12-hour ride from this capital city..."). At some point, they'll say something like, "Well, that's a wonderful thing you're doing." And there it is. Our in with just about anybody. We all *want* to do wonderful things, we tend to praise people who even *try to do* wonderful things, and in the back of our minds, we all really wish we actually *were* wonderful!

I have a choice to make right then and there. I confess, occasionally I deflect the praise, thank them for that, and tell them, "Really, it's an incredible privilege to be able to spend my life doing this." And I mean it of course. But that's usually an end to the conversation, so that I can then proceed to selfishly catch up on some sleep or watch a movie (or three!) or even read a book that I've had with me for the entire trip and still haven't managed to finish. But my other option is to engage more fully—gently, but keeping the doors open for more conversation. It is a long flight after all. Certainly I want to know why they're on this flight, too. Sometimes that reveals the next reply or question that's most natural. Or I can ask if they've ever thought about doing things like this (a short-term volunteer service opportunity). Or maybe they know someone who has? I can feel them out for where they are spiritually, religiously, or socially.

Eventually—but sometimes almost immediately after the first compliment (that's a wonderful thing you're doing)—I will continue with something like this: "You know, it really *is* a wonderful thing we're doing, but I want you to know, I'm not doing this because *I'm* such a wonderful person. In fact, most of my life, I was pretty self-absorbed. But I do this because I have come face to face with a command from Jesus to love and serve the poor, and I realized it required something more from me. I don't know what your experience has been with Christians; but if its anything like most people's, it's not very good. I hope people can see the Jesus I've found in the Gospels, one who came to seek and serve and love people, by looking at my life."

You'd be amazed at what usually happens next. I give them a little open door to talk about their lives and their experiences with Christians—which are often filled with distrust, pain, bitterness and disillusionment—and they'll talk, and talk, and talk. They'll vent, in fact. And I can often corroborate and affirm their experience! But in the end, I can almost *always* say, "But that's not who Jesus is. Would you take another look at Jesus?" or "Can I show you who Jesus is and what He says about himself?" Occasionally—especially in the case of disillusioned, post-Christian thinkers—I might even be able to remind them of some biblical and historical proofs to rebuild a confidence in the resurrected Jesus. And of course, often, I ask for their forgiveness for how they have been wronged by people who supposedly profess to follow Jesus.

Our actual work on the ground in cities and villages all around the world does the same. A common series of questions when we arrive in local villages is "Who are you?" "Where have you come from?" "What are you doing here?" We are immediately distrusted as foreign strangers, and rightly so. But with some dialogue, they are almost always turned from suspicion to acceptance, as they come to realize we have come with no agenda but to serve their community as we hope to develop a hospital to care for their health needs, or a school to teach their children, or an orphanage to rescue at-risk babies. And when they find out that we are volunteering our time and services and no one is paying us, almost all defenses fall.

We come from halfway around the world to serve, and in so doing, build an identifying connection with people very different from ourselves. This is a difficult hurdle to overcome, especially for the short-term mission effort. Now that short-term missions work has been on the scene for about 50 years, some excellent books have been written on the subject, and I'll quote a few of those along the way here. There are some great benefits—and great liabilities—in serving the world through short-term missions. This is where EMI began, and this is the EMI I joined in the mid-'90s, only a little more than a dozen years into EMI's development as an international missions organization. But almost immediately upon my joining EMI, God spoke to Glen Woodruff (you'll remember he's the senior staff member who recruited me for my first volunteer mission trip). Through a frustrating experience of poor communication with a missionary partner in India, and the resulting missed deadline, he distinctly heard God speaking to his spirit saying, "Go there and do there what you do here."

Within a couple years, Glen relocated his entire family to India to live and work and *be* among them—exponentially increasing the depth of identification with the people he served. Within a few months of living and working in India, in close contact and relationship with his mission partners and the Indian church, Glen said, "I wish I could go back and change everything I ever designed here up till now." He found such a new and deeper understanding of and identification with people and culture and the constraints within which they lived. Having a first-hand understanding of the requirements our designs and construction projects had to meet completely changed his perspective and equipped him to better serve our mission partners and the Indian church. He found where he fit in God's plan to reach the world!

Serving the Church around the globe has also built incredible perspective in all of us regarding the power of identification. One of the greatest benefits of EMI's commitment to the short-term mission model has always been our commitment to bolster the local church and enhance our partner ministry's effectiveness by simply backstopping their mission with the missing resources needed to continue advancing their vision. Today, we have eleven international offices and still conduct many short-term mobilizations into the areas of the world where there is no office. We will continue in that same vision through this two-pronged approach for many years to come. We don't own these works; we don't take control from our local partner; we simply want to be the silent partner providing the missing piece to see the vision fulfilled. Fikkert and Colbert, in *When Helping Hurts*, explore the benefits of mutual inquiry and learning (a process of moving into deeper understanding of one another through curiosity, engagement, and vulnerability) as a path to better participatory development.[3] Our goal is to build up the local church and see the kingdom of God come to the hearts and lives of the people whom our on-the-ground mission partner is serving. In so doing, we reinforce the incredible value and importance of their direct connection, relationship, and identification with their local people.

Binora is a missionary to his own people in Ethiopia. We had joined him with an EMI team to design a new water system that could carry water from mountain springs some 17 km away to three local villages in a region called Gewada. In the course of working together (and the many advance months of planning this partnership together) Binora and I became friends. He asked me if I might preach a word of encouragement to the local church the following Sunday.

The building was pretty large, considering it was made of mud brick and heavy wood beams for its roof structure. There were hundreds of people seated inside and more peering in through the windows. I chose to preach to this church the message of standing in the gap on behalf of the land, emphasizing the subject of identification. As I began describing the critical importance of identifying with the people to whom you are trying to build a bridge, the thought suddenly came to me to invite a little child to come up and give me a hug. I hadn't really thought through the consequences, but found myself quickly surveying the audience and wondering if it was such a good idea? If someone comes up—as I expected—I *thought* I might know what to do or what to say. I was ready to talk about how it was not enough to send design advice or books or resources or money. We had to come physically to be with them and to lead the way, to study their villages, the countryside, to get to know how they lived, the limitations they faced and the challenges that prevented development of water systems up till now.

But what if no one comes up to me, then what? I hadn't fully thought it through, even as I dared to make the invitation. I asked a second time. Not one little brave child budged, and not one parent, having sympathy on me, appeared to even *try* to nudge a child to come forward! That left me with the follow up that was somewhat unrehearsed, but exactly what God had for them at that moment. I quickly changed gears and drew on their own unfamiliarity and distrust of me in order to help them see that it is only *they* who can reach the villages of the Gewada people. We as skilled and trained Westerners can come alongside them with all the hope we have to

Identification

offer: *physical* hope in terms of knowing how to design a 17 km water pipeline to serve three villages, and *spiritual* hope in the message of the Gospel that we share; but the people cannot receive directly from us because we are not "of them," a part of their lives, or familiar with their communities, their history, or their personal struggles. Only these Gewadan Christians assembled that morning could effectively stand in this gap, uniquely fit to them. Will they rise to the call? I cannot do it for you, no matter how much I might desire it or try to force it. Two weeks is just not going to be enough time to convince anyone that I truly care for them and can be trusted. Later, by email, Binora sent word that—for weeks afterward—the people were still talking of that message that challenged them to see how much they can help, how much they can give, and how much they can be a part of God's plan to reach their part of the world.

David Dann had a clear vision from God of what he wanted to do before emigrating to the United States. After completing his studies, David's vision was to return to his native country, Liberia, to help his countrymen. Unfortunately, David's vision was shattered when a civil war broke out in which his father and other relatives were brutally slaughtered by rebel factions. Two civil wars over an eleven-year period devastated Liberia and claimed the lives of 250,000 people. "I have no reason to go back to Liberia since the rebels had killed my parents and relatives," David said. He was infuriated by the deaths of his relatives and the destruction of his beloved country.

But this is not the David Dann I had the privilege of serving with, only a few years later. It was 1999, and with the first signs of the country opening up after a ceasefire had been established, I led an EMI team in to assess the situation with David. David, like Nehemiah in the Old Testament, went back to his home with the heart to help them rebuild. He couldn't deny his tremendous identification with the struggle of his countrymen, and the opportunity to be a catalyst for whatever God might have for him to do—he knew he was "uniquely positioned" by God for this hour. (I will talk more about David Dann and Liberia in Chapters 7 and 8.)

This was how we found Liberia. Years of war had wreaked havoc on their cities and roads, their economy, and their society; nothing of their old way of life seemed the same or intact. Reaching out to people with any kind of encouragement was incredibly difficult. Hearts were broken or hardened. We found human bones in the high grasses where we surveyed land, the grizzly remnant of hand-to-hand massacres across the land.

But dozens of villagers gathered to walk through the jungle with us as we did our first site visit, and children especially would run after our survey team and follow them for hours at a time. Later in the week, ministering to scores of children was the assignment for much of our team at the Sunday church service. The determination on the face of the pastor as he shared with us his faith and vision for what God could do in response to their nation's hopelessness was inspiring.

Some young African men from the families working on the radio station compound where we were staying would join us each evening for our times of worship and devotions. In their early twenties, they were just trying to finish high school since there was no school during most of the '90's due to the war. One 24-year-old (described later by his friend as being particularly bright) said, "If it weren't for the Holy Spirit, I couldn't get up in the morning because I'd have no hope." His friend also said, "I've asked God, 'Why did you make me a Liberian?'" EMI finds itself in the thick of this type of situation all the time...that's who we are, what we do, and why we do it! But these young men captured my heart in a way I hadn't experienced since Trinidad, my first trip with EMI as a volunteer, with the Cuban refugee Orlando.

As we joined the people for their Sunday morning church services, team members shared testimonies and several of us led them in worship. When I came to the pulpit to preach, I was impressed to first exhort them from Ezekiel 22:30. EMI describes itself as "coming alongside missionaries who are struggling to meet the physical needs of the impoverished communities to whom they are bringing the Gospel." Well, that's why God made them

Liberians! From among them, they are uniquely fit and qualified to stand—just as they are indeed standing today in faith and power *and identification*—on behalf of their land. EMI, I said, is like the mortar that holds them in place, a brace from either side of the wall (referencing Nehemiah again) to help them stay fast. Let me tell you, preaching that day to a group who has suffered long and calling them to persevere in their pursuit of God provides an entirely new perspective from preaching at home.

The power of identification with people cannot be underestimated, but it can also happen in all kinds of smaller ways. I had taken a team to Joao Pessoa, the easternmost point in the Americas, on the Atlantic coast of Brazil. We were serving Isaac and Betania Seboia and their YWAM team on a campus they were building out to host training camps, conduct outreach, serve the local community, and to rescue boys from the street life of gangs, drugs, and prostitution. There were boys ranging in age from 8 to 18 living there, and they hung out with our team regularly. As we shared in devotional and worship times together—struggling through the English to Portuguese language barrier—we began to build connections.

Who could've imagined the kinds of things in our own stories that might build identification with these young boys who had already seen such hardship and pain in their lives? My intern, Mark, told them about how as a young boy, his family home burned to the ground and about the pain and loss of being left with nothing. Another young man, who today is an electrical engineer in the Silicon Valley area, told of how he grew up in such rural poverty in the Midwest that his home had floors falling in and rats running in the walls. These boys who had nothing but the clothes on their backs drew hope from their stories of God's faithfulness through their struggles.

The staff living and working where we've planted EMI offices—Latin America, Africa (North, South, East and West), the Middle East, India, and Cambodia—are some of the best I know at discovering and building identification connections for the sake of the Gospel witness going forward.

Chad and Shanthi Gamble have established both our Uganda office and our Cambodia office. They have adopted two Ugandan kids. They have lived in both countries for several years each, and India as well. They've learned new languages, crossed cultures, and given their lives for people who are not their own, but God's. Matthew Coffey went to India with me as part of my short-term team, and I left him to stay in our office there for a term as an intern after our trip was over. He extended that one term, and then after a short time, took over as the office director in our North India office! I always stayed in touch with him over the years and followed closely along with his prayer updates and ministry reports. I joked with him that "I left you in India, and you never came home!" After several years, he was learning Hindi so that he could preach and connect with north Indians better, he was wearing the traditional Indian clothes, and he had grown his hair and beard rather long. Our Indian friends joked that he was more Indian than they were!

I was in Kenya one year training another new project team leader when a serious revolution broke out in another country where we maintain an EMI office. While I have navigated some tense times while overseas when riots and sieges clamped down cities and airports, I had never experienced anything quite so widespread. I was in contact with the other members of our leadership team back in Colorado, while we were in touch with our staff team on the ground in that country. Many other Christian ministry workers and NGO staff were being quickly evacuated. But our team in-country felt too much investment in the lives of their community members and neighbors to just get up and leave, just because it might be safer. As they saw it, they were all at risk. In the end, as they stayed through the whole ordeal, they built even stronger identification with their neighbors (who were quite shocked that our team would stay and defend their homes and families right alongside their neighbors). Relationships were deepened while identification built true connection where friendships could truly be forged.

Identification

EMI's current CEO, John Dallmann, and his wife Gala lived in Africa for decades, learning languages, raising their 5 children in multiple countries and in over 25 different homes! In the desert of northern Kenya, God spoke to him when he was young, "John, I want you to win people for Christ as a water resources engineer that no one else could touch." He built a life around that call and today describes himself humbly, saying, "I'm a water guy who loves to bring clean water to villages. I love Africa and Jesus is at the center of my life." John and Paula Sauder, part of the original Uganda office planting team 20 years ago—and a brilliant and creative long-time office director there after Chad—have bought land and designed and built their own little home (John is an architect, of course). John continues to serve in Africa using his extensive cross-cultural experience as EMI's Global Programs Director. I expect them to remain there for the rest of their lives. That's identification!

Our staff truly live out Jesus to the world wherever God has planted them, and just as John Dallmann says he "loves Africa," they all love the people of the new cultures to which God has sent them. I understand what he means. I love the people in all the places where God has sent me, though I joined EMI before we had international offices where we could send expat staff to live and work longer-term. At that time, our full-time EMI staff team was less than 10 people!

I became a part of the leadership team a quarter century ago, and often joked that we were "EMI, the Next Generation." We knew that we were laying the foundations for EMI's future growth. Together with Glen Woodruff as CEO, and Craig Hoffman as my fellow Vice President, we strategically planted several overseas field offices, raised up and trained the new staff, sent them there to figure it out, and then repeatedly visited many times. As part of that leadership team for EMI, I carried the heart of the people of EMI more than anyone (Glen was the visionary, and Craig the quintessential analytical strategist). I've led about 50 teams and have worked in over 40 countries, but never lived overseas for more than a summer in one place. While our new full-time overseas staff can put down roots, learn the language, adopt children, and become assimilated into the local church and community, I have worked on 5 continents; logged thousands of hours on planes, trains and automobiles; learned bits and pieces of a dozen or more languages; and get myself easily confused three months later in yet another new country!

I am regularly asked, "What's your favorite place, project team, or country?" I'm not usually asked, "Who were your favorite people?" but that's the heart of the matter. The people everywhere are the precious gems hidden so often beneath the world's hardened crust of poverty, war, famine, drought, sickness, and filth. And as all people are created in the image of God, they have all been precious to me. My identification has been a global one, and a privilege. There are many more stories of course, too many to tell here. But they all have at their core a missionary heart, that heard God's call when He went looking, and through relationship has built an incredible identification with the people we serve.

Even when it is unwittingly discovered, appropriate identification can still be effective in building partnerships for the Kingdom. I was leading a team to Burkina Faso in West Africa, in the Sahel region between the coast and the Sahara Desert. After overnight flights from the states, we had a very long layover in Casablanca, Morocco, and I figured I would take my team into town to see some sights (I had heard that the tallest mosque in the world had been built there). From the airport, we had boarded a bus to take us to a nearby hotel where we could book a room for the day to refresh the team. Even as we left the airport, I could see that my little bit of French that I knew was more than anyone else on the team and we would be quite challenged by the language barrier as we tried to spend the day the way we had hoped.

During the bus ride, I noticed my volunteer architect, Mark George, a middle-aged white man from Kansas, striking up a conversation with a young African woman as they stood close together—too close, I thought. Inside, I'm cringing at all the possible things that could be going wrong in this inter-personal, cross-cultural communication and was wishing he hadn't engaged her. Mark talked in enthusiastic tones as he explained where we were headed and why (as I've explained, it's always a door for sharing more with people). I could hear most of their conversation, and it was casual and comfortable—too comfortable, I thought. With her accent, it was clear she was fluent in English, but French was her heart language from her home in Rwanda (or was it Burundi?). She was receptive and conversational; she had a father working in government in Burkina Faso and was headed there herself to visit him. Mark was a father (the incredible depth of this man as a father I only learned later, as his story includes raising three sons with severe disabilities); he connected with her as a daughter who missed her father. I was witnessing identification at heart level in a matter of moments.

In the end, since she was planning the exact same activity for her day with the same schedule as us, she volunteered to help escort us around town! We hired three separate taxis to fit us all, toured the city making several stops including the mosque and the oceanside beach, and ended up back at the hotel before we had to return to the airport. We covered all her costs for her that day since she was such a valuable member of the team now. And she even fought with the taxi drivers—in French—who were trying to triple-charge us for their services for the day! It only happened because an American dad identified with an African daughter.

Not far from there, in the early 2000's, I was the guest of Nigerian President Olusegun Obasanjo, and his daughter, Iyabo, for a partnership to design and build a specialty women's hospital in Nigeria. Obasanjo was a believer who was seeking to unite the Christian and Muslim factions. His support for this project won over the governor of the state where the new women's hospital would be, and he was giving 50 acres of land to use for this mission. This trip served to lay the groundwork for the full team that I would bring back later that year, and that's where this story concludes later in Chapter 11. For now, let me focus on Iyabo's identification with the plight of young women in her country and elsewhere in Africa. She recognized her position of privilege, especially magnified during her father's presidency. She saw the plight of the bush women suffering from fistula. She saw the struggle for survival of village women. She identified with women, young and old. And to that end, she was using the voice and platform that God had divinely provided to her for however long this season might last.

Fistula is an all but unknown injury in the West but is estimated to afflict nearly a million young woman across the Sahel region of Africa (more on that in Chapter 11). Iyabo hosted Dr. Steve Arrowsmith and me to research the possibility of designing a hospital specifically enabled to provide surgical interventions and healing from this terrible injury to young, primarily Muslim, women. As a missionary surgeon, Steve was a part of the first ever established work among fistula patients in Ethiopia years earlier, which led to a successful small addition to an existing hospital in Jos, Nigeria, on the other side of the continent. He was now hoping to invest his years of experience in a full-sized new hospital—that EMI would design-build—on the new land. Every time I heard his name, I thought of Steven Tyler of Aerosmith. Not to be confused, two *very* different people. Surgeons, by the way, have their own set of inside jokes just like engineers and architects ("you put your life in other people's hands, and I put my hands into other people").

From the minute I landed in Abuja, I knew this was no ordinary EMI ministry trip. We were met by Iyabo's personal driver and bodyguard. The bodyguard was a skinny guy and no taller than me, but he had more than his shirt tucked into his belt, and he carried an Uzi in his soft leather briefcase! I don't think I've ever felt safer on an EMI trip. We were ushered through several guarded entries onto the Presidential compound and were the guests of the President for the night. Though it was 11 p.m. and I was jet-lagged, Iyabo, suggested in a familiar Nigerian accent, "Why don't we go say hello to my dad before it gets too late?" My first thought was, *"Before* it gets too late?"

As we wound around the estate gardens—looking something like the White House lawns—the gardens overflowed with vibrant colored flowers and broad-leafed plants unlike anything at home. The manicured lawns were wet with dew and the humidity hung in the air. As we neared the front door of the Presidential Palace, we met an entourage coming up the driveway around the lushly landscaped circle in front of the main hall's entrance. They were walking and beating ceremonial drums announcing the arrival of an Asian dignitary. We got rather mixed up in their party as we were checked through a metal detector and security guards, but managed to squeeze ahead of them just in time to greet President Obasanjo as he reclined in his sitting room. With a brief hello, welcome, and handshake, he thanked us for our interest in serving the people of their country and beyond. And then he excused himself and we left, rushed out because of his evening appointment. So much for my first meeting with arguably the most powerful man in Africa. It left me reeling with biblical images of appearing before kings and princes that filled my head, and then were gone almost as fast as my eyes scanned the palace rooms and the security team of men standing in strategic places.

Before we embarked on our long drive up into the north of Nigeria on Sunday, we received an early morning escort to the President's private chapel on the grounds of the estate. Once again, we were directed through tight crowds and metal detectors. In the hectic and crowded melee in the foyer, I got separated from Iyabo and opened the back door of the nearly full sanctuary and stepped in all alone—the lone pasty white guy in the middle of all these black faces. Intimidating? Yes, but I was being beckoned by a finely dressed Nigerian woman way down at the front. It was one of those classic moments where you make a furtive glance around and ask yourself, "Is she motioning to me?" before you do something really stupid and publicly embarrass yourself. (Not that it has ever happened to me, but I've heard that it happens to other people). Apparently she *was* looking at me, and had a special seat waiting, along with about twenty other white people being very obviously specially treated.

As the special guest just two rows in front of me got up to speak, it dawned on me that I was erroneously assumed to be a part of the special entourage that accompanied Jimmy and Rosalyn Carter to Nigeria! He was there the same weekend for a national and continental symposium addressing health care solutions and interventions pertaining to the African HIV-AIDS crisis and its victims, along with Bill Gates, Sr. representing the Bill Gates Foundation with about 25 million dollars of grant money. Carter was the guest preacher that morning and my intrinsic identification with that group made a way for me! Later, after the service was over, I was asked by several of them who I was and what I was doing there. Obviously, they knew I was not a member of their group, but it gave me a chance to witness for the Lord about what I was doing there and why, and mention EMI.

A similar thing happened afterward, when I was invited to attend a lunch served in the palace dining room with all the department ministry heads (like our American Presidential Cabinet). Iyabo escorted us over to a side entrance of the palace. In we walked, up through another beautiful garden and courtyard and into the formal dining room—with a hand-carved wood table that seated 30. At the end, the president was already seated and being served by several waiters dressed in crisp white service uniforms, flanked by his minister of health, special advisor, minister of transportation, and the minister of the chapel, all dressed in fine, colorful African robe-like suits. Iyabo's seat was waiting for her at his right hand, and the rest of us took our seats immediately next to the others further down the table and proceeded to be served in the finest of manners. Most of the meal I spent silent, dutifully listening to humorous unofficial banter between the President and his daughter. Once she referred to me, I was able to address the full group and briefly introduce myself, EMI, and how we serve people in the developing world in Jesus' name. After being asked similar questions as back in the chapel, I could bring glory to God with my testimony before this illustrious group of Nigerian leaders—and my mind took me back to the woman who spoke prophetically at a small gathering introducing me to Elim ministers years before, that I would stand before kings and princes!

One last unintentional moment of hysterical identification: a considerable crowd had gathered outside the entry gates to the palace adjacent to the chapel. As we were trying to move through the crowd for the Presidential luncheon, security was questioning Iyabo as to who was allowed through with her. After trying unsuccessfully to single out a small handful of us as she pointed around to the crowd from a position up on the stairway, she finally just blurted out, "All the white people. All the white people are with me!"

Regarding Carter's message—and I don't care which party affiliation you have or which way you lean politically on this side of the ocean—it was truly an Ezekiel 22:30-inspired idea and resonated powerfully with me and the Spirit of God! He quoted the Bible and summed up the absolutes of Scripture and the Ten Commandments, saying this was the cure for the crisis... but in a voice of tenderness, he asked, "But as a Christian, what must our response be to the victims?" He proceeded to introduce this Jesus whom we all love and that he obviously personally knows, and referenced his mercy and compassion, calling us to the same in service and outreach and *identifying* with the desperate needs of people. I tell you, it was powerful! And as soft-spoken as he was, his message was played on national TV over and over that day carrying enormous impact! Even the staunchest conservative would've had to approve.

CHAPTER 7

RESTORATION

"...who would build up the wall ..."

> *"I looked for someone among them* **who would build up the wall** *and stand before me in the gap on behalf of the land so I would not have to destroy it, but I found no one."*
> *Ezekiel 22:30*

Restoration. The word rings of peace, wholeness, and newness. It means "returning to a former good," or "becoming like new." Something that once was whole, right, useful, or beautiful had been somehow broken, marred, or made unable to fulfill its original purpose. The wall in broken ruins is the picture before us. It's a picture of the work that God will do to restore his people, returning them to their former state. In this context, healing and repairing are good synonyms. Once again, protected and led by their God—and willingly choosing his rule and reign—his people will become like new. And this is where we now take our discussion of the work of *restoration* that God does in his creation and in our lives, as well as the work of God's people in the world.

To review, Ezekiel was one of the exiles taken prisoner during the first Babylonian attack on the city of Jerusalem. The city was, by and large, spared at this time. Ezekiel would have visions and hear from God a few years later during his life as a refugee in Babylon. He prophesies that Jerusalem and the Temple all face imminent destruction from another attack. Israel's idolatry has caused the glory of the Lord to leave the Temple, but in Chapter 11, Ezekiel sees the glory of the Lord there with the remnant in Babylon. God promised that He hasn't abandoned his people, and that a remnant will one day return with new, transformed hearts. This is a small glimmer of hope, before the final judgment on the city comes. The city does fall, and the Temple is destroyed during the time of Ezekiel's prophesying. Chapter 22 occurs in the midst of several parables and allegories representing unfaithful Israel and focusing on God's judgment.

The picture that Ezekiel paints in 22:30 is that of the broken wall, with a breach in it. The wall of course represented protection in ancient times; and for Israel, God's divine role in Jerusalem's protection. A gap in the wall would allow the enemy through, and indeed that is what happened during the attacks that led to the exile. To defend the city, the people would need to flood into that location to defend the breach against the enemy. We know the wall was left in rough shape from the account of Nehemiah's calling to go rebuild it: "The wall of Jerusalem is broken down, and its gates have been burned with fire" (Neh 1:3).

With the exile and the ruin of Jerusalem as a backdrop, God is speaking in spiritual terms regarding the heart of his people, their sin, the judgment they have earned, and his plan for ultimate restoration. By the time Ezekiel is prophesying restoration in Chapters 47-48, he's using imagery that appears in both the Garden of Eden in Genesis 1 and 2, and the new heaven and new earth (a restored Eden) in Revelation 22. In Ezekiel's vision, a stream flows from the new temple, which quickly becomes a rushing river that brings life to everything it reaches. The river is teeming with life and creatures of all kinds and trees along its banks. Full of hope and a new future, it foreshadows the "river of life, as clear as crystal, flowing from the throne of God and of the Lamb," (Rev 22:1). It reminds us that God's plan has always been to restore humanity and all creation back to his life-giving presence, under the rule and reign of God.

Scripture is replete with the theme of restoration and God's commitment to it. The psalmist writes, *"Restore us, O God*; make your face shine upon us that we may be saved" (Ps 80:3). "The Lord is my shepherd, I lack nothing. He makes me lie down in green pastures, He leads me beside quiet waters, He *restores my soul*" (Ps 23:2-3). Implicit in the hearts of his people is an understanding that God is the one who restores; He alone can bring the real restoration that the human heart—indeed, all of creation—groans for. Isaiah prophecies repeatedly of the salvation of the Lord and restoration. "… In the day of salvation I will help you; I will keep you and make you to be a covenant for the people, *to restore the land* and to reassign its desolate inheritances, to say to the captives, 'Come out,' and to those in darkness, 'Be free!'" (Is 49:8). In prophesying of the Lord's favor, he gives us a powerful picture of who God is, and in turn who we can be to a world hungering for restoration.

> The Spirit of the Sovereign Lord is on me,
>   because the Lord has anointed me
>   to proclaim good news to the poor.
> He has sent me to bind up the brokenhearted,
>   to proclaim freedom for the captives
>   and release from darkness for the prisoners,
> to proclaim the year of the Lord's favor
>   and the day of vengeance of our God,
> to comfort all who mourn,
>   and provide for those who grieve in Zion—
> to bestow on them a crown of beauty
>   instead of ashes,
> the oil of joy
>   instead of mourning,
> and a garment of praise
>   instead of a spirit of despair.
> They will be called oaks of righteousness,
>   a planting of the Lord
>   for the display of his splendor.
> They will rebuild the ancient ruins
>   and *restore the places long devastated*;

they will renew the ruined cities
that have been devastated for generations.
> Instead of your shame
>> you will receive a double portion,
> and instead of disgrace
>> you will rejoice in your inheritance;
> and so you will inherit a double portion in your land,
> and everlasting joy will be yours. (Is 61:1-4, 7; emphasis mine)

And finally, as if meant for just this architect who was struggling with the humanistic futility of his profession, the verse that EMI chose as their conference theme the year my wife and I joined them as volunteers was:

> …if you spend yourselves in behalf of the hungry
>> and satisfy the needs of the oppressed,
> then your light will rise in the darkness,
>> and your night will become like the noonday.
> The Lord will guide you always;
>> He will satisfy your needs in a sun-scorched land
>> and will strengthen your frame.
> You will be like a well-watered garden,
>> like a spring whose waters never fail.
> Your people will rebuild the ancient ruins
>> and will raise up the age-old foundations;
> you will be called Repairer of Broken Walls,
>> *Restorer of Streets with Dwellings.* (Is 58:10-12, emphasis mine)

Like Ezekiel, Jeremiah prophesies:

"This is what the Lord says:
"'Your wound is incurable,
   your injury beyond healing.
…I have struck you as an enemy would

Restoration

and punished you as would the cruel,
because your guilt is so great
   and your sins so many.

…'"But all who devour you will be devoured;
   all your enemies will go into exile.
Those who plunder you will be plundered;
   all who make spoil of you I will despoil.
But *I will restore you to health*
   and heal your wounds,'
     declares the Lord,
'because you are called an outcast,
   Zion for whom no one cares.'

"This is what the Lord says:

"'*I will restore the fortunes of Jacob's tents*
   and have compassion on his dwellings;
the city will be rebuilt on her ruins,
   and the palace will stand in its proper place.
From them will come songs of thanksgiving
   and the sound of rejoicing.
I will add to their numbers,
   and they will not be decreased;
I will bring them honor,
   and they will not be disdained.
Their children will be as in days of old,
   and their community will be established before me;
   I will punish all who oppress them.
Their leader will be one of their own;
   their ruler will arise from among them.
I will bring him near and He will come close to me—
   for who is He who will devote himself
   to be close to me?'
     declares the Lord.

"'So you will be my people,
and I will be your God.'" (Jer 30:12, 14, 16-22)

And Zechariah prophesies of restoration as he announces the coming king of Zion:

Rejoice greatly, Daughter Zion!
  Shout, Daughter Jerusalem!
See, your king comes to you,
  righteous and victorious,
lowly and riding on a donkey,
  on a colt, the foal of a donkey.
I will take away the chariots from Ephraim
  and the warhorses from Jerusalem,
  and the battle bow will be broken.
He will proclaim peace to the nations.
  his rule will extend from sea to sea
  and from the River to the ends of the earth.
As for you, because of the blood of my covenant with you,
  I will free your prisoners from the waterless pit.
Return to your fortress, you prisoners of hope;
  even now I announce that *I will restore twice as much to you*. (Zec 9:9-12, emphasis mine)

And Amos joins the collective voice of the prophets, "I will restore David's fallen shelter—I will repair its broken walls *and restore its ruins*—and will rebuild it as it used to be, so that they may possess the remnant of Edom and all the nations that bear my name," declares the Lord, who will do these things," (Am 9:11-12, emphasis mine).

Peter also testified about God's plans for restoration:

But this is how God fulfilled what He had foretold through all the prophets, saying that his Messiah would suffer. Repent, then, and turn to God, so that your sins may be wiped out, that times of refreshing may come from the Lord, and that He may send the Messiah, who has been appointed for you—even Jesus. Heaven must receive him until the time comes *for God to restore everything*, as He promised long ago through his holy prophets. (Acts 3:18-21, emphasis mine)

Humble yourselves, therefore, under God's mighty hand, that He may lift you up in due time. Cast all your anxiety on him because He cares for you.

Be alert and of sober mind. Your enemy the devil prowls around like a roaring lion looking for someone to devour. Resist him, standing firm in the faith, because you know that the family of believers throughout the world is undergoing the same kind of sufferings.

And the God of all grace, who called you to his eternal glory in Christ, after you have suffered a little while, *will himself restore you* and make you strong, firm and steadfast. To him be the power for ever and ever. Amen. (1 Pet 5:6-11, emphasis mine)

The theme of restoration from the prophets in the Old Testament to Jesus and the apostles in the New Testament is hard to understand absent the kingdom of God and his rightful authority over heaven and earth, his people and their land, and our very hearts and lives as its foundation. The whole Gospel hinges on this. In the face of all creation groaning in brokenness, we can often lose sight of God's Kingship and his Kingdom. The Bible describes God as an eternal King. "The Lord is King forever..." (Ps 10:16). It also declares that He is sovereign over all things (Ps 103:19). He is everywhere. At every time and place, throughout the vast reaches of his universe, God has been in full control. He has never compromised his supreme prerogative of his godhood. To do so would make him less than God.

It is essential to recognize his undiminished sovereignty if we are to have a proper view of his kingdom. His work of creation, with all the apparent risks involved, was the work of his sovereignty."[1]

In references to restoration made by the prophets, God is always referring to the land. It has always been a part of his covenant blessing, the importance of which stretches back to the creation story. God made a covenant with Adam, and commanded him to be fruitful, subdue the earth, care for it, and cultivate it. A king and kingdom are nothing if they have no authority to act on behalf of the land with power, protection, and provision. Much of this has been lost in contemporary, Western Christian culture. For us in America, our experience is so far removed from a monarchy that we would be hard pressed to think of God's kingdom in any context besides the British monarchy, and even then, only as an observer, not as someone subjugated to it. And I might add, it's mostly for entertainment's sake.

This is a far cry from what the gospels tell us: "And this gospel of the kingdom will be preached in the whole world as a testimony to all nations, and then the end will come!" (Mt 24:14). "And from the time John the Baptist began preaching until now, the Kingdom of Heaven has been forcefully advancing, and violent people are attacking it. For before John came, all the prophets and the law of Moses looked forward to this present time" (Mt 11:12,13 NLT). "The Law and the Prophets were proclaimed until John. Since that time, the good news of the kingdom of God is being preached, and everyone is forcing their way into it" (Lk 16:16).

Scholars struggle to completely agree on the essence of verses like these, but suffice it to say, there is a work to be done in entering into the kingdom of Heaven. There is opposition from the enemy and a broken, wayward humanity bent on spiritual rebellion. With both verses from Matthew and Luke, we can get the picture that Jesus is saying that there will be a battle as the kingdom of Heaven advances in the world. One doesn't have to look very far to find men and women working hard against God and his church. But as people "lay hold of it," the glory and power of God's kingdom is revealed in people who are released from Satan's power (the "kingdom of this world").

> "Something has been missing in the message and the life of the Church, and this has caused many men to walk away. That missing something has been the Gospel of the Kingdom, the message of a victorious King who reigns evermore and whose kingdom was inaugurated, is being advanced, and will be consummated at the end of the age. I believe that that missing something is about to be *restored*."[2] (emphasis mine)

The reduction of the gospel in the last few generations to an altar-call-driven, secret (every head bowed, every eye closed) conversion experience that guarantees the sinner an eternity in heaven completely loses sight of the bigger story of God's work from the beginning to end of the Bible, and our part in it! We have lost the sense of the kingdom of God and the authority of his rule and reign over all creation.

> Jesus is the conquering King, and the region He has conquered is the [entire] earth. All authority on the earth, after all, has been rendered unto Jesus (Mt 28:18-20), and He is presently reigning over the affairs of man (Eph 1:21-23). Through his Church, He is working to bring all things under his lordship (Mt 28:19-20, Eph. 2:10) and to bring all things into rightful submission to his name (Phil 2:10, 11). At some point in the future, Christ will return to earth, abolish death, and consummate his reign, at which time He will also turn the kingdom back over to his Father (1 Cor 15:24-28).[3]

The gospel without a kingdom restoration message doesn't make sense. Jesus was always talking about the Gospel of the Kingdom, from his first sermon (Mt 4:17) to his last (Mt 28:18-20) and much of his ministry in between! Restoration in the earth is a demonstration of the character, nature, and ultimate plan of God. Jesus taught us to pray, "Your kingdom come, Your will be done, on earth as it is in Heaven" (Mt 6:10). There is something of the paradise in Heaven that was being replicated here on earth in the creation story; and it has become, like John Milton's epic from 1667, a *"Paradise Lost."* As I said earlier, Ezekiel's prophecy carries themes from Genesis to Revelation, with the true restoration of the land looking like it did from the very beginning—a Paradise regained! Pastor and theologian Tim Keller writes,

> When we look at the whole scope of this story line, we see clearly that Christianity is not only about getting one's individual sins forgiven so we can go to heaven. That is an important *means* of God's salvation, but not the final end or purpose of it. The purpose of Jesus's coming is to put the whole world right, to renew and restore the creation, not to escape it. It is not just to bring personal forgiveness and peace, but also justice and *shalom* to the world. God created both body and soul, and the resurrection of Jesus shows that He is going to redeem both body and soul. The work of the Spirit of God is not only to save souls but also to care and cultivate the face of the earth, the material world.[4]

If we don't begin and end with these—the beauty and magnitude of creation, God's kingdom having come to earth, and the climactic scenes of Revelation where we see and experience final restoration of all things in his Kingdom—then we have what Gabe Lyons refers to as only half the story. He puts it as well as anyone I've heard or read. In our typical Western experience, it seems

> ...that the beginning (God's goodness throughout creation) and the ending (the restoration of all things) of the greater story have been conveniently cut out, leaving modern-day Christians with an incoherent understanding of the Gospel.

> Many are bound to a Gospel story with a climax that feels actually quite boring. "Go tell others how to escape from Planet Earth" doesn't feel like a compelling mission to them. Sure, they want to help others come to know the way of Jesus, but they believe their story should affect real lives and situations now. Not just in the afterlife.
> Although technically accurate, [that] misses the larger point. This telling of the Gospel only includes half of God's story. By truncating the full narrative, it reduces the power of God's redeeming work on the cross to just a proverbial ticket to a good afterlife. *Is this all there is to Christianity? Did Jesus die only so we could get out of this place and go somewhere else?*
> ...Half story versions begin abruptly in Genesis 3, where the separation of humanity from God is the opening scene. This story starts with everyone as corrupted sinners, with little rationalization given for non-Christians who still do good works. All the evidence suggests that this version of the story isn't connecting with the next generation. It not only begins with a judgmental tone but also seems to miss some element of truth postmodern seekers have experienced—namely the human compulsion to do good.[5]

Whether it's your neighbors in the post-Christian world we now find ourselves, or the poor around the world, or those marginalized in any other way, I'm convinced that you fit into God's plan to reach them! If that's true—and if you've stayed with me this far into the book, I know you believe that it is—then something deep within you is screaming for meaning in this earthly life of living out the restoration plan of God in your life and in other people's lives. It's not enough of a purpose to simply get up every day knowing you have eternal life without acting on the powerful truth of that reality.

We must then seek to live as Jesus lived, to work as God has worked, and become a part of his work of restoration in people's lives. How can we go on living as we do when "people are perishing?!" (Jackie Pullinger, at the moment of her conversion).

We must get involved in the rescue work of orphans and widows, of the homeless and sick, of the trafficked and the abused, the forgotten and neglected—these are not just concepts, but huge numbers of people around the world desperate for restoration in their lives.

> Christ's death and resurrection were not only meant to save people *from* something. He wanted to save Christians *to* something. God longs to restore his image in them and let them loose, freeing them to pursue his original dreams for the entire world. Here, now, today, tomorrow. They no longer feel bound to wait for heaven. Instead, they are participating with God in his restoration project for the whole world.[6]

We have the privilege and the compulsion to wake up every morning with this as our prayer, "The Spirit of the Sovereign Lord is on me, because the Lord has anointed me to proclaim good news to the poor. He has sent me to bind up the brokenhearted, to proclaim freedom for the captives and release from darkness for the prisoners..." (Is 61:1).

> Two thousand years after the Christ event, people are still on earth and the hope [that began in Christ] is not diminished. Paul tells us in Colossians 1, that Christ's shed blood began a restorative work affecting the eternal things of heaven as well as the here and now events on earth. More than simply offering us a postmortem destination, God commissioned us to share his whole story and become conduits for him to bring healing to earth and its residents. Like a capstone to the story of God, Christians are called to partner in restorative work so that the torch of hope is carried until Christ's return.[7]

And like Luis Bush spoke the very words of God—and the world—to me ("The poor of the world are crying out 'send us your

Christian design professionals!'"), let me be that voice to you today. The people of the world—from the Eastern hemisphere to the east side of your town—are crying out for you to find your unique fit in God's plan to *restore* the world!

For me, a design professional, I resonate of course with EMI's vision statement which is simply "People restored by God, the world restored through design." We believe that we bring our lives and our gifts to the altar as an offering to God to use and to grow and play our part in bringing restoration to people's lives in the name of Jesus. I have had the privilege over and over of seeing restoration come to broken lives and broken communities around the world. This need is never more obvious than in the war-torn nations of the earth. In the years following the horrific genocides of Rwanda and Cambodia, the army and rebel-led civil wars of Liberia and Sierra Leone, the brutal despotic military regime of Uganda's Idi Amin, and countless other conflicts around the world, EMI has been called into such places with critical restoration needs.

In 1994, nearly a million innocent people were viciously murdered in Rwanda's horrifying genocide in its first 100 days. Before it was all over, the number had reached well past a million. Ethnic Hutu extremists had been driven to such evils by a myriad of malevolent factors, but they targeted the minority Tutsi community, as well as anyone who might have been seen as a political opponent. I learned more about this tragic story than any Western news agency provided by coming alongside Anglican Bishop John Rucyahana, who was working in the aftermath for both the physical and spiritual restoration of Rwanda and its people. In valiant efforts to support restoration work in a country that had torn itself apart, socially, physically, and spiritually, EMI sent multiple teams to work with the Bishop and his partners over the course of several years.

During that time, I had grown used to having nightmares as a result of the gruesome stories I heard. I came to know people—like the Bishop—who saw friends and family members murdered or had miraculously narrowly escaped their own extermination. We in the West just watched from remotely distanced positions, as governments—ours included—refused to call it genocide and thereby relieved themselves of any burden to intervene with a united response from the international community. In fact, as I became more and more aware of the history, I realized that in the spring of 1994, our country was captivated by a slow-speed police chase of OJ Simpson down a California highway (that ended in his equally nationally absorbing arrest, trial, and acquittal), yet barely aware that the Rwandan massacre was taking place. It still leaves me feeling guilty, self-absorbed in my own foolish cultural morass.

In Bishop Rucyahana's book, *The Bishop of Rwanda: Finding Forgiveness Amidst a Pile of Bones*, he brings us back to the kinds of questions we all seek answers to in the face of such hardship and pain. After affirming that man has free will, yet at the same time, God did not want such a horrible thing, he says,

> We cannot understand God's mind, and ultimately the only answer is that God is God and does what He wills. He is the giver of life, and He is the only one who can *restore* life.... God is the giver of eternal life, and He can bring great good out of any situation. He raises the dead; He can also raise the broken. He can *restore their hearts and minds* and lift their spirits to renewed life.
>
> In my country God is doing this today by the thousands. There is so much pain here, so many real tears, and so much guilt that our ministry is like preaching hope from the top of a pile of bones. From atop a mountain of mutilated bodies, we are stretching a hand upward to proclaim a message of transformation and recovery. And it is happening! It is my intention to show you this miracle—the miracle of God in Rwanda.[8] (emphasis mine).

I can hardly say much more, other than buy his book! But I warn you, if you do, and if you dare wade into the biggest swamp of human need you might witness in this lifetime—it'll leave you in a state like *the Missionary Heart*—"the first thing God will do is to force through the channels of a single heart the interests of the whole world." And again, it'll crush you. I have witnessed the most intense feelings of sorrow and loss—and guilt and shame—from Rwandans as they recount their experiences. I have walked among the somber monuments of the genocide museum in Kigali. And I have made my commitment to the Rwandan people to never forget the desperate need for restoration in their country and in the hearts of its people. I have counted it among the greatest privileges of my life to be some small instrument in the hands of God to help bring restoration to a country in such brokenness.

The ministry of John Rucyahana with which we have partnered is living the scriptural prophesy from the prophet Jeremiah:

"This is what the Lord says:

"'Your wound is incurable,
    your injury beyond healing....
I have struck you as an enemy would
    and punished you as would the cruel,
because your guilt is so great and your sins so many....

"'But all who devour you will be devoured;
    all your enemies will go into exile.
Those who plunder you will be plundered;
    all who make spoil of you I will despoil.
But *I will restore you to health and heal your wounds,*'
    declares the LORD,
'because you are called an outcast,
    Zion for whom no one cares.' (Jer 30:12-17)

"Here is a poor African country, ripped to pieces by hatred and unfathomable cruelty, which I believe God is raising up as a shining example of what happens when a nation turns its hearts to Him.[9] Scripture makes it clear that God wants to use the broken pieces. Then, whatever He does in our lives, we cannot take credit for it."[10]

The nations of Liberia and Sierra Leone in West Africa share much of the same history, with warring factions rising up against their own citizens, and when it was all over, hundreds of thousands of lives were lost, both countries' infrastructure devastated. In the successive years of their wars, each country traded hundreds of thousands of refugees as they flooded past their shared borders. I already shared the state in which we found Liberia, and Sierra Leone was no different.

The overwhelming sense of hopelessness was everywhere; a country that had known a certain degree of development more than much of Africa now struggled in the dark without municipal power or water services, without the national wealth or ingenuity to rebuild the infrastructure; virtually nothing was left that didn't require rebuilding—and I'm not just talking about infrastructure! The human bones we found in the high grasses where we surveyed land were the first inescapable reminder. Whenever we travelled to the countryside, we'd see the usual little stick-built stands for selling vegetables or firewood crowded next to each other along the roads, illuminated in the evening by only a small candle on each table. If it weren't for the tragedy of all power lines having been stripped during the war for the metal's resale value, it would almost feel like a romantic improvement compared to the harsh glare of bare fluorescent lights. We found whole families smashing rocks by hand in the shadow of huge rock-crushing machinery that no longer had power or owners to operate it; a young man made four trips twice a day to a well to fill up the large buckets in our guest house bathrooms.

For my part in coming alongside my Liberian friends, believing for restoration in the land, I once again come back to Isaiah 58:10-12:

> ...if you spend yourselves in behalf of the hungry
>   and satisfy the needs of the oppressed,
> then your light will rise in the darkness,
>   and your night will become like the noonday.
> The Lord will guide you always;

> He will satisfy your needs in a sun-scorched land
>   and will strengthen your frame.
> You will be like a well-watered garden,
>   like a spring whose waters never fail.
> Your people will rebuild the ancient ruins
>   and will raise up the age-old foundations;
> you will be called Repairer of Broken Walls,
>   Restorer of Streets with Dwellings.

Elsewhere around the world, we find broken vestiges of age-old missionary ventures or the latent failings of imperialism from generations ago. Just as in the aftermath of war, peoples' lives are impacted by a bleak future struggling to get out from under a long-developed brokenness.

"When the white men came, their vision was to reach the Zambian people in the remote areas, building a hospital and a secondary school. The vision is still there, but we cannot do this on our own. When the white man left, there was a gap to fill." Lt. Col. Frazer Chalwa, the Salvation Army Director of the Chikankata mission station, summed up the challenge we came to help him face.

As I walked the mission station over the course of several days, people often called out from their front porches and gates, "How is the dam?" Children regularly followed me on the road, as they often do. Our team would share in the evenings about our interactions with the people. We were a team of engineers and planners in the heart of Zambia at a 70-year-old mission hospital, assessing its local water reservoir (a large lake behind a man-made earth dam). To the local people, the reservoir and the dam were one and the same. The water supply was dwindling, and we were told ahead of time that "the dam" was the problem.

Day after day, I was primarily studying the sprawling facilities and the site layout while our engineers were assessing the power and water supply. I was constantly amazed at the size of it all: 225 acres with 2000 people living, working, and going to school here. I had to retrace my steps daily because of how much I would miss each day in my research and observations.

Over and over I wrestled with the enormous vision that had founded such a campus in the middle of very rural Zambia, and the fact that today it was crumbling all around us. Lt. Col. Chalwe also told me, "The white farmers [in the area] were in full support but are no longer there. The whole design was by a missionary, not a Zambian. Going deep into the interior was not easy. The vision of 1947 is still there. EMI has come to do the research to match the time we are at now."

He was right of course. Where they are today is as if they were frozen in time 50 years ago, except that the deterioration of facilities has progressed. Today, we recognize the pitfalls of missionary outreach and international relief and development, often creating western dependency when the west mobilizes vast resources. We at EMI are embracing our role as "silent partners," bringing only the resources that are missing from the local Body of Christ as they desire to own the vision to minster to their own people and communities. In all our international offices, and on all our short-term teams, we recruit local design professionals to add to our teams. In this way, we see balance come to the process of shared resourcing and responsibility in all our partnerships, to realize restoration on a sustainable level.

But at this moment, that seemed completely unattainable. Over the years there has been a breakdown of mission and vision transfer—and subsequent ownership of the stewardship responsibility. But as Col. Chalwe spoke, he was referring to the need for the Church to work around the world to replace colonial domination. "Where there is no vision...," he partially quoted Proverbs 29:18, knowing that I knew the end. He simply said, "We need renewed missionary vision to carry us further." He labors under the tremendous weight of the difficulties faced by the Zambian church that we usually don't see or understand. He had just returned from the funeral of his father-in-law, saying that his wife was not well enough to meet us.

Little did we know what that meant—we got word weeks later that she had passed away.

And so EMI comes in the role of a servant, to undergird and "lift up the arms" of a weary national church and team of workers who don't know what they don't know. The problem was not so much with the dam, it was the broken facilities that needed restoration…from the water treatment tanks to the inadequate storage and distribution systems all over the campus. And with rolling black-outs, not enough water was being pumped and stored to meet the daily demand of 2000 people.

As our team of engineers provided this initial assessment, we created a benchmarking tool to begin a long process of partnering with the Zambians of Chikankata Mission to "rebuild the ancient ruins and restore the places long devastated; they will renew the ruined cities that have been devastated for generations" (Is 61:4).

We have dozens of similar experiences where wholesale destruction of communities has occurred, not just from man-made disasters like war, but also natural ones. I have led teams around the world responding to earthquakes and floods. EMI's beginnings go back to an experience in Saipan, where EMI's founder, Michael Orsillo (a civil engineer) providentially found himself chaperoning a youth mission trip to that country shortly after that little South Pacific island nation was recovering from damages sustained in a recent typhoon. As he studied the effects, documented issues for redesign, and gave advice, God birthed the vision of mobilizing engineers and architects to serve missionaries and the Church around the world.

In 2010, an earthquake epicentered at Leogane, Haiti, leveled half of the buildings in the region and claimed over 225,000 lives in just over 45 seconds. When I led a team of structural engineers into the devastation, we could not escape the weight of it all. Coming in as soon as the airport was able to reopen, we travelled from Port-au-Prince to Leogane and Carrefour. In the capital, you couldn't go a few hundred feet without encountering a damaged building, badly listing or twisted or crushed like stacks of pancakes. Multistory buildings now occupied the space of one story, all containing bodies. It was grim, and we were shaken. The cruel reality was that something could have been done ahead of time to mitigate these terrible losses. The country—like so much of the developing world—has a history of corruption in the government that allowed poor design and construction practices that greatly contributed to such a catastrophe.

Out in Leogane, a short distance from the capital, nearly every other building was leveled or severely damaged. The scene looked like something out of an apocalyptic movie, with piles of rubble cascading into the streets, preventing passage. The power lines and poles were toppled or hanging over the roads. Roads had been literally torn apart, with giant fissures down their lengths, one half of the pavement now two feet higher than the other. Tenuously hanging on to exposed steel rebar, whole sections of concrete floors or walls were dangling over pedestrian's heads as they tried to make their way in the streets below. The usual smell of burning trash was overpowered by the construction debris and dust clouds that hung in the air, and occasionally the strange smell of death.

We camped in the back lot of the Compassion International headquarters, only occasionally entering the damaged 4-story building. We could feel the building vibrate in response to aftershocks. We traveled all day in teams of two to assess buildings from which CI conducted their child-sponsorship programs. In the evenings we would return to design retrofits (if possible) to save structures we hadn't deemed irreparable. Our small team would debrief and pray and spend some time encouraging each other and found ourselves helping to encourage the Haitian people we were there to serve. Our efforts to serve them focused on creating hope that restoration could be possible—*would* be possible. No one with whom we talked had escaped losing someone they knew, often people who were very dear to them: family members, friends, coworkers—everyone was shouldering the pain and the loss. The hope of restoration kept them going.

And speaking of hope, much closer to home there are many works in which Christians can get involved. Eight Days of Hope (EDOH) is a ministry similar to EMI's international disaster response program, founded by my friend Steve Tybor. It all started in 2005 with a phone call from a father to a son after the devastation of Hurricane Katrina. The idea was for a few people to take a trip to the Gulf Coast to rebuild a home or two. What ended up happening was nothing less than astounding: it became a volunteer effort of 684 people loving and serving 84 families—something, truly, only God could do!

From that simple beginning, it has become a movement through which God has touched thousands of people's lives and impacted communities forever. The number eight means "new beginnings." When they considered the real reason they were going to the coast, it wasn't just about rebuilding the damaged homes—it was about sharing the hope of our God. Hence, the ministry "Eight Days of Hope" was born.

Since then, EDOH has done 18 rebuilding events. Through trips that occur within months after a disaster, they include roofing, carpentry, electrical, painting, and more. In 2014, EDOH started a Rapid Response arm to respond 48-72 hours after a disaster strikes with tasks such as gutting homes and tarping roofs. In 2016, EDOH added distribution, feeding, shower, and laundry ministries. The distribution ministry serves as a conduit for large companies to donate products that are no longer being used, which EDOH then provides to churches for free to help their communities. The feeding, shower, and laundry ministries often accompany rebuilding and rapid response trips, but the trailers are also available for churches to use when they are not being utilized by EDOH.

In 2018, EDOH put plans in place to build a national headquarters in Tupelo, Mississippi. The headquarters opened in May 2019. Eventually, a Northeast satellite was established in Buffalo, NY, and a Midwest satellite in Cedar Rapids, Iowa. In the fall of 2019, EDOH launched the newest arm of its ministry: building or remodeling safe houses for survivors of human trafficking.

I have witnessed EDOH teams on site and in makeshift dorm rooms we've shared in an old school building. They are not all skilled tradesmen. They are whole families of people who simply want to be a part of restoring lives and homes and communities. Anyone can do this! And there are so many more opportunities in our culture at home to do similar things—outreaches of all kinds to any persons at risk for many different reasons—food scarcity, homelessness, addictions, mental illness, and disabilities. When our children were small, my wife would involve them in making sandwiches to be distributed through Hearts for the Homeless, a local street ministry back in Buffalo. These ministries and many more are forever looking for more workers, partners, donors—people!

Now, put restoration back into the story [as the appropriate book end]. Instantly you've created millions of jobs for all the "unemployed" and bored Christians in the church—jobs they can get excited about. Now there is work to do for people who want to make the world a better place in the meantime. Instead of simply waiting for God to unveil the new heaven and the new earth, the rest of us can give the world a taste of what God's kingdom is all about—building up, repairing brokenness, showing mercy, reinstating hope, and generally adding value. In this expanded model, everyone plays an essential role. In this way, relearning [restoration] becomes exciting and personal.[11]

"I looked for someone among them who would build up the wall..." Today you can be found in works of restoration near you! And being a part of restoration gives the world a glimpse of the heart of God and the possibility of a different future—for them, for us, for all of his creation!

CHAPTER 8

INTERCESSION

"... and stand before me..."

"I looked for someone among them who would build up the wall **and stand before me** *in the gap on behalf of the land so I would not have to destroy it, but I found no one."*
Ezekiel 22:30

Every culture of the world knows there's something broken about us in our human existence. That's why we long for restoration. We long for things to be good or set right, without really knowing why or how. Everyone is trying to reach the place of peace, wholeness, and "oneness" with whatever or whomever can make it right. "He has made everything beautiful in its time. He has also set eternity in the human heart; yet no one can fathom what God has done from beginning to end" (Eccl 3:11). Don Richardson does a thorough and masterful job recounting thousands of years of folk history and religious tradition in *Eternity in Their Hearts* that bears out this fact.

> Clearly the Abrahamic Covenant did not mark the first time God revealed himself to men...Others [in the biblical record]...had received direct communication from God. All of these prior revelations center around (1) the fact of God's existence; (2) creation; (3) the rebellion and fall of man; (4) the need for a sacrifice to appease God and the crafty attempts of devils to make men sacrifice to them; (5) the great Flood; (6) the sudden appearance of many languages and the resulting dispersion of mankind into many peoples; and finally (7) an acknowledgement of man's need of some

further revelation that will seal man back into a blessed relationship with God. These seven major facts which were known before Abraham's time are still included among the main components of folk religions worldwide.[1]

The seventh will be the focus of the next two chapters.

Today, every culture has a solution—generally an endless process that includes performance of interventions of some kind or another. Those solutions comprise the religions or other systems of thought from those cultures. I love to study the basic strategies that come out of world religions, compare and contrast their basic tenets with Christianity, and even learn them. That is beyond the scope of this book; but we will, however, cover some of those basic ideas in Chapter 9.

For now, let us simply agree: Jesus stands in stark contrast to every one of them. Our God's solution is not a system, an outline, or a map; nor is it an endless list of things to do or duties to perform or improvements to make upon the human condition. It is a person. A person with whom you may have a life-changing experience and a life-long love affair. More on this, too, in the next chapter.

But still, answering the how and the why becomes a salient point to our understanding of the whole story. HOW is it that Jesus has become the literal solution to our struggle with brokenness? And WHY should we want a lifelong relationship with him? That's the heart of it. We each have a relationship with Jesus quite simply because He and the Father are one, and He has come to stand between us and the Father, and bridge the gap that was created by sin, disobedience, brokenness, and shame. *He always lives to intercede for them* Heb 7:25, emphasis mine). *That's the HOW.*

Intercession means to be standing in the place of someone who can't, acting as a representative of someone who needs help, or speaking on behalf of someone who doesn't even know their need. At its core, for believers everywhere, it is praying for and on behalf of others. Intercession (*pagha`* in Hebrew) means "to strike upon," "to assail anyone with petitions," or "to urge," on behalf of another.

We see this word used often in the Old Testament: In Ruth 1:16, we see the *urging* of Ruth's impassioned plea to Naomi to not send her away; in Jeremiah 7:16, God refers to their *pleas and petitions* and in 27:18 we see the prophets are instructed to *plead their case before the Lord Almighty*; In Genesis 23:8, Abraham asks the people to *intercede on his behalf.* Job 21:15 asks the question, "What do we gain by *praying to him?*" (The Almighty); When we engage in intercession—or "intercessory prayer"—we gain access to God on behalf of another.

God himself has fulfilled this role. From the beginning of creation He knew what would be required: He clothed himself in humanity and became a servant, the very vehicle of intercession for mankind. "...For He bore the sin of many, and *made intercession for* the transgressors" (Is 53:12, emphasis mine). "Therefore He is able to save completely those who come to God through him because He always lives to *intercede for them*" (Heb 7:25, emphasis mine). There are plenty of verses that speak to God's initiative: before we try to do anything on our own, God has proven his heart, his character, and his nature...and *demonstrated* for us what is to be done! "...Christ Jesus who died—more than that, who was raised to life—is at the right hand of God and *is also interceding for us*" (Rom 8:34, emphasis mine).

And if Jesus is forever now living to make intercession for us, how can we do any less? To this you were called, that you should follow in his steps. I have seen Jesus call individual believers to join him in intercession most often and most powerfully in the lives of our missionary partners with whom I've worked all around the world. So often, it begins in the heart of just one man or woman (remember, God is looking for s*omeone* —even just *one*!) as God's heart begins to grow in them. They cannot escape the incredible burden of intercession they are drawn into on behalf of friends, families, countries or people groups.

In Chapter 6, I introduced you to David Dann and his incredible calling by God to return to Liberia, his devastated homeland. Fifteen years of civil war claimed the lives of 250,000 people and had all but destroyed David's ties to his homeland with the deaths of his family and friends. But God gave David a new heart—a missionary heart— to intercede for his people.

The EMI team arrived in Liberia after days of travel delays. As we taxied in on the Monrovian runway, wide lines of people had assembled by a chain link fence, perspiring profusely in the intense midday sun while waiting for arrivals. Then I saw the obvious reason they were there, waiting in the steaming heat. The two-story concrete terminal building stood in blackened, burned-out ruins, a monument to what once was. The building in which we were processed as foreign visitors was just a small, concrete block barracks-like structure, far too small for all the impatient people trying to get their bags and leave. The pushing, shouting crowds and pungent odor made navigating baggage claim and customs chaotic.

David received us, along with his church leaders, and finally we were on our way, packed tightly with all our bags and too many people in an old van. I could tell this was a place unlike any other I had seen when we came to a roadblock check point just minutes from the airport. These ubiquitous road checks would become routine in a few days—each with its sandbag and chain-link walls and guards who appeared to be young teenagers, semi-automatic weapons in hand and stoic looks on their faces. "What horrors lay beneath the stares?" I wondered.

As we learned more history and heard the personal stories of hardship from David's friends and ministry partners, it was painful to see how the oppressed became the oppressors. The freed Africans from the United States and the Caribbean who colonized Liberia in the mid-19th century dominated the native Liberians for decades, and ultimately brought destruction upon themselves and their country.

Each day would see us packing tightly into our van and heading down the blockaded roads. We'd return after long days in the jungle sun to our guest house on the Liberian coast—quite nice accommodations really, though without power or running water—on the grounds of the ELWA (Eternal Love Winning Africa) radio station compound. All the white missionaries had left the country during the war years, but the nationals remained and persevered to rescue this facility, the only radio outreach for the city of Monrovia.

A particularly exciting time was a live interview we did at this radio station. A church member told us later that he heard us on the air and felt the conviction of the Holy Spirit confirming, "These men and women have been sent by God."

Sharing a room—and literally the only bed—with David in a little house on the shores of the Atlantic allowed me to see why and how we were sent by God. Every morning I would wake early while it was yet dark to the quiet mumblings of David in prayer, on his knees at the side of his bed. The reason EMI was there at all was in direct response to the work of intercession to which he had been committed for years. He was well-organized and prepared to facilitate the work our team needed to do each day; but nothing was done that didn't begin in simple intercession for his people and his land, before his God who had called David to stand before him.

Before we ever reached Liberia, however, the EMI team had its first significant intercessory prayer need in a neighboring country. As I reached the door of the plane to descend the long metal stairway to the asphalt below, the now-familiar blast of humidity that blanketed me seemed like the greeting of an old friend saying, "Welcome to Africa—once again." It was dark again after more than 36 hours of planes and airports. Walking to the customs entry across the dimly lit airfield, I noticed the airport sign of Cote d'Ivoire. We were here in the Ivory Coast just till we could catch the flight to Liberia tomorrow. Only God knew what delays awaited us there.

After passing through the French-speaking customs check there in Abidjan, we waited in the baggage claim area only to find that four bags with our survey equipment, tools, (and all my clothes & supplies!) had not made it. It took more than an hour to arrange to have our bags traced and forwarded, since we would have to leave for Liberia the next day before the next Air France flight would arrive. There were mountains of unclaimed bags from previous flights piled near the baggage carousel—I left that night with little confidence that I was ever going to see those bags again. We were the last ones to leave. What was earlier a loud, intimidating, foreign place was now almost desolate, and equally intimidating. As we walked out of the last customs gate, we were greeted by one familiar face, June Mathias.

You might say June came in May! June was my old friend from Buffalo, New York, sent by our home church into her mission calling. She had been working with Wycliffe Bible Translators for nearly 10 years in Burkina Faso. When I learned that I would be in Liberia, just two small West African countries away, I emailed her. She told me that at the time I'd be there, she would be taking some vacation leave time away from Ouagadougou because it typically is about 125 degrees there that time of year (and this was only May!). Well, as God would have it, she did meet us down on the coast there in Abidjan and joined me and my team for the entire trip. Speaking fluent French, she was an invaluable member of our team—especially for the next few days.

The next day we returned to the airport. *We prayed fervently as a team, asking God to intervene on our behalf somehow.* Committing our missing bags to the Lord, we boarded the Ghana Airways plane to Monrovia, Liberia's capital. We couldn't have imagined what God would do! The small commercial airplane felt more like a bus, with bench seats, and rudimentary interiors, not inspiring confidence in its capabilities. As we got over Monrovia—just an hour away—there was a severe storm. There were no lights on the runway and radio contact with the airport was lost, so they turned the plane around and returned to Abidjan! The next flight would not be for two more days. *That night* we got two bags in from Paris and *the next night* we got the last two—I felt like we had to apologize to all the rest of the passengers *for how God intervened on our behalf and answered our prayers so miraculously!* It meant we were a bit more rushed during the rest of the trip but what we found at the airport in Monrovia more than convinced me that God was in control all along.

Over and over again, I could recount the stories of miraculously answered prayer as we put ourselves out there on the edge of the frontier of faith, where we are completely powerless to make anything happen on our own and we must fully depend on the divine working of God on our behalf and on the behalf of those we serve and for whom we are "standing in the gap." But so often on the other side of the ocean, instead of a vibrant call to a prayerful life of intercession in every believer, it seems like the Church believes it's the job of a specially called group of people called to intercessory prayer. It's for "those people." Over there. Not here. "I could never do what you do," is something I've actually been told—and more than once! Really? What is it that I do that's so unique or special? I would say nothing, but attacking the core of the American dream is not nothing! If we are to see the kingdom of Heaven come to earth, we must all embrace the entire heart of God—and that begins with intercession.

The apostle Paul, in discipling the young pastor Timothy, reminds him, "I urge then, first of all, that petitions, prayers, intercession and thanksgiving *be made for all people...*" (1 Tim 2:1, emphasis mine). A little historical context here is helpful to understanding this scriptural mandate for the Church. The context reveals that as important as the actual acts of prayer and intercession are, it is equally as important to do it for *everyone*. The church had fallen prey to some factions already in its infancy, and numerous times the apostle Paul had to address these in his letters to the churches. In this case, the Body that Timothy was shepherding in his early days as pastor was picking and choosing who they'd like to pray for! Paul goes on "...for all people—for kings and all those in authority, that we may live peaceful and quiet lives in all godliness and holiness" (1 Tim 2:1-2). All people? That's certainly going to be a long list. It's likely that is going to take *every member* of the Body of Christ fully engaged in the work of intercession to do that!

And if "for all people" isn't clear enough, there are many more Scriptures that provide insight into how and for whom we should offer prayers, not just those in authority:

- enemies (Jer 29:7 and Mt 5:44)
- Jerusalem (Ps 122:6)
- friends, especially when they have acted foolishly (Job 42:8)
- ministers or those who need rescuing (Phil 1:19)

- the sick (James 5:14)
- those who forsake us (2 Tim 4:16)

That about covers it, doesn't it? Where could we ever have gotten the idea that this kind of prayer can or should only be done by a special few within the Body of Christ that are somehow "called" to intercessory prayer? These Scriptures—and the whole story from beginning to end of the Bible—should make it abundantly clear that it is a job and calling for every believer; any follower of Jesus must do as He did—and does. The real problem lies in our detachment from people in need, and our preoccupation with the busy lives we lead. So even though praying for the needs of others is often a part of our things-to-do list, thoughts that take us there and to the desperate needs of others are often pushed aside.

I've already recounted Jackie Pullinger's testimony that the missionary's heart response was practically instantaneous for her at the moment of her conversion. That knowledge always haunted me, as I wrestled with the question, "Why must you stay?" Once I answered the call to go, I finally began the process of letting go of the things that had constrained me—held me—in the grip of my western materialism, and created so much distraction from the fundamental call to all believers, "Go make disciples of all nations…" And when that becomes your primary purpose, you can't help but intercede for people when you engage God in prayer. Nothing else really matters anymore. God is still looking for someone among the faithful to stand up for the sake of the faithless, the lost— those who are still blinded in sin, caught in the trap of the Enemy who is at work seeking to "steal, kill, and destroy" their lives. God is looking for his people to step out from the crowd instead of blending in, separating, coping, or just surviving. He wants us to intercede for the masses struggling under the weight of sin and brokenness.

It was Israel's faithlessness that resulted in exile, where God's people were living at the time of his message through Ezekiel. Faithlessness is the normative condition of today across most of our everyday culture. At best, most of western culture is no longer interested in nor satisfied with the Christian message. At worst, your friends, family, and neighbors have been abused, abandoned, or battered by it. We are often at a loss as to where to go when confronted today with such a polarizing opposition to the message. But intercession is the greatest act of love—and the greatest tool for change—that can be shared by *every* believer! Dietrich Bonhoeffer wrote, in *Life Together,*

> Therefore, spiritual love proves itself in that everything it says and does commends Christ. It will not seek to move others by all too personal, direct influence, by impure interference in the life of another. It will not take pleasure in pious, human fervor and excitement. It will rather meet the other person with the clear Word of God and be ready to leave him alone with this Word for a long time, willing to release him again in order that Christ may deal with him. It will respect the line that has been drawn between him and us by Christ, and it will find full fellowship with him in the Christ who alone binds us together. Thus this spiritual love will speak to Christ about a brother more than to a brother about Christ. It knows that the most direct way to others is always through prayer to Christ and that love of others is wholly dependent upon the truth in Christ.[2]

The greatest thing we can do for another is to "speak to Christ about a brother more than to a brother about Christ!" I can hear the prophet Samuel saying, "As for me, far be it from me that I should sin against the Lord by failing to pray for you" (1 Sam 12:23).

> *Intercession is the greatest act of love—and the greatest tool for change—that can be shared by every believer!*

Another critical idea to draw from Bonhoeffer's writing is this: as we desire to connect with and intercede for people, the overwhelming possibility exists that we might hurt or control or manipulate in the process. To prevent that, and at the same time to facilitate successful intercession (and later intermediation, which we'll discuss in Chapter 10), Jesus comes as both the line that separates us (to protect each other from our own sinfulness) and the bond that unites us (once we've come into God's family and have fellowship on a playing field that is leveled).

So, why do we still fail to pray? There are as many reasons as there are people to debate this, but here are several very common ones. We have *defined* intercession in such a way—as I've already stated—that we believe it's a special gift for a special few. We have heard the condemning voice of our enemy and believe we are not worthy to pray for big things, hard things, or things we still long for ourselves. We don't really know what to pray for. We don't have the time. We don't think we have the personality for that kind of praying. We think, "Isn't this for ministers or missionaries, Jesus freaks, grey-haired grandmas, or retirees with lots of time?" We're defeated before we even begin, thinking "What difference can one prayer really make?" Ultimately, we don't have faith and don't understand our power in prayer or believe that we have it. Whatever the reason—and there are more than these—Romans 8:26 reminds us that "In the same way, the Spirit helps us in our weakness. We do not know what we ought to pray for, but the Spirit himself intercedes for us."

It was April, ahead of a fall no American will ever forget. I stood on the rooftop porch of a missionary's home high in the mountains of North India—in the foothills of the Himalayas—praying with a small group of people for a country of which I had seldom thought. Our host provided us with prayer journal entries made by a group of women who had journeyed to the country months earlier to learn first-hand how to pray with more insight and to "ask God for the nations." Our host had also made an outline of the country in yarn on the floor with candles lit at the major cities—Kabul, Kandahar, Jalalabad...names I'd never heard before. As we interceded for a darkened nation, our little group cried for the oppressed and prayed that the forces of the enemy would be bound and overthrown. At one point, I sensed God would have us step into the outlined land, in a prophetic demonstration of claiming, receiving, and taking it for the kingdom of God. I never imagined the future events that would unfold.

The following January, only a few months following September 11th, 2001, EMI's CEO, Glen Woodruff—my boss, mentor, and friend—led an EMI volunteer team that met with high-ranking government leaders in Afghanistan. EMI was partnering with another Christian organization that had been doing disaster relief and community development in Afghanistan for years. Their director said, "We have been building bridges of trust [for years] so that the trucks of salvation might cross over." Glen remembers:

> Our first trip we flew into Peshawar, Pakistan. We checked into a guest house while exploring options for travel to complete the final leg of our journey—Kabul. We explored all options; quickly, there appeared to be no options. During our wait, one of the team members shared Matthew 11:12, "From the days of John the Baptist until now, the kingdom of Heaven is forcefully advancing, and forceful men lay hold of it." I wondered if the Church was up for the battle. Were we up for it? After three days we hired a caravan of cars and trucks led by a pickup packed with six or seven men in turbans with guns and RPG's. Locals called them "security." We left Peshawar early on a Saturday morning and we arrived in Kabul just as the sun set. The next day, Sunday, we attended an expat church service—as far as anyone knew, the first church service in many years in Afghanistan. Had we joined in the advance?

EMI returned a couple months later and again in October with two full teams of volunteers who began infrastructure assessment and specific design and rebuilding projects. Imagine...EMI a part of leading the way to reach this country. We hardly knew where to begin, but their officials offered us office space in Kabul in which to set up and get started! In awe of God, we titled EMI's National Conference that year "IMAGINE: Building the kingdom in the 3rd Millennium." Dan Batchelder, the ministry leader who had been investing relationship-building efforts for so many years in a country then ripe for harvest was our keynote speaker and shared a model for reaching the closed world.

I'm reminded of Ezekiel's reply to God when He asked him in verse 37:3, "Son of man, can these bones live?" I [Ezekiel] said, "O Sovereign Lord, you alone know." You know the rest of the story. God commands him to prophesy—speak what He commanded—and God does the supernatural work.

Even in saying, "O Lord, you alone know," I wonder if Ezekiel imagined the outcome? A preacher along on one of our trips at that time encouraged all those in attendance at a worship service with this thought: "If you can imagine it, God can do it." I appreciate that thought simply for the vision that it speaks of: "Is there anything too hard for Me?" says the Lord. No Lord, of course not... but then do I go out and live my life based on that profession of faith? We can change the world if we do.

The importance of this kind of foundational prayer at the core of evangelism and outreach cannot be overstated. Like David Dann at his bedside each morning—faced with the prospect of overwhelming devastation all around him—we see it as fundamental to everything to which God would have us put our hands for the sake of the Kingdom. And every day, we can intercede with these same kinds of foundational, strategic prayers in every situation in which we find ourselves. It should be a great comfort and encouragement that we all can do this, and that we would all take part in the privilege of partnering in the Spirit to do so!

If we're going to pray for people to be set free from sin and darkness and brokenness, we've got to understand the dynamics of spiritual power—not just emotionalism, not wishful thinking, but genuine power! Ephesians 2:6 says, "And God raised us up with Christ and seated us with him in the heavenly realms in Christ Jesus." All through the first chapter of Ephesians, Paul explains how much power Jesus has, and He has this power for the Church! Does any Christian question the power of Jesus himself? No! So what about Ephesians 2:6? Here Paul is talking about God having put us in a position in him so that we can exercise that power. Talk about being "positioned" by God! Anything that we do in life that's good is because we abide in Christ. Christ is in us; we are in him. We are nothing: we have absolutely no hope outside of Christ. But in Christ we can do all things because He strengthens us! (Phil 4:13). If we can really understand the strength of Christ, and what it means to pray in the name of Jesus, then we can do everything we need to do in the spiritual realm.

When we pray and we say *in the name of Jesus*, that means we are praying in the stead, position, and nature of Jesus; as an ambassador, co-laborer, and representative of Jesus—one who *intercedes!* When we say "in the name of Jesus," it's not just some random line we tack on at the end of our prayers to identify ourselves as Christians. It's a point of power—a place where we say we're doing this as a representative of the Son of God, not independent, impotent agents acting on our own. We're not doing it on our own; we're doing it because Christ indwells us. With this understanding, we have a much clearer picture from Jesus as He replies to Philip:

> Philip said, "Lord, show us the Father and that will be enough for us."

> Jesus answered: "Don't you know me, Philip, even after I have been among you such a long time? Anyone who has seen me has seen the Father. How can you say, 'Show us the Father'? Don't you believe that I am in the Father, and that the Father is in me? The words I say to you I do not speak on my own authority. Rather, it is the Father, living in me, who is doing his work. Believe me when I say that I am in the Father and the Father is in me; or at least believe on the evidence of the works themselves. Very truly I tell you, whoever believes in me will do the works I have been

doing, and they will do even greater things than these, because I am going to the Father. And I will do whatever you ask in my name, so that the Father may be glorified in the Son. You may ask me for anything in my name, and I will do it. (Jn 14:8-14)

Christ has positioned us at the right hand of God the Father, so when we pray something in the name of the Lord Jesus, we're speaking it as an ambassador of the King of Kings and Lord of Lords—we're speaking it as an ambassador from Heaven! So we don't actually pray from earth. We pray from heaven, seated with Christ! Your kingdom come, your will be done, on earth as it is in Heaven. If we pray from our position on earth that means it's a position under sin—a position under the curse, under depression, under disease, under failure, under biological results and the survival of the fittest. But when you stand up and you pray in Jesus' name, you've received his nature, his mind, his name, his authority, his righteousness, his word. And as a person in that position, you are a brand-new creation yourself!

I know we have trouble believing all this, "but Jesus beheld them, and said to them, "With man this is impossible, but not with God; all things are possible with God" (Mk 10:27). I love John Piper's thoughts on this from his book, *Desiring God*: "In front the words give hope, and behind they give humility. They are the antidote to despair and pride."[3] This is where every believer can grow a new excitement about embracing our invitation to partner with Jesus himself in intercession.

Our work in Nepal demonstrates John Piper's commentary on this, as I reported to our supporters many years ago, with some input from my intern, Andy Rice. A missionary born in Siberia and raised in South Korea, God has chosen Emmanuel Lee to be a church planter in the difficult regions of North India and Nepal. Humble and small in stature, he speaks a dozen languages (but only six fluently!). He fought in the Viet Nam War with the U.S. Army's Special Forces and for decades has devoted himself to missionary work in India and Nepal.

Intercession

Christian missionaries have long been restricted from Nepal; today they are permitted strictly for humanitarian work. Churches are not illegal, but evangelizing in public is forbidden. Several years ago, The Nepal Theological Seminary University (NTSU) was *miraculously* approved by the Nepali government as an educational institution. Emmanuel operates this small seminary for training young men to be pastors and church planters in Gospel-hostile areas such as India and Nepal, and most of these young men believe they are called to martyrdom.

Our EMI team was there to help him plan an expansion with new land and new structures added to an existing building that was a 300-year-old former palace. If you had looked at the EMI file we had on Emmanuel and his work developing this seminary, you would likely have been discouraged. We were committed to partnering with a missionary with no real home, no substantive support (following the Asian market collapse), who couldn't write very well in English, and had just a handful of students that he was training. You might have thought his work and calling were of no real consequence. One would have never guessed that this individual could have been used so mightily by God over the years. It took a fair amount of prying for our team to learn many of these details. Our intern Andy Rice writes:

> My first impression of NTSU was dismal. I could not understand how the word "seminary" could be used to describe a place in this condition with only seven students. As time passed while we were there, I learned that each student stays there for 3 years. They study Greek and Hebrew each semester along with other biblical and evangelism courses. Their day starts at 5:30 a.m. with worship (I heard it each morning; we lived in the same building) and finishes at 10 p.m. During the day they have 6-7 hours of class time, with professors coming from India, Nepal and Korea to live at the NTSU compound for various semesters. The students share the routine tasks of cleaning,

laundry, upkeep and food preparation. They also have regular devotion and study times throughout the day. The students are required to keep a rigorous schedule to say the least.

Nepal was a place that seemed hopeless. My problem-solving mind constantly thought "If we could just give them better housing or clean water, we could do...whatever." Obviously, what they need is the light of the Gospel, but when you see women along the road that had just filled their urns with muddy water where earlier that morning at dawn people had just relieved themselves along the shores, this architect can't help but think of meeting physical needs. Everywhere in the local villages, along the road mixed with the homes were shrines, altars, and idols, freshly painted from that morning's worship. And next to them are cesspools of sludge and filth—a word picture of physical filth to go with the spiritual. Permeating every level of society, Hinduism appears only to contribute to the perpetual poverty and hopelessness. But into this seemingly forgotten land comes God's partner in the gospel, Emmanuel Lee—sent by God, "invited to the dance," and making something beautiful out of the "mud puddles of human need."

Every evening he would join us for our worship and devotions (all our trips end each day with a couple hours of worship and devotions). He would generally be quiet through much of the discussion time, but at the end he'd have a few profound comments and the team would be left in awe to ponder this man's life and work and his relationship with his God. When describing how so many things have been accomplished, all he says is that he *prays, and God does the rest.*

Remember the significance of the early church model? I believe it had to be missional by its very nature and what it was all about. In fact, Emmanuel Lee's small band of students in his "Theological Seminary" had the look and feel and functional mission and ministry that I imagine was very much like the early church:

> They devoted themselves to the apostles' teaching and to fellowship, to the breaking of bread *and to prayer*. Everyone was filled with awe at the many wonders and signs performed by the apostles. All the believers were together and had everything in common. They sold property and possessions to give to anyone who had need. Every day they continued to meet together in the temple courts. They broke bread in their homes and ate together with glad and sincere hearts, praising God and enjoying the favor of all the people. And the Lord added to their number daily those who were being saved. (Acts 2:42—47, emphasis mine)

Do we see ourselves that way as a local church in our community? Hardly ever, I dare say. But today we can resolve to embrace that very same mission that is ours as the Church today and devote ourselves to prayer.

Recently, I had the opportunity to spend 5 days with a group of fellow evangelists (The Forge team of speakers, with Dwight Robertson, their leader) on the campus of the Billy Graham Evangelistic Association in Charlotte, North Carolina. We attended workshops and participated in the launch of the Evangelism Intensive with BGEA leadership and took part in the museum "experience" that chronicles Billy Graham's life. I will never forget an interview with Billy Graham by news commentator Greta Van Susteren. The interview was being played on a loop in one of the last halls of the museum exhibit, and in it Greta asked Dr. Graham (who was 92 at this point), "If you were to do things over again, would you do it differently?" I was struck by his response. He said, "Yes. I would study more. I would pray more. Travel less. Take less speaking engagements. I took too many of them, in too many places around the world…If I had it to do over again, I'd spend more time in meditation and prayer." To clarify, he went on to say that he wouldn't have spoken less at the stadium events (focused on the Gospel message being preached where thousands of decisions to follow Christ were made), but more the conferences and other things where he was invited to speak. Nearer to the end, Greta asked him, "If you have any advice for young preachers today, what's the advice?" Without any hesitation, he replied and reiterated his earlier thought, "Spend more time in study and prayer." For this busy Christian worker, that is a sobering call! If Billy Graham—who has preached to millions all over the world—feels like he did not pray enough for the people to whom he was called to bring the message, then how can I justify any more lost or wasted time in my life that ought to be devoted to more time with God in prayer? We must embrace the critical role of prayer—often, extended, purposeful, strategic and prevailing—if we ever hope to see the glory of God at work in our lives and the people to whom we are called to serve.

I know it's difficult to read this chapter and believe you could make a change instantly. But coming through and out of the cultural morass of the global Covid pandemic, John Eldridge has written two new books (*Get Your Life Back* and *Resilient*) that are great resources for busy people who want to connect—or reconnect—with God. One simple tool that he has produced is his *One-Minute Pause* app. It reminds us on a timer to pray, "Lord, I give everyone and everything to You." If you can devote more than one minute, you can build from there. But with or without the app and your cell phone, you can embrace the simple idea that I've put forth and begin to orient yourself to more time praying for the world. Set daily reminders, make your prayer simple, and determine to refocus away from all the distraction and to the "One Who Knows."

CHAPTER 9

RECONCILIATION
"...in the gap..."

"I looked for someone among them who would build up the wall and stand before me **in the gap** *on behalf of the land so I would not have to destroy it, but I found no one."*
Ezekiel 22:30

As I began focusing on "in the gap" in Chapter 2, the meaning of this little portion of Scripture in the original Hebrew is "to be in between." As we see it used only a small number of other times in the Bible, it refers to a repairing, a mending, or harmonizing of two sides or two positions, bringing them back together in *reconciliation*. When used in physical terms, it would be a refilling or rebuilding; in more spiritual or emotional references—such as in relationships—it would be reparation or making amends. A biblical idea here that is synonymous is atonement. Perhaps nothing is more important to the believer than this.

> But God demonstrates his own love for us in this: while we were still sinners, Christ died for us.
>
> Since we have now been justified by his blood, how much more shall we be saved from God's wrath through him! For if, while we were God's enemies, we were reconciled to him through the death of his Son, how much more, having been reconciled, shall we be saved through his life! Not only is this so, but we also boast in God through our

Lord Jesus Christ, through whom we have now received reconciliation." (Rom 5:8-11)

We have been reconciled to God! This is Good News! And even better news is that it was 100% initiated by God! It did not depend one iota on us! As I stated in Chapter 8, this in and of itself is what makes Christianity stand out uniquely against all other world religions. *Every* other religious system in the world sets out a rigorous set of rules or standards that one must achieve *before* one can expect to arrive at forgiveness, peace, wholeness, or any other place that reconciles us, elevating us above our struggle with brokenness. Most approach the problem of our brokenness with the first assumption being that we are inherently good, but need to work hard on our weakness and ignorance in order to find the answers we all seek. I'm not just speaking from study, but also from the experiences I have had sitting with people around the world, observing and hearing about their lives and cultures and faiths.

> Well-meaning people eager to avoid controversy commonly insist that all religions are different ways of comprehending the same truth. This is an erroneous view, although it contains an element of truth...There is a common morality that the great religions of the world share. Also, the monotheistic religions are attempts to worship the one God and therefore the same God. They differ however, in their understanding of why man needs God and how man can find him.[1]

It's not my purpose to go very deep into a study of world religions here—and it's certainly not my intent to vilify any of the precious people I have met who are living in these religious belief systems—but for now, let's just encapsulate some of what I'm talking about.

Islam has its 5 Pillars—the profession of faith, prayer, almsgiving, fasting, and pilgrimage—all good things, at least at face value. Even if the most faithful adherent performed each one as perfectly as he could, there's still no guarantee this is enough to please the unknowable and capricious Allah. Cab drivers—who I've engaged from time to time—have literally said, "Well, we do the best we can." Islam offers no chance of reconciliation or relationship. I met over lunch one afternoon in Ethiopia with some very gracious Muslim professionals who worked in Addis Ababa government offices tied to building and construction permitting and legal practices. It became clear as they shared their stories with me that they were educated for most of their childhood in private, foreign missionary-run, Catholic schools. I asked how they viewed themselves, their own Muslim faith, and their place in the multi-faith religious life in which they were raised. The answer was "we are very tolerant Muslims." My impression was that meant they were quite secularized. I spoke up with perhaps more boldness than I should have, and said, "I respect that and am thankful that you welcome us here [to do the development projects we were designing in Ethiopia], but I want you to know that we love and follow Jesus who commanded us not to just tolerate people, but to "love your enemies." I do not call you my enemy, but I am used to being seen myself that way. Thank you for tolerating me." It was actually amusing and disarming, and the lunch went on easily. I'll come back to the importance of this later, but suffice it to say, true reconciliation is unknowable for the Muslim.

Buddhism has the 4 Noble Truths and the 8-Fold Path. The 4 Noble Truths are all about suffering: its causes, ending, and solution to free us and the world of it. The 8-Fold Path is a series of statements about understanding, intentions, speech, action, livelihood, effort, mindfulness, and concentration—again, all good things. I often wish Christians would invest this kind of thought into the examination of their own lives and behavior as Paul admonishes the church at Corinth to do in 2 Corinthians 13:5! So many of the tenets are practical and good for everyone to attain to, but I have never known anyone to get this all right—and I've asked monks at shrines if they had. Of course, no one has. And as good as they might seem at face value, their fruit in people's lives all around the world is not usually so.

I once sat down to dinner with an American Catholic who converted to Buddhism. He prayed over our meal of salads that we would be forgiven (by whom exactly is unknown) for taking life, because all food is a life. My immediate thought was, "What good is a religious system that requires you to ask for forgiveness for doing something you fully intend to do—indeed, *must* do—again and again every day for the rest of your life?!

I had the opportunity to meet another Buddhist on a church-planting mission in Thailand. As the village witch doctor, he was the most respected man in the village. He invited us in to share tea with him and, as we sat in his little elevated smoke-filled straw hut, we could see he was quite drunk. He had walked us back to his place, his arm around my 16-year-old son Zac. He was a very friendly and warm drunk but drunk just the same. Over and over again, I've seen that the search for enlightenment often leaves a void that adherents try to fill with the use of drugs and alcohol.

It is almost impossible to give a brief summary of Hinduism here. It is a boundless universe of gods and goddesses, sacred texts and laws accumulated by different people at different times over thousands of years that form various collections of writings about spiritual and earthly knowledge. It is believed that the ancient holy men of Hinduism developed a "consciousness" that enabled them to hear the truths about the universe, the nature of god, and life. Unlike Buddhism, which does not have a concept of God or an afterlife with or without him, the endless practices and rituals that accompany a faithful Hindu life are accompanied by a philosophy of karma and an attempt to appease the gods (reconciliation) and to impact one's future reincarnated status for the better (though this can never be guaranteed). But like Buddhism, Hinduism similarly addresses the problem of selfishness through meditation that attempts to wipe out the "self," since that is at the root of the problem of the human condition. Essentially, the goal is to become nothing. I agree with Dinesh D'Souza, who says,

This is a supremely difficult project. Among Buddhists, only the monks claim to even approach nirvana. I believe the awareness of the chasm separating holiness from human weakness has produced, in Hindu and Buddhist cultures, their distinctive fatalism. Many Hindus believe fate will decree whether they reappear as a prince, a dog, or a flea in the next life.[2]

Admittedly, as an outsider looking in, I see it usually only oppressing people, but I've learned much from the writings of E. Stanley Jones, a 20th century Methodist missionary who worked extensively across India and Africa without attacking any religion (including Hinduism, Buddhism, and Islam). He began his work with the lowest in the caste system but caught the attention of the high castes in the process. He also helped support practical ministry-related institutions that would help thousands of people to have better lives through health care, social programs and education. He had a way of sharing the Gospel without the trappings of Western culture attached to it—simply the way of Jesus. It is exactly how I try to reorient people who I meet in my travels—just take another look at Jesus. Not everyone would agree with Jones of course, but they might just say we can certainly all try to be like Jesus.

Even some forms of worship that have incorporated Christian elements—especially sacramental forms—have devolved into hopeless attempts to find peace and reconciliation, offering little assurance of salvation to the faithful: "...having a form of godliness but denying its power" (2 Tim 3:5). In much of Latin America, it's heartbreaking to see the results of an ancient culture of pagan superstition and idolatry overlaid with a "form" of Christianity—a tightly woven tapestry of tradition and rituals. It's no less pagan, superstitious, or idolatrous than the daily offerings made along the village roads of India! Its hopelessness is pervasive, seeming to forget the victory of our risen Lord, who died once, for all, for the forgiveness of sin, to bring us into real, life-giving reconciliation with God if we would but put all our faith in him and him alone. And it's dark. You could easily sense demonic strongholds—as easily as walking the streets of Nepal amidst the Hindu and Buddhist shrines. It's the same spiritual oppression that contributes to keeping people in poverty and robs them of the joy of walking in the freedom of the Light of the World, as they continually and faithfully perform the deeds through which they are hoping for true reconciliation.

After a team project serving an orphanage in the rural desert area of Guatemala (for more on this, see Chapter 10), we found ourselves in Antigua—the former capital of all of Central America—surrounded by mountains and volcanoes. The history and the architectural ruins were fascinating of course, and life on the streets looked pretty much as it might have for generations. But if I had seen one more satin-clothed, bleeding wax Jesus in a glass coffin at the back of a huge basilica, I would have been compelled to run screaming through the streets, "He's not dead, He's alive! He has risen!"

In addition to these dominant religious systems of the world seeking a path to reconciliation, there is another that cannot be ignored as we find ourselves attempting to give an apostolic witness of God's work of reconciliation to the post-Christian culture in the Western world. Since the early 1800's, when radical secularists coming out of the Enlightenment committed to reforming society, they openly declared war on the Gospel and the need for us to be reconciled to God. In so doing, they conveniently redefined our "problem," and firmly established secular humanism as a new worldview the likes of which had never been seen before. The problem, as I have stated and that somehow inherently all cultures of the world have known or sensed down through the millennia of human history, is that something is broken and we long for it to be fixed.

> To the humanist the Church was wrong in placing such unfettered emphasis on God and his sovereign rule. The emphasis, they held, should be on the more important issues of humanity, such as human accomplishments, human needs, human passions, and human potential. In their way of thinking, the Church's perspective of reality

Reconciliation

was backward in that it placed God and his reign instead of mankind at the center of the belief system.[3]

As we are surrounded by this prevalent belief system today, it is certain that it is exactly that—a belief system. Every bit as much as any of the other religions of the world, it has tenets by which its adherents must live. In denying the sense of longing deep within every human heart, it must find something else to assuage our deepest need, namely relief from the guilt and shame of the brokenness we sense and struggle to repair. They found it in in the mid-1800's in Charles Darwin's theories of evolution, a new and radical "faith" in the "survival of the fittest." Darwin published *The Origin of the Species by Means of Natural Selection or the Preservation of Favored Races in the Struggle for Life* in 1859. It paved the way for a philosophy that held that man was the product of random chance, self-directed and self-developing, apart from any action of God. God—if indeed He exists at all—was completely separate from man's self-sufficiency. Nietzsche's writings followed, further reinforcing these ideas as he trumpeted his "God is dead" assertions, philosophically condemning all absolute perspectives and values.

In the absence of a Kingdom-centered worldview, mankind is left to determine morality and ethics for himself. In this scenario, with no absolutes, everything to do with law, morality, or values becomes dynamic, always evolving or relative to the person or the situation of the moment. For every hundred people, you could have a hundred different definitions of right and wrong. Why do I say that? If there are no longer any absolutes to govern a worldview, then every person is left to themselves to determine what is right or wrong—for them—and each acting as his or her own judge. "Everyone did as they saw fit" (Judges 21:25), describes the kingless Israel ignoring God and his commands and instead following their own will and desires. The pervasiveness of this in all channels of our culture today is now undeniable, over 150 years later. The Western educational system was wholly turned over to secular humanists with this agenda from the mid-1800s and, since the early 1900's, as each generation since was inculcated in the system through education, our churches were filled with these minds and subsequently even the Church has embraced more of a man-centered worldview. Interestingly, however, there still exists a powerful "moral argument" for the existence of God, because deep in the hearts of men there remains an acknowledgement of an absolute morality that we just can't seem to shake.

While the humanists were advancing their message and goals, Christians seemed poised and ready to withdraw.

> Despite the Church's succumbing to the secularizing of society through the public school system, our defenses had already been weakened by an earlier form of religious humanism called pietism. The pietists of the late eighteenth and the early nineteenth centuries held that the Christian should focus on spiritual things and the inner man. Contemplation of such secular foci as politics and the arts were regarded as pagan activities. This pseudo-spiritual emphasis caused much of the Church during this time to abandon the belief in the comprehensive reign of God in human affairs.[4]

Just as with the theme of restoration (Chapter 7), as we lose sight of God's Kingship and his Kingdom, the message of reconciliation in the heart of every man and woman is lost.

Mother Teresa—very much aligned with Jones's methods—once said a fascinating thing in an interview. The interviewer had asked if they (Hindus) should love Jesus too. She replied, "Naturally, if they want peace, if they want joy, let them find Jesus. If people become better Hindus, better Muslims, better Buddhists by our acts of love, then there is something else growing there. They come closer and closer to God. When they come closer, they have to choose."[5]

Without any exaggeration, I have meditated on that quote for hours. What exactly did she mean? How does becoming a better

Hindu or Muslim or Buddhist lead them closer to God? And as they get closer, what will make them choose? I have come away with this conviction, and two things are at play here. First, I've actually had people tell me, "Well, I'm not actually a very *good* Hindu (or Buddhist, or Muslim). I don't do everything I'm supposed to." None of us can! Unless they've faithfully executed all the do's and have faithfully avoided all the don'ts that are required (which we've already determined is not possible), they'll never get to the point of seeing that it doesn't really work. It will never work. But unless they work the system hard, they will never know that, and always have the excuse to fall back on, that, well, if I had tried harder, it would've worked. And we could add secular humanism to this too. The endless task of self-improvement to dispel ignorance is just that: endless!

Secondly, if they can see and understand Jesus from a new perspective that they've never known because of our acts of love and service to them—unconditionally and self-sacrificially—then they truly have seen Jesus and they have something to which they can compare their own experience. If they can be honest in their evaluation, then they might really be convinced to choose Jesus! I have become convinced in my many years devoted to missionary service—which in turn has led me into being a student of cultures and people—that the vast majority of people we assume have rejected Jesus have never actually met him! They've never seen Jesus! (Remember? I always ask people, "Would you take another look at Jesus?") What they've seen is the weak, selfish, bastardized version that we've given them! So have they *really* rejected Jesus? It seems not.

Especially in the context of reconciliation and all the work that the world's religions—including secular humanism—require to find peace, spiritual enlightenment, or self-actualization, the uniqueness of Christ cannot be overstated. He does not *have* a way for us to reconcile our brokenness to God. He *IS* the way!

Then Jesus declared, "I am the bread of life. Whoever comes to me will never go hungry, and whoever believes in me will never be thirsty. But as I told you, you have seen me and still you do not believe. All those the Father gives me will come to me, and whoever comes to me I will never drive away. For I have come down from heaven not to do my will but to do the will of him who sent me. And this is the will of him who sent me, that I shall lose none of all those He has given me, but raise them up at the last day. For my Father's will is that everyone who looks to the Son and believes in him shall have eternal life, and I will raise them up at the last day." At this the Jews there began to grumble about him... (Jn 6:35-41)

John, who wrote his Gospel later than the others (likely nearer to the end of the first century, so perhaps up to three decades later), sums up all the Gospel writers' purpose as this: "...these are written that you may believe that Jesus is the Messiah, the Son of God, and that by believing you may have life in his name" (Jn 20:31). And over and over, what Jesus said about himself is recorded by John, so that we might understand that He was not just *showing* us the way to the Father (and thereby to peace and reconciliation); He was showing us that He *is* the way, and by believing in Him, He *becomes* our path to reconciliation with the Father!

When Jesus spoke again to the people, He said, "I am the light of the world. Whoever follows me will never walk in darkness, but will have the light of life." (Jn 8:12)

"I am the gate; whoever enters through me will be saved. They will come in and go out and find pasture. The thief comes only to steal and kill and destroy; I have come that they may have life, and have it to the full." (Jn 10:9-10)

"I am the good shepherd. The good shepherd lays down his life for the sheep. The hired hand is not the shepherd and does not own the sheep. So when He sees the wolf coming, He abandons the sheep and runs away. Then the wolf attacks the flock and scatters it. The man runs away because He is a hired hand and cares nothing for the sheep. I am the good shepherd; I know my sheep and my sheep know me—just as the Father knows me and I know the Father—and I lay down my life for the sheep." (Jn 10:11-15)

Jesus answered, "I am the way and the truth and the life. No one comes to the Father except through me. If you really know me, you will know my Father as well. From now on, you do know him and have seen him." (Jn 14:6-7)

"I am the true vine, and my Father is the gardener. He cuts off every branch in me that bears no fruit, while every branch that does bear fruit He prunes so that it will be even more fruitful. You are already clean because of the word I have spoken to you. Remain in me, as I also remain in you. No branch can bear fruit by itself; it must remain in the vine. Neither can you bear fruit unless you remain in me." (Jn 15:1-4)

With the work of reconciliation firmly established and provided in the person of Christ Jesus, the Apostle Paul goes on from there to expand the ministry of reconciliation to his followers.

For Christ's love compels us, because we are convinced that one died for all, and therefore all died. And He died for all, that those who live should no longer live for themselves but for him who died for them and was raised again.

So from now on we regard no one from a worldly point of view. Though we once regarded Christ in this way, we do so no longer. Therefore, if anyone is in Christ, the new creation has come: The old has gone, the new is here! All this is from God, who reconciled us to himself through Christ and gave us the ministry of reconciliation: that God was reconciling the world to himself in Christ, not counting people's sins against them. And He has committed to us the message of reconciliation. We are therefore Christ's ambassadors, as though God were making his appeal through us. We implore you on Christ's behalf: Be reconciled to God. God made him who had no sin to be sin for us, so that in him we might become the righteousness of God. (2 Cor 5:14-21)

And though all of Paul's New Testament letters were addressed to particular churches across the Mediterranean world and usually addressed very specific issues those believers were facing, this theme is repeated in almost the same language to the church in Rome.

You see, at just the right time, when we were still powerless, Christ died for the ungodly. Very rarely will anyone die for a righteous person, though for a good person someone might possibly dare to die. But God demonstrates his own love for us in this: While we were still sinners, Christ died for us.

Since we have now been justified by his blood, how much more shall we be saved from God's wrath through him! For if, while we were God's enemies, we were reconciled to him through the death of his Son, how much more, having been reconciled, shall we be saved through his life! Not only is this so, but we also boast in God through our Lord Jesus Christ, through whom we have now received reconciliation. (Rom 5:6-11)

The critical thing to remember as we take up the responsibility of being ambassadors for God and imploring people to be reconciled to God is this: while we were yet sinners, Christ died for us. In spite of ourselves and in the face of our hatred toward him, God still moved—entirely of his own initiative and driven by his boundless love—to reconcile all things to himself.

> For God was pleased to have all his fullness dwell in him, and through him to reconcile to himself all things, whether things on earth or things in heaven, by making peace through his blood, shed on the cross.
>
> Once you were alienated from God and were enemies in your minds because of your evil behavior. But now He has reconciled you by Christ's physical body through death to present you holy in his sight, without blemish and free from accusation.... (Col 1:19-22)

So if truly we are to follow in his steps in bringing this message of reconciliation to the world, it must be from a place of God's *hesed* lovingkindness to the world. A covenantal, committed, unwavering, selfless love. Sadly, the world has rarely seen this. Instead, they see judgment. Instead, we live as Separatists. Instead, we remain firmly entrenched behind our walls of comfort, defensiveness, or worldly distractions. Expecting people's behavior to line up with the Ten Commandments—when there is no longer a shared worldview underpinning them and before they have believed in Jesus and embraced the power of the Holy Spirit to help them do so—is not appropriate or helpful in a post-Christian culture, where we now find ourselves.

We need a new kind of apostolic witness. New to us, but not new to the Christian church from antiquity. We must start with the loving response of a Savior who died for a world while it was still separated from God by its own rebellion, step into the "mud puddles of human need," and risk getting ourselves a little dirty in bringing the message to them. "When [Jesus] saw the crowds, He had compassion on them, because they were harassed and helpless, like sheep without a shepherd" (Mt 9:36). This is precisely where the pastor of the small church in *In his Steps* finds himself—having come face-to-face with his own prejudices and parochial notions of how we "do" church, he has a heart-change at that moment. Love and compassion well up within him for the desperate visitor, and he finds an intrinsic identification with the apostle Paul: "I have become all things to all people so that by all possible means I might save some" (I Cor 9:22). That's how Paul put it.

Shortly before I heard Jackie Pullinger's message, when I was growing frustrated with my choice of careers because of its incompatibility with my worldview, I found a book called *The 100: A Ranking of the Most Influential Persons in History* by Michael Hart. I have never been able to forget the stinging indictment he brought against the followers of Jesus. He ranked Jesus third, behind Sir Isaac Newton and Muhammed. He had his reasons. He talked about how Newton's scientific theories were universally held, and that Muhammed influenced society on every level—not just religious, but secular.

After giving his reasons, and also stating that the successful spread of the Gospel had as much to do with the Apostle Paul's ministry as that of Jesus, he said:

> The impact of Jesus on human history is so obvious and so enormous that few people would question his placement near the top of this list. Indeed, the more likely question is why Jesus, who is the inspiration for the most influential religion in history, has not been placed first.[6]

After referencing the Sermon on the Mount, Hart goes on:

> Now, these ideas—which were not a part of the Judaism of Jesus' day, *nor of most other religions*—are surely among the most remarkable and original ethical ideas ever presented. If they were widely followed, I would have had no hesitation in placing Jesus first in this book. But the truth is that they

are not widely followed. In fact, they are not even generally accepted. Most Christians consider the injunction to "love your enemy" as—at most—an ideal which might be realized in some perfect world, but one which is not a reasonable guide to conduct in the actual world we live in. We do not normally practice it, do not expect others to practice it, and do not teach our children to practice it. Jesus' most distinctive teaching, therefore, remains an intriguing but basically untried suggestion.[7]

Until we are truly overcome with a missionary heart—that work of the Holy Spirit indwelling us that crushes us—we will never be drawn into people's need bearing the message of reconciliation. And until they see us living lives of sacrificial love—walking as Jesus walked—they cannot receive it.

Years ago Stephen Colbert offered a stinging rebuke to a remark made by Fox personality Bill O'Reilly about the United States being a Christian nation: "If this is going to be a Christian nation that doesn't help the poor, either we have to pretend that Jesus was just as selfish as we are, or we've got to acknowledge that He commanded us to love the poor and serve the needy without condition and then admit that we just don't want to do it."[8] Wow. Couple that with Hart's indictment and we have a double whammy coming against the Church's testimony and witness. Not only do we not love those who are "outsiders" (and that's typically where we lump our enemies), we do not give our lives in service to the needs of others. You've heard it said, "People don't care how much you know until they know how much you care!"

A long look back into Scripture gives us more understanding of reconciliation with another example of that original Hebrew phrase translated as "in the gap." In Numbers 16, we read about the story of Korah's rebellion, along with two other Levite priests and others—250 Israelite men in total. They challenge Moses' authority in hearing from God, claiming that they too, ministering before the Lord in the Tabernacle are qualified to stand before him. They were even blaming Moses for their wandering in the wilderness. In the end, after presenting offerings before God, the ground opens up and swallows them and fire goes out "from the Lord" consuming the 250 men. I guess we know how the Lord felt about that! The next day the people grumbled against Moses, blaming him for the deaths of their friends! The cloud covered the Tabernacle and the "glory of the Lord appeared." God was ready to put an end to the assembly of people, but "Moses said to Aaron, 'Take your censer and put incense in it, along with burning coals from the altar, and hurry to the assembly to make *atonement* for them. Wrath has come out from the Lord; the plague has started.' So Aaron did as Moses said and ran into the assembly. The plague had already started among the people, but Aaron offered the incense and made *atonement* for them. He *stood between* the living and the dead, and the plague stopped" (Nm 16:46-48).

Aaron is an example for all of us in the Church today! He stood in a place where on one side were rebellious people and on the other was God's righteous presence, power, and judgment. He stood as an "ambassador of reconciliation" to bring healing to the side of the rebellious and allow God's lovingkindness to flow once again. Oh, that we would get in between on behalf of the world, that the plague would stop in our generation!

This is the work of God through Christ, established from the beginning and brought full circle to the reconciliation of his creation back to himself.

> The Son is the image of the invisible God, the firstborn over all creation. For in him all things were created: things in heaven and on earth, visible and invisible, whether thrones or powers or rulers or authorities; all things have been created through him and for him. He is before all things, and in him all things hold together. And He is the head of the body, the church; He is the beginning and the firstborn from among the dead, so that in everything He might have the supremacy. For God was pleased to have all his fullness

dwell in him, and through him to reconcile to himself all things, whether things on earth or things in heaven, by making peace through his blood, shed on the cross.

Once you were alienated from God and were enemies in your minds because of your evil behavior. But now He has reconciled you by Christ's physical body through death to present you holy in his sight, without blemish and free from accusation.... (Col 1:15-22)

And since we have such a great gift, we have work to do ourselves—not toil as in the cursed work of the garden at the Fall—it's a privilege!

Therefore, brothers and sisters, since we have confidence to enter the Most Holy Place by the blood of Jesus, by a new and living way opened for us through the curtain, that is, his body, and since we have a great priest over the house of God, let us draw near to God with a sincere heart and with the full assurance that faith brings, having our hearts sprinkled to cleanse us from a guilty conscience and having our bodies washed with pure water. Let us hold unswervingly to the hope we profess, for He who promised is faithful. And let us consider how we may spur one another on toward love and good deeds, not giving up meeting together, as some are in the habit of doing, but encouraging one another—and all the more as you see the Day approaching." (Heb 10:19-25)

We each have a unique place where we can stand, holding unswervingly to the hope we profess, as we step into the world bringing the message of reconciliation. You alone are the Esther that might stand for your family members. You alone are the "priest" of your own household. You alone are the one who rubs shoulders every day with the same group of co-workers or fellow students, or community members or neighbors. And you alone—perhaps—are those about whom the poor of the world are crying out, "please send them to us!" We must be willing to stand, as Aaron did, and as Jesus did when He came from heaven to stand between us, the lost, and the Father. There He raised himself up from the earth on the cross—like Aaron's censer—and reconciling us to God, the judgments of God were forever stayed in our lives. Do you see it? This is how you can fit in God's plan to reach the world!

Jayson Georges has produced a great resource for anyone seeking to be ambassadors of the message of reconciliation, framing the Gospel in any culture, called *The 3D Gospel*.

> Three moral emotions have become the foundation for three types of culture: (1) *guilt-innocence cultures* are individualistic societies (mostly Western), where people who break the laws are guilty and seek justice or forgiveness to rectify a wrong, (2) *shame-honor cultures* describes collectivistic cultures (common to the East), where people shamed for not fulfilling group expectations seek to restore their honor before the community, and (3) *fear-power cultures* refers to animistic contexts (typically tribal), where people afraid of evil and harm pursue power over the spirit world through magical rituals.[9]

He goes on to describe in detail the elements of those cultures and worldviews, and how to best tailor the Gospel using their primary worldview metaphor, namely, and respectively, Courtroom, Community, and Combat. We can connect with people in powerful identification when we can skillfully tell the Biblical story of the Gospel in the context of these three metaphors, and using the Scriptures that demonstrate them.

> For example, Paul wrote the book of Ephesians to explain "the unsearchable riches of Christ" (3:8), which involves each of these three components of salvation (italics added below).

Guilt-Innocence—"In him we have redemption through his blood, the *forgiveness of sins*" (1:7a). God "made us alive in Christ even when we were dead in *transgressions*" (2:5).

Shame-Honor—"In love He predestined us to be adopted as his sons through Jesus Christ" (1:5). "You are no longer *foreigners* and *aliens*, but *fellow citizens* with God's people and *members* of God's *household*." (2:19, cf. 2:12-13)

Fear-Power—"That power is like the working of his *mighty strength*, which He *exerted* in Christ when He *raised him* from the dead and seated him at his right hand in the heavenly realms, *far above all rule and authority, power and dominion*" (1:19-21). Be *strong* in the Lord and in his *mighty power*. Put on the *full armor* of God so that you can *take your stand* against the devil's schemes." (6:10-11)[10]

The reason I want to mention this here, is that I believe we are seeing a powerful shift in Western culture as a result of the impact of 150 years of secular humanism eroding an ethic of absolute morality (even though it is written on every human heart). The courtroom metaphor is applicable only to societies that can actually embrace the idea that we've broken a higher moral law. That conviction in Western society came from the religious and societal foundations having been formed in Jerusalem and Athens. The further we move away from those underpinnings, the harder it is to make sense of that kind of Gospel presentation. Western society is firmly in the era of post-Christian culture, and as such, fewer and fewer people believe—or *feel* (remember, three moral *emotions* have become the foundation for three types of culture)—that they have broken any serious law, so the idea of being reconciled to God through justice or forgiveness is growing foreign to them.

What is interesting, however, is this moral oxymoron. While the secular humanism of the day claims moral objectivity in media, entertainment, art, politics, sports, and education, it never ceases to recognize shameful acts of every high-profile character within those spheres. It seems we know and feel shame universally, even when we are reluctant to define an absolute morality! Within this reality, I believe we must now tailor the Gospel in Western culture more often as if it were Shame-Honor based, not Guilt-Innocence. In this way, instead of presenting the Gospel with the Four Spiritual Laws strategy and related Scriptures such as the Romans Road, we would be better to focus on Jesus' parable of the lost son, wherein God is depicted as our gracious Father, waiting "on the porch" to receive his wayward son back into the family.

When I retell that story, I stress the idea that the Father is always looking (*initiating*), always waiting, anticipating the day his son might come home, because the Scripture says, "But while he was still a long way off, his father saw him and was filled with compassion for him; he ran to his son, threw his arms around him and kissed him" (Lk 15:20). It's as if the father gets up every day with the hope of reconciliation in his heart, and looks, seeking for his son from the porch. Tim Keller, in his book *The Prodigal God*, reminds us that the definition of prodigal is actually "lavish" or "extravagant." The lost son went off and lived in lavish extravagance to be sure, but Keller's point is that our God is the one who lavishes his grace upon us extravagantly. This is a message that can reach many with God's gift of reconciliation!

Our continual challenge to live out the message of reconciliation dates back to the early Church. The new church was made up of many different peoples and cultures. They, too, struggled to properly live out the message among their own members and a rift formed between the Gentiles and the Jews. It still happens today in the Body of Christ, in families, and in nations. It's always happening because in the spirit of the world there is a nature of rebellion, and some will always want to rise up. But the two groups here—Jews and Gentiles—are representative of "all peoples," and therefore illustrate the truth of God reconciling *all men* to himself through the cross!

> Therefore, remember that formerly you who are Gentiles by birth and called "uncircumcised" by those who call themselves "the circumcision" (which is done in the body by human hands)— remember that at that time you were separate from Christ, excluded from citizenship in Israel and foreigners to the covenants of the promise, without hope and without God in the world. But now in Christ Jesus you who once were far away have been brought near by the blood of Christ.
>
> For He himself is our peace, who has made the two groups one and has destroyed the barrier, the dividing wall of hostility, by setting aside in his flesh the law with its commands and regulations. His purpose was to create in himself one new humanity out of the two, thus making peace, and in one body to reconcile both of them to God through the cross, by which He put to death their hostility. He came and preached peace to you who were far away and peace to those who were near. For through him we both have access to the Father by one Spirit.
>
> Consequently, you are no longer foreigners and strangers, but fellow citizens with God's people and also members of his household, built on the foundation of the apostles and prophets, with Christ Jesus himself as the chief cornerstone. In him the whole building is joined together and rises to become a holy temple in the Lord. And in him you too are being built together to become a dwelling in which God lives by his Spirit. (Eph 2:11-22)

I related the story of Rwanda's restoration as seen through the eyes of Bishop John Rucyahana in Chapter 7. He went on to say, "God has always used the broken, and He is using this broken nation to manifest his grace and power. He is taking the brokenness caused by evil and using it for a greater purpose—a great *reconciliation* in a nation the world had not only given up on, but given over to the devil, and its own evil."[11] (emphasis mine)

Reconciliation was and is the critical precursor to restoration. You won't hear about this part of Rwanda's recovery on American news channels. The world would not believe it. Reporters would speculate. Politicians would debate reparations. Intellectuals and philosophers would get caught up in thoughtful study and empathy. And in reading the gut-wrenching accounts of how the gendarmes used machetes to mutilate, disembowel, and slaughter mercilessly, I confess I could hardly imagine forgiveness and reconciliation ever coming to this nation. But I worked closely with people who shared the truth of the story at a ministry campus where the almost-forgotten paradise of the *Land of a Thousand Hills* and *Gorillas in the Mist* was seemingly reborn.

> Rwanda as a nation sought God because it was desperate, and God answered because He is a loving God. That is what is behind our healing and the power of our reconciliation, and it is available to the entire world. The God who is healing and blessing Rwanda wants to heal and bless the entire world if it would but call upon Him.[12]

John Rucyahana also notes:

> The steps that we are using in Rwanda for reconciliation and healing can be applied to other communities in the world. There is no barrier that cannot be overcome and no division that cannot be healed. What could be worse than the violence that happened in Rwanda? If the Rwandan situation can be amended by repentance and forgiveness, and the people here can be reconciled enough to live together again, it can happen anywhere in the world. Perhaps differences in culture may require different applications of these methods, but the principle is the same.

The principle is that God can and will heal a human mind no matter how much pain it has seen or caused. God can transform that mind. If a perpetrator of the genocide in Rwanda, a person who tortured and killed many innocent people, including women and children, can repent and cry out for forgiveness to those he wronged by killing their family members, then any offender, anywhere, can repent the same way. If a woman who was raped and beaten and forced to watch as her husband and children were tortured and killed before her eyes can forgive in the name of Jesus Christ those who did such a horrible thing, then any victim, anywhere, can forgive the same way. It is through repentance and forgiveness that people can relate again. They can live life together again. No one believed that this could happen in Rwanda. Everyone said, "It's impossible. These people cannot be together again." It is hard, but it is not impossible—we are doing it![13]

Reconciliation Among the Haitians

Haiti was...Haiti. Long before the destructive earthquake of 2010, the signs of a broken country were visible at every turn. As much as anywhere I've been (and I've served with more ministries there than anywhere else in the world), Haiti struggles under a spiritual oppression that forces its people to daily engage in battle. As I planned and ran this particular project with our ministry host, we encountered spiritual opposition in numerous ways. Unrest in the country threatened to derail our mission. Excessive heat and water shortages challenged our hosts and our team. And I came down with a terribly debilitating cold that required me to disappear for hours at a time and just sleep.

The environment of crumbling infrastructure personified the plague of spiritual attack, demonic strongholds, and evil, despotic leaders that have oppressed the people for decades. There was no escape from the ubiquitous, sickly-sweet, pungent smell of burning trash day and night; the cloying humidity; the cavernous ditches eroded across the roads; the running sewage along the curbs; or hours-long power outages.

> *We visited and observed a school in a rural community near the coast. It was as simple and poor as anything I've ever seen anywhere...stick huts with cardboard and sheet metal walls, thatched roofs, rocky mud roads, naked little children, and one central water pump for all washing, bathing, and drinking water.*
>
> *But the people of Haiti...now there's the real story! Their smiles still welcomed us and their worship was unrestrained. No confusion here between the God who redeemed them and the world around them that was still so yearning for reconciliation. And our team joyfully engaged with people, and pressed into God, bore up under spiritual attacks, and picked up the slack caused by my illness.*
>
> *During the week, a pastor taught us the words in Creole (the native language, a hybrid of French and Spanish) to the chorus "I Have Decided to Follow Jesus." Our team played and sang it in the churches we visited on Sunday. Not me of course, I could barely croak out a tune, but one of my interns—Jackie Wong—took over and led the team. I barely managed to give the message, and then laid myself out on a bench afterwards as everyone else visited and fellowshipped.*
>
> *We had heard from our ministry partners that life is so often directly impacted by Spiritism and the occult, a deep-rooted counterfeit system of atonement. In those churches, I preached a message of intercession, reconciliation, and restoration to congregations of Haitian Christians who live amongst the most pagan of cultures, steeped in what the world calls its "spiritual roots"—voodoo. It was my greatest burden and my highest priority to encourage the churches in their path to true reconciliation with God, the one who holds supreme power over the devil and demons in the spirit world of the Haitian.*

CHAPTER 10

INTERMEDIATION

"...on behalf of the land..."

"I looked for someone among them who would build up the wall and stand before me in the gap **on behalf of the land** *so I would not have to destroy it, but I found no one."*
Ezekiel 22:30

Intermediation picks up where intercession and reconciliation leaves off. Or perhaps we should say intermediation is the culmination of both intercession and reconciliation. To conduct intermediation—to *be* a mediator—one must embrace the arbitration role as both lawyer and ambassador. It is so akin to intercession that you might think them one and the same. But for the sake of the lives of believers everywhere seeking to find where they fit in God's plan to reach the world, I draw this one very important distinction: intermediation will nearly always carry us further in, deeper into those "mud puddles of human need." "On behalf of the land" implies that we are showing up where no one else is able or willing.

Jackie Pullinger:
And then I said to God, "You really didn't finish the job, did you? The other two, when they believed in God they got off instantly, what about him?" And so we found that I had to take another step for them, which involved having a place for them to live. I lost my ministry; I couldn't be a street preacher anymore. The house got full of them, I had to look after them. I'm not a nanny, I'm not a house-matron type person, I'm a street preacher, it's much more glamorous. But for 10 years I had to stick inside a house with this

> bunch of people that kept trying to run away. They'd jump out of windows, prophesy one day, and fall back the next. If anybody had seen us they would have seen death. I didn't wear sleeping clothes for four years. I slept on the sofa I was so used to police phoning in the middle of the night.[1]

It is possible to conduct intercession in both prayer and physical interventions, but with intermediation, we must almost *always* "go there and do there what you do here," as Glen Woodruff clearly heard God telling us we must do as EMI grew. We can pray from the other side of the ocean. And we must. We can mobilize and send financial resources from a distance too. And again, we must. But we cannot lay our hands on the sick (or carry them into the hospital as I did for a teenage girl recently in Uganda); hold a crying, soaking wet baby (as we did in Guatemalan orphanages); or speak to "kings and princes" (or presidents and village chiefs as we did in Nigeria or Ghana) from our prayer closets. Our team has done all these things because we *went* and mediated. We must *not stay*.

After the Apostle Paul had instructed Timothy on the urgency of intercession and prayer being offered to God on behalf of all people, he immediately followed up with, "For there is one God and one mediator between God and mankind, the man Christ Jesus, who gave himself as a ransom for all people" (1 Tim 2:5-6). If indeed we are to "follow in his steps," then it also follows that we must leave—at least to some degree—a place of our relative and personal comfort, safety, security, or convenience. Even if this does not mean—like Abraham—packing up your family and belongings and going to "a land that I will show you, to a people who are not your own," it most certainly means stepping out from the crowd—no matter how intimidating that might feel—and standing "on behalf of the land." I have heard Paul Johansen say, "All through our lives, you will have things that—when you are worshipping God—He will speak to you, that will never be yours unless you put boots on the ground."

Intermediation

Another Scripture reference where that original Hebrew phrase for standing "in between" occurs is Job 9:33: "If only there were someone to arbitrate between us, to lay his hand upon us both." It can hardly be any clearer than that word picture! Job, in his misery and pain, is crying out to the Redeemer who he knows lives but cannot seem to find at this moment. He needs a mediator. His friends and even his wife had all kinds of unwanted advice that was not helpful! Instead, he paints for us the most powerful image of one who would—with one hand in the hand of God himself, in the riches of all of heaven—stretch between him and God and lay his other hand on a hurting world.

My friend, this might be the most critical idea of this whole book! Abraham *moved* to Canaan. EMI *moved* to India. And Jesus came *from* heaven *to* earth, to be raised up *between* heaven and earth, to make his life a sacrificial offering to reconcile us to God. You might say, He *moved!* We must move off our couches, come out from behind our desks, and get our heads out of our electronic media, and *move out* for the sake of intermediation! There's just no other way to do it without getting into those mud puddles, personally and physically, living Jesus to a world who otherwise may never see him, hear him, or know him.

The cry of the world has not changed since Job. If only there were someone, someone who could bring us together! You might be the only Jesus the world around you will ever meet! E. Stanley Jones (I introduced him to you in Chapter 9) said, "An individual gospel [without a social gospel] is a soul without a body; a social gospel [without an individual gospel] is a body without a soul. One's a ghost and the other's a corpse, you can take your choice. I don't want either one. I want both."[2] Wow. The Individual Gospel is a call to repentance with the gift of salvation, restoration, and reconciliation being offered to every person. The Social Gospel is the kind of work that Jones was known for, investing in the improvement of people's lives for the sake of Jesus' name and reputation. He saw the two as inseparably linked as the breath in a living human being—and he uses such shocking personification to demonstrate that.

They are both equally troubling, too. A corpse has no life, so what is it able to do or communicate? That's the very real limitation of reaching out only with a Social Gospel: it is often done by the Blenders and Philanthropists from Gabe Lyon's Christian categories, or the thousands of NGO's working around the world. They are attempting to do great work of intermediation, but without the breath of the Spirit of the Living God in it. I once heard a missionary say, "If you give a cup of cold water (Mt 10:42) to a dying man without sharing the Gospel, you've just sent a hydrated man to Hell." I've never forgotten it.

And what of the ghost? The image of the ghost is just as dead, but has the appearance of life—though vacuous, changing, or invisible. This is like the Separatists, Insiders, and Evangelizers who are consumed with preaching the Good News of Christ (the Individual Gospel) but stop short of any meaningful intermediation. Like the apostle James wrote,

> What good is it, my brothers and sisters, if someone claims to have faith but has no deeds? Can such faith save them? Suppose a brother or a sister is without clothes and daily food. If one of you says to them, "Go in peace; keep warm and well fed," but does nothing about their physical needs, what good is it? In the same way, faith by itself, if it is not accompanied by action, is dead. (James 2:14-17)

Jackie Pullinger:
I was in a nation country a few months ago, and I was speaking with some pastors, and I said to them, talking about what God in his mercy has done amongst us and begging them, if they would, to find their own prostitutes and their poor, and to welcome them into God's love. I said "if you will do this it will be very slow to start with, nobody will understand, the rest of the church will not. Don't expect them to. You need to know this before you start. It doesn't look as if it grows quickly. It's painful and it's exhausting, and people may treat you like they treated

Job, with introspective Bible studies instead of comfort. They will not understand.

And it will be slow, and it will be painful, and it will be lonely, and you may see none won to Christ and your friend's church down the road may be multiplying greatly whereas yours, well your people won't remember the Tuesday Bible study because they don't know it's Tuesday. They can't come to your church anyway for they have no wheels, and no bus fare. They forgot to get up or they were beaten in the night, and they slept through. That's what it's like with the poor. They can't make our times and they don't understand our services. You have to go to them. You can't wait in your church for them to come to you. But then neither did Christ." And I said, *"You may do this, you may love one unlovely man for five years, you may pour your life out for him. You may share everything you've got, and he may cheat you at the end of five years and it still will be worth it."* And a pastor looked at me and he said, *"Could we speak about this more later, I have never heard this before."*

Whoever claims to live in Christ must walk as Jesus did. How come he'd not heard before? *The temptation that Jesus had early in his ministry was to have an instant ministry. To have and to use his power for himself, to use his power for effect, to use his power for instant results. And He could have done it. But He chose to do the will of his father. What a strange way to win the world. Who would think of that? Who would think of winning the world by having your son killed? What a strange plan to be sure. He was crucified in weakness, yet He lives by God's power. Likewise, we are weak in him, yet by God's power we will live with him to serve you. Examine yourselves to see whether you are in the faith, test yourselves. Do you not realize that Christ Jesus is in you? Unless of course you fail the test.* And Paul wrote this, he said, *"we always carry around in our body the death of Jesus so that the life of Jesus may also be revealed in our body. For we who are alive are always being given over to death for Jesus' sake so his life may be revealed in our mortal bodies so then death is at* work in us but life in you." And that's what the gospel does, you see, it always kills the donor and gives life to the receiver, always. And it will be no different for you, there is no cheap way of giving the gospel, it will kill you. But who wants that old life anyway?[3]

"Pray that I see water in Gewada or die trying!" This was the response I received from Binora when I asked him how our team could pray for him as we were planning for our project trip and partnership. Binora Dado is the Ethiopian missionary with whom I had become friends as we planned a 17 km water pipeline project. He was called by God as intermediary on behalf of the land. We were headed to Gewada, Ethiopia, to serve a cluster of three small villages that did not have access to clean drinking water.

Binora, the son of the village witch doctor in a remote Ethiopian bush village, told us his story late one night by the dim table lamp. Our team was exhausted by our day's work, but mesmerized by his story. Fleeing the Marxist regime as a teenager, he committed his life to Christ when he encountered an evangelist. He found his way into a Sudanese refugee camp, and ultimately immigrated to Toronto, Canada, where he experienced the comfortable lifestyle of North America. But several years later, the Lord convicted him to return to Ethiopia, where he worked there as a missionary. A dozen years later, EMI joined him.

He continued,

> But there's something inside of me, and has been for the last eleven years, that convinces my whole being that I am doing the right thing. This is where happiness is and where a sense of purpose in life is for me... because now I see that I simply stutter the Gospel to people and they're accepting the Lord! I have become the most joyous person because I see people who are in darkness coming to light... and the liberation of every person who is listening to the Gospel. Then there are development programs happening here and there a little bit, that even draw people like you to Ethiopia. And I tell you, that makes me a joyful Christian.

Besides the call to preach the Gospel, Binora could not escape the tremendous need for clean water. In every way he embodied what we in the evangelical world of relief and development call "integral mission." Like James' discourse on faith and works, it's the coupling of the Great Commission to "Go make disciples in all nations" (Mt 28:18-20) and the Great Commandment, to love God and love people (Mt 22:36-40, Mk 12:28-31).

When he returned after his long absence, Binora could see that nothing had changed in the ancient tribal village. These local villages never had basic services such as a medical clinic or communication with the outside world. They were completely isolated; it was over 12 hours from the capital to the nearest and last outpost of civilization—the Konzo Hotel (and I use the term hotel *very* loosely!). From there, we launched out every day to get to the villages another hour away. Because of such isolation, the incidence of disease is high; many children die before 10 years of age. Over and over, Binora saw his neighbors needlessly succumb to diseases that could have been prevented if only they had clean water. The villagers hiked twice daily—an hour each way—to fetch murky, contaminated water from a river. River water sources like this are common across the developing world, where animals relieve themselves and everything and everyone is washed in it upstream.

Attempts at drilling wells had failed for a number of reasons related to sustainability, such as lack of power and failed equipment. Binora had grown consumed with finding a solution. He asked if it might be possible for EMI to design a low-tech water pipeline system (using gravity alone) from a spring that he knew of high in the mountains. We walked and surveyed 17 km of mountainside as we descended from the spring to the villages, and Binora was with us the whole time. As we walked and worked and talked, I reminded him of what he told me before we came, as we were planning together: "Pray that I see water in Gewada or die trying!" He replied quickly, "And I mean it, Gary!" He knew where he fit in God's plan to reach the world. God used Binora as his mediating agent on behalf of little-known villages to bring EMI together with them to provide a sustainable solution to their needs!

By the way, one day Binora invited me and a few others (including Scott Powell) into his small, dark mud hut. We crawled under a tarp and bent down low to enter the opening and found ourselves inside—you guessed it—the vision I had of an African hut so many years ago as I sat in silent darkness settling some things with God! We joined hands and laid our hands on Binora and asked God to continue to use him as the servant He has positioned to intermediate for the people of Gewada, and committed ourselves in service to God, Binora, and the Gospel proclamation.

Our EMI team serving in Ethiopia got a powerful reminder of the impact the Body of Christ has – or does not have – in intermediation on behalf of the world. We had come in and out of the capital of Addis Ababa three times. We first arrived with one team of volunteers that we took out to the bush hundreds of miles away for the water pipeline project with Binora. We then returned with them to send them home, and received a second team to serve an entirely different ministry to train teachers in the immediate area of the capital. The Ethiopian Hotel became our familiar rest stop... sounds upscale, but it was not...yet it was the best option around, and despite fleas in the beds, many international guests were there among us.

In the streets of Addis there were more people with disabilities camped out at intersections, street curbs and store fronts than I had seen anywhere. At the entrance to the hotel—but just off the edge of the property—stood a meek young woman every day in clear view of all those who would come and go from this hotel. Always in a pretty, sleeveless dress, you could see she had a malformed arm and was missing a leg. She stood with the help of a simple wooden crutch. Her point of course was to make sure we saw her body, and thereby saw her need. It was emotionally convincing and convicting, and the team needed to debrief about it.

I was always drawn in by her appearance and expressions, which were gentle and pleading, showing her longing "to be seen."

As awkward as we felt looking at her, that was the point. She wanted us to look, see, and be drawn in to respond. And how could our hearts not be touched in this exchange of looking, feeling and understanding? Yet, the plight of the beggar universally around the world never comes with easy solutions like money or addressing social evils. It's always bigger than that, and in debriefing with my team, I wanted to know where their hearts were in responding to the emotions they had—and they ran the full gamut from sorrow and pity, to compassion and empathy, to anger and frustration over the manipulation. All very real and very fair responses.

We talked for a while one evening, shared different perspectives, and prayed that God would clearly lead each one to respond as their consciences would lead them. Later, I was left to quietly meditate on it all. I've reconciled my own heart response and my own actions pertaining to beggars long ago (I always try to have small change in my pockets for the kids who so often run after us, but beyond that, I do not give money away), but I recognize that this was all very new for most of my team. We discussed the issue of James' challenge of faith without works being dead and how it can be challenging to combine and balance the two. But most of the time in circumstances like these, you don't get the chance to share Jesus clearly. I certainly didn't want our Gospel witness to be either a ghost or a corpse!

As I sat alone contemplating this woman whose disabled body frustrated her life, I felt God gave me some insights into who we are as the Body of Christ. Why is the Body of Christ such a powerful concept for us as his ambassadors of reconciliation to the world? I immediately had these two thoughts: first, our bodies are how we get things done; and second, they are how we present ourselves to the world. The Body makes intermediation possible. Let's dive into this then.

If our bodies are missing members or connecting members improperly, we are like this woman's disabled body. And we are so often like this young woman! We as the Church have many members who are missing—missing in action!—who have never been properly joined into the Body. They have never discovered their proper "fit" in God's unique design for us all to be together, work together, and perform works of ministry—especially intermediation! Some members are supposed to be paired because we are more effective with two rather than one—we are bilaterally symmetrical beings for good reason! Other members are alone as they work to serve the Body. Some are out in front; some are reserved or private. Some are seen, some are unseen. Paul does a great job describing this interplay of the members in 1 Corinthians 12. Regardless of function or role, no one can be missing without it impacting the whole body's effectiveness and appearance!

What is the effect of missing or improperly connected members? A dysfunctional body! The body is how we accomplish anything that the mind, soul, and spirit inspire us to do. It is also how we present ourselves to the world—it's how we recognize one another! So when we are missing members or are connected improperly to the body (such as this woman's missing forearm, such that her hand is directly connected to her elbow), not only are we less effective, but we're shockingly strange, unattractive, or "disfigured" to the world around us. We elicit contempt: "that doesn't really work; they're just wrong; they don't do anything good for the world…" Or we elicit pity or shock or repulsion, because what we've presented to the world is some sort of abnormal, unattractive mess. We are seen as some sort of bastardized, illegitimate representation of Jesus.

If members are missing, others are forced to do a job they weren't designed for, and the jobs they were designed for might not be accomplished at all. For instance, it's possible for me to walk on my hands (at least it was when I was a younger man), but forcing my arms to act like legs will exhaust my arms and the rest of my body very quickly. Meanwhile, the arms can't perform what they uniquely were designed for—reaching, grabbing, holding, hugging—and the legs can't even pretend to perform that function. They're left on their own, flailing around just trying to keep the body from falling over, their real strength for lifting, walking, and running left unused.

I can hear some of you reacting right now, saying, "Gary, doesn't God use all of us in our brokenness, in spite of it all? Doesn't He welcome everyone into his presence and send his Spirit to live in each of us, making each of us his temple and his holy vessels to be used by him for reconciliation and restoration regardless of all that?" Yes, that is absolutely true. Individually, we do have the promise that "we have this treasure in jars of clay to show that this all-surpassing power is from God and not from us" (2 Cor 4:7). We are "jars of clay"—fragile, cracked, imperfect, but beautifully and individually handmade! "We are God's handiwork, created in Christ Jesus to do good works, which God prepared in advance for us to do" (Eph 2:10). The Greek word for handiwork is *poema*, from which we get our word poem. We are each a beautiful, creative expression of our God's initiation and design.

But that is not what I'm talking about here. The ultimate witness we have for the world is our mediation not as individuals, but as the Body of Christ. The restoration of creation and his kingdom is at stake! "And God placed all things under his feet and appointed him to be head over everything for the church, which is his body, the fullness of him who fills everything in every way" (Eph 1:22-23).

When the members of the Body of Christ are all accounted for, connected, and working together—regardless of our weaknesses or flaws—then we make up for each other's lack of ability in other areas. Indeed, we were not all designed the same, and for good reason. In her autobiography, *The Story of My Life*, Helen Keller said, "Thus it is that my friends have made the story of my life. In a thousand ways, they have turned my limitations into beautiful privileges, and enabled me to walk serene and happy in the shadow cast by my deprivation."[4] If one of the most famously challenged Americans who ever lived could say that about those around her, I know we can all aspire to be that kind of image to the world for the sake of Christ as well!

When the Body of Christ is working at its best and all members are cooperatively respecting and supporting one another for the singular purpose of achieving the plan of God to reach the world, it's a beautiful thing to be sure. Intermediation of all kinds can be accomplished when the whole body jumps into the "mud puddles of human need." But a commitment to abandon our own agenda for God's is the heart of intermediation. It's the missionary heart at work, crushed for the world's sake and for the sake of reaching the world. Showing up where no one else is. Taking on challenges that no one else will. God is in all these difficult places and stories, and He's inviting us to come into them with him.

It's difficult to be sure. Sometimes it is very challenging. It's hotter and stickier "there" than anywhere I've ever been—I wouldn't know unless I went. It's long jet-lagged workdays from sunup till sundown—I wouldn't know I could do it until...I did! I once logged over 175 hours of planes, trains, and automobiles in India for just three days of ministry work time in the mountains of Siliguri near Darjeeling. The food is strange, and I have the world's most sensitive digestive system. It's true—I call it God's practical joke on me. There's a travel book brewing in me over that one!

I've often found myself in scary, intimidating, unknown and unforeseen circumstances – but I'm here today telling you about it, aren't I? Ask me someday about Venezuela, with tanks and rocket launchers in the streets looking very much like a military coup; the schizophrenic volunteer who wigged out on me, almost making it impossible for me to get him home; the city-wide rioting in Cochabamba, Bolivia, answered by a military martial-law-mandated curfew, with rubber bullets spraying in the crowds, tire fires at city intersections as high as two story buildings, and tear gas in our guest house; the car accident where our Indian driver hit a child in a small village near Darjeeling and the swarm of the crowd around us; the broken down vehicles on the sides of isolated African roads; and the Brazilian airline that went bankrupt as we flew home on our first leg in Brazil, effectively stranding the team in Rio when we landed mid-trip. The conclusions of those stories make up more miracles to tell you about! It is precisely in those things that are bigger than us that God can meet us there and glorify himself! Still, He asks us to be his hands that can serve, his feet that can take us into the presence of others, his arms that can give a loving hug, and his voice that can speak encouragement; in every way, the Body of Christ and his love personified in the middle of those "mud puddles of human need." We just *can't* stay!

Very early on, my wife joined me as we were developing the next phases in an orphanage village-like community in rural Guatemala. We were so excited for her to join me, knowing there would be lots of ways for her to be God's hands and feet and heart, interacting with the children who lived there. From the moment we set foot in Zacapa, a desert region of Guatemala, we could see the challenges we faced: the white-knuckle car rides across the country from Guatemala City; bats, rats, and lizards; and beds full of dust and mold (to which Judylynn is allergic).

Two days into the trip, I saw the difficult living conditions I had unwittingly invited my wife into and asked myself and God, "What have I done?" It was one thing for me to endure the hardships, another to subject my wife to them. I spoke to the missionaries about how surprised I was at the condition of the compound. The last EMI team stayed at a little hotel in Zacapa and that's one of the reasons I thought this was a good opportunity to invite my wife. They then explained to me that when the last team came about a year earlier, this same compound was under eight feet of mud and water from Hurricane Mitch and they had spent most of the last year cleaning it up. I briefly alerted them to my possible need for Judylynn's sake to get her out of there, and they graciously offered to perhaps make arrangements for us at the hotel. Later when we talked though, she wanted nothing to do with that, recognizing that it would not be much of a team-player attitude or appearance. And how would I be able to properly oversee things if I was dealing with traveling to and from the hotel every day. She said, "Let's just see…" We prayed, and I fell asleep that night counting the number of days that we would have to be in this place.

Early in the trip we visited a government orphanage in the evening after a long workday in the heat. The building we were in had one room, dimly lit, for about twenty children—infants, toddlers and a few teens—with beds and cribs ringing the perimeter of the room. From under the mosquito nets, you could smell the urine from the babies sitting in their drenched rag diapers. Judylynn almost immediately picked up a baby who was alone in an infant seat sucking at his bottle. Her heart going out to this little one, she easily saw how detached he was from the one holding him. Already, without love and physical affection, these little children had fallen into the defense mechanisms of detachment and fearfulness of loving, caring touch and communication. My wife's initiative stirred the rest of us to do the same. My two young interns—Geoff McMillan and Sheldon Smith—unreservedly held and fed these babies, whose soaking wet cloth diapers soaked their own shirts. Undaunted, they loved on those little babies perhaps for the first time ever (for both the baby and the intern!), happy to shower once they got back to the compound.

We saw first-hand the difference between a government-funded and run orphanage and the one we came to serve—House of Hope. Where the world's solution is dark, depressing, and fearful, House of Hope stands in stark contrast: bright, encouraging, and, well, *hopeful*! There is indeed a future and a hope in our Lord, and these children are living in it! The House of Hope Orphanage team, whom we were serving, stands in polemic defiance to the status quo. They are determined and committed to their children living in clean and comfortable houses, with loving "house parents," and they go to school, do homework, take naps, and play. Our missionary hosts have dedicated their lives to running the orphanage and have a love for these kids that inspires them to call them "our kids." They have a vision to rescue *all* those kids from the government orphanage, and to raise them knowing their potential in Christ!

Judylynn became a veritable ambassador of goodwill, faithfully pumping herself full of allergy medication morning and night, and never once breathed a negative word. She continually encouraged the people of our team and those around the compound and, working through the language barriers as well as she could, got to know the women there, mediating for them more than anyone else on our team: the woman who brought us meals every day, the Guatemalan wives of American missionaries, the missionary family, and the children. Judylynn's faith and perseverance opened the door for God to bless not just those children, but the team, the missionaries we were there to serve, the members of the community...literally everyone she encountered!

One last piece of the story in Guatemala: we also got to know a young Korean man who —like the Bible school students in Nepal— believes he will be martyred for Jesus in a Muslim country one day! Now that's a gift I confess I haven't sought after, but as he embraces the ministry of reconciliation, he is willing to pay the ultimate price in intermediation. I later remembered the words of Jim Elliot, who was martyred in Ecuador: "He is no fool who gives what he cannot keep to gain what he cannot lose!"

Nowhere does the missionary heart look more like God's heart than in serving orphans around the world. EMI has served countless missionary efforts to rescue orphans and abandoned children. But children with disabilities exponentially compound both the compassionate response and the challenges. EMI has seen children with disabilities basically caged inside of cribs, without enough caregivers or resources to properly and safely care for them. Other children are abandoned and left to die, because the challenges of caring for them are insurmountable, or superstitions or social pressures force their parents into such desperate acts.

On one of my trips to Uganda a few years ago, I served with two such ministries. One group—Imprint Hope—was headed by a remarkable young American woman who had already adopted two Ugandan boys of her own. Our team developed the design for a training center for families with children with disabilities on land she had purchased. The lives of these children are bleak, and even if they have loving families, they are often powerless to care for these children. Imprint Hope teaches and trains families with an on-campus, in-residence, multi-week program to care for their own children, instead of leaving them in desperation.

The other ministry—illustrative of how I personally fit in God's plan to reach the world—is the Gem Foundation. As a little girl, Dwight Saunders' daughter Emma's heart was broken for special needs orphans. At just 6 years old, she began to pray that God would pick her to take care of orphans in Africa. On her eighth birthday, her parents recorded a video of her saying she was moving to Uganda to help take care of the orphans. At 13, she began taking mission trips to Uganda. In January 2013, Emma moved permanently, and her dream had now become a reality. Soon after moving, she began the lengthy and arduous process of registering and opening The Gem Foundation. Eighteen months later on July 10th, 2014, the first eleven Gems arrived; they were home forever!

In 2015, Emma married her high school sweetheart, Josh. They were married at The Gem Foundation, surrounded by the children and her staff. Emma and Josh are truly a team. The Gem has been open for several years now, and they have had the privilege of caring for more than 70 Gems. God has been faithful every step of the way, and neither Emma nor Josh can take credit for what He has done! And in Emma's words: "I am humbled that He chose to use me. Today my husband Josh and I, together as a family with our [five] children, have the joy of caring for our most precious Gems! We love living in Uganda and loving our Gems! There is truly nowhere else we'd rather be." They know where they fit in God's plan to reach the world.

Thirty-five years ago Emma's parents, Dwight and Linny Saunders, brought home their oldest son from Asia. Over the years they would lovingly gather ten more children from around the world and have a few biological children, as well. Now, married for over four decades, their six oldest have launched from the nest and they are expecting their 15th grandchild! Of their fifteen grands, five are adopted. One of their greatest joys is that they are a multi-generational adoptive family.

As beautiful as each adoption was, they were burdened remembering the ones left behind. Dwight and Linny knew they had to do more! So with their hearts all in and their lives demonstrating what they passionately believe, they committed to making a tangible difference in the lives of waiting orphans by founding their own non-profit, International Voice of the Orphan (IVO). They began the ministry by providing medical care and life-saving surgeries, as well as meals to the orphans. IVO has fed approximately two million meals to orphans and their staff around the world.

Their daughter Emma and her husband Josh have dedicated their lives to serving the broken-bodied orphans of Uganda. As "The Gem" needs continued to grow, IVO narrowed its focus to advocate and support the special needs orphans at the Gem, and the two ministries merged. Together, they proclaim that *every child with special needs is a Gem from the heart of God!*

I held the babies, sat on the living room floor to help feed or play with them, and served meals on the porch of the Gem Foundation home even as EMI was designing the new campus that they have now moved into. Clearly, it is Emma and Josh who are the Gems!

Of all the incredible stories of rescue work that have come out of these powerful testimonies of intermediation, one has become a book called *Rescuing Ruby*, by Linny Saunders, chronicling the story of Ruby's adoption. Leading a team with her father, Emma found an emaciated and dying baby girl in the darkened corner of an orphanage. Struggling for life, her big brown eyes seemed to be pleading, "Please! Will you help me?" Emma ran to her dad, Dwight, calling, "Daddy! Daddy! Come quick! This baby! She's dying! We have to do something!" Following Emma to the darkened corner of the room, he was stunned at what he found, words inadequate to describe. Emaciated. Mere skin draped over her protruding bones. Her sweet head was much larger than her boney exposed limbs. He gasped. "Dying" was the only word that really could describe her. And at that divinely God-orchestrated moment, Almighty God broke his heart for her. One baby girl, but a picture-perfect representative of the millions and millions of orphans globally in desperate need of someone to care for them. Emma and Dwight learned that day that this baby girl was just over a year old yet weighed barely six pounds. She truly was dying! Their rescue of little Ruby is truly the substance of divinely led, inspired, and empowered *intermediation.*

God's work of positioning me and Dwight Saunders for the intermediation of the Gem Foundation spanned four decades! Here's the story as I shared it in a newsletter a few years ago:

It begins with a 16-year-old kid, who met a guy on the city bus he used to ride every day to get to school. That kid said a prayer the day before to a God he hardly knew was real. He wondered if he even meant a word of it. Today he can testify that God showed up that very day with some amazing proofs that He was indeed real, and He had, indeed, heard his prayer. One of those proofs was the guy he sat down next to: a messenger from God who just happened to be reading his Bible. He was in law school at the time, probably around 23 years old, and was helping lead a youth group at a local church nearby. A conversation started, and the young man made sure to get that kid's phone number before they said goodbye. After weeks of faithful calling and being turned down, the kid finally agreed to attend a youth meeting. He had never seen anything like it: young people loving God and each other, happy to be followers of Jesus in their everyday lives! Thus began a friendship that has lasted over four decades.

Their lives intertwined and overlapped and separated for seasons over the years, but were marked by significant connections. That guy became a lawyer, and that kid became an architect. The two of them pursued their careers, served in the local church, and raised their families; until one day, each on his own separate journey, they heard the call of the Master to leave it all and venture into full-time ministry. The lawyer was several years ahead of the architect in pursuit of the ministry. In his first year at seminary he received a postcard about a small international ministry that mobilized engineers and architects to partner with missionaries to design development projects to serve and reach the poor. He sent it to the architect, who—nearly headed for burnout and having absolutely no heart for such a thing at the time—did not throw it away but dutifully filed it away out of the respect he had for the one who gave it to him. A few years later, when the lawyer was already serving as a pastor, the architect heard the missions call and knew exactly where that brochure was. He dug it out and within a few months of calling that ministry organization, was on a plane traveling overseas for the first time in his life, discovering the very reason he was made!

Over the years, their two ministries never connected, though God was calling them each to the needs of orphans over and over again. The lawyer—now pastor—and his wife began adopting children from all over the world, and the architect began serving orphan communities and designing orphanages, also all over the world! In recent years, the lawyer told the architect that he was seeing a focus on orphan ministry develop in Uganda, and one of his daughters was establishing a work there. The architect had begun training new team leaders and had spent the bulk of the month of June for the last three summers there. Father and daughter began looking for land, raising up child sponsors, and caring for orphans, all the while dreaming of how the lawyer and the architect could come together one day and design an orphan home community.

Thirty-nine years after meeting on that bus, EMI's Uganda office designed the initial master plan for the project for this "lawyer/minister/missionary" guy and his daughter and her husband. At the exact same time a few hours away, the kid who has now been an "architect/minister/missionary" for over twenty years was back in Uganda training a new project leader for the EMI Uganda office. Coming together that week, for the design review and trip reports of each team at the EMI office, the two men spent some time together reflecting, thanking God for what He had done, and marveling at "such a time as this!"

The architect's favorite prayer is, "God, may Your kingdom come, and Your will be done, on earth as it is in heaven." In and through and all around their two stories, God has used them. But they know this isn't all about them, as much as they are in the center of it, mediating between God and men. Two men with changed lives because of the loving God at work in their hearts, desiring to see that same transformation in the lives of hundreds and thousands of kids. Even as they have been positioned by God, the architect prays that he doesn't get in the way!

These are such inspiring stories of "standing in the gap" intermediations, yet the Bible makes it clear and strangely simple: "Religion that God our Father accepts as pure and faultless is this: to look after orphans and widows in their distress..." (James 1:27). All over the world, there are not nearly enough government-sponsored services like those found in North America. Most governments can't —and shouldn't —take the place of the Church. From healthcare, to education, to orphan care, and more, the Church and its missionary efforts around the globe fill in the gaps as mediators between God and men. Even here at home, there is still great need for the Church to rise up as mediators to intercede for people in great need— children, families, single parents, the trafficked, the addicted, the homeless. The list goes on and on, and becomes a literal prescription for anyone who is seeking the answer to the question: "Where do I fit in God's plan to reach the world?" Intermediation provides the tangible and physical expression of God's love for people and opens the doors to share the very hope of the Gospel: *redemption.*

CHAPTER 11

REDEMPTION

"...so I would not have to destroy it..."

> *"I looked for someone among them who would build up the wall and stand before me in the gap on behalf of the land* **so I would not have to destroy it,** *but I found no one."*
> **Ezekiel 22:30**

In declaring this—*not wanting* to destroy the city—God reveals his Father's heart for his people even then. He's looking for someone from among his people who would, in faith, step into partnership with him so that his judgment might be stayed. God's own "missionary heart" that is poured out in power to save and to rescue is on full display. His redemption of humanity and all creation is a mission of recovery and reclamation. Throughout the Bible and this book—from beginning to end—we see God's redemptive plan unfold. And from the beginning clues of creation—with its beauty and splendor—we know instinctively that things are not right when we see them, and long to see restoration through the redemption of broken things and broken lives.

When it comes to novels or movies, I most enjoy redemption stories. The greatest triumphs, the most endearing love stories, the best "come-back-from-the-brink" rescues are all about making up for past sins, mistakes, or wounds. They are usually those where the protagonists must somehow come back from heartbreak, cynicism, hurt, or anger in order to be whole again, to love again, to be open to the love of someone else again, or to realize their full potential in their calling. Our hero or heroine is redeemed from the pit: the pit of loneliness, rejection, judgment, or their own living hell.

It's no wonder really, because the inherent attraction relates directly to the problem of our own brokenness, screaming from within us to be redeemed. We know the good we ought to do, but so often choose selfishness or faithlessness—out of fear, ignorance, or foolishness. The books we read or the movies we watch give us the hope that broken lives can indeed be redeemed. I love these stories so much that I don't even mind stopping on an old movie as I'm channel surfing to just catch the last 20 minutes! That's just enough time to refresh my memory of the hero's battle through brokenness, experience the climax, and revel in the redemptive denouement. It makes my poor wife crazy, but this way, I don't have to vicariously re-live all the hero's pain—just the celebration of the feel-good ending! That's a win-win!

King David was a man with just such a story. He was a man who knew a special kind of closeness to God, certainly a rarity in Old Testament times. The Bible describes him as a "man after God's own heart." He had perhaps the most meteoric rise as a hero. But he also stands as a fearsome reminder of just how totally broken we are and the deeply redeeming work we all need. Talk about a story of desperately needed redemption after the absolute worst of sinful and evil choices leads him to a climax none of us ever saw coming! Even Hollywood couldn't have come up with a more wicked sinner's redemption story. David forced himself on a married woman named Bathsheba. After learning she was pregnant with his child, David plotted to have her husband—a loyal soldier called Uriah the Hittite—murdered. But he didn't do it himself...he ordered Uriah's commanding officer to do the deed by moving him to the front lines of battle then withdrawing the rest of the warriors! It pains me every time I review the story.

David thinks he's gotten away with all this sinful intrigue, "but the thing David had done displeased the Lord" (2 Sm 11:27). That's putting it mildly! God sends Nathan to speak his judgment, and David is completely undone by the prophet's words (2 Sm 12:1-9) and God's punishment: "Now, therefore, the sword will never depart from your house, because you despised me and took the wife of Uriah the Hittite to be your own" (2 Sm 12:10). In Psalm 51, in the face of utter ruin, we hear the depth of David's sorrow and longing for redemption. "Create in me a pure heart, O God, and renew a steadfast spirit within me. Do not cast me from your presence or take your Holy Spirit from me. *Restore to me the joy of your salvation* and grant me a willing spirit, to sustain me" (Ps 51:10-12, emphasis mine). He pleaded for God's redeeming love to return to him.

Indeed, the work of saving people is at the heart of the Gospel message, to restore what was lost, to give back value to something that was ruined or thought to be worthless. We are so valuable precisely because God has created us and redeemed us! It is not that we were so valuable that God *had* to redeem us, but that we were *so chosen* by God that He committed to the work of redemption from the start, thereby placing his stamp of value upon us! God had chosen David from the start, the last of Jesse's sons. Do you think David's fall from grace took God by surprise? Hardly. Just as in the beginning, when He created us in his own image knowing that our rebellion was going to color the rest of the story and require his great redemptive plan to be set in motion, He still *chose* David, knowing that one day "the lust of the flesh, the lust of the eyes, and the pride of life—[that] comes not from the Father but from the world"—would seriously complicate things (1 Jn 2:16). Remember the power of being chosen, according to Ann Voskamp? "When you trust that you're chosen by someone good, you can trust that you're always being taken to good places. The chosen are simply the ones approached by an enamored God who can't stop thinking about you."[1]

When it comes to redemption, God just can't stop thinking of us! In the full story from creation to restoration, the critical moment—the pinnacle of the story—is his redeeming work. In the cross of Christ, we see and find full redemption: "For God so loved the world that He gave his one and only Son, that whoever believes in him shall not perish but have eternal life. For God did not send his Son into the world to condemn the world, but to save the world through him" (Jn 3:16,17). But it's revealed in God's heart and plan much earlier in the biblical record. Repeatedly throughout the Old Testament, the profession of the faithful is that God *will* redeem, *is* their redeemer, and *will complete* the work of redemption. It's the hope of Israel, and the promise of God from the beginning.

Years later, after David had personally lived the redemption of God in his life, he heard from God that he must not be the one to build a temple for the Lord, but his heir would. He goes on to extol God and his singular act that reveals his *hesed* lovingkindness toward his people.

> "There is no one like you, Lord, and there is no God but you, as we have heard with our own ears. And who is like your people Israel—the one nation on earth whose God went out to *redeem* a people for himself, and to make a name for yourself, and to perform great and awesome wonders by driving out nations from before your people, whom you redeemed from Egypt? You made your people Israel your very own forever, and you, Lord, have become their God. (1 Chr 17:20-22, emphasis mine)

God redeemed a people for himself! He chose his people in *hesed* lovingkindness. If there was ever any doubt as to where the value lies, this clears it up. For himself and for his glory and name, He redeemed a people. And through that people for centuries, He displayed his power, his wrath, his love and his ultimate purposes in redeeming that people. The Psalms proclaim the power of God's redeeming love: "O Israel, put your hope in the Lord, for *with the Lord is unfailing love and with him is full redemption. He himself will redeem Israel from all their sins"* (Ps 130:7-8, emphasis mine). And Isaiah proclaims and celebrates all this prophetically: "But now, this is what the Lord says—He who created you, Jacob, He who formed you, Israel: 'Do not fear, for I have redeemed you; I have summoned you by name; you are mine'" (Is 43:1).

> "Remember these things, Jacob,
>   for you, Israel, are my servant
> *I have made you,* you are my servant;
>   Israel, *I will not forget you.*
> I have swept away your offenses like a cloud,
>   your sins like the morning mist.
> *Return to me,*
>   *for I have redeemed you.*"
>
> Sing for joy, you heavens, for the LORD has done this;
>   shout aloud, you earth beneath.
> Burst into song, you mountains,
>   you forests and all your trees,
> *for the Lord has redeemed Jacob,*
>   He *displays his glory in Israel.* (Is 44:21-23, emphasis mine)

Redeeming a people for himself was all for one purpose: the salvation of the entire human race, the redemption of *all* mankind. God made this very clear as He covenanted with Abraham, declaring that all people would be blessed through him (Gn 12:3). Through his work in his people Israel, God made room for the stranger and the alien. From the design of the world with Eden at its center, to the Tabernacle, and then the Temple, the three-part design was consistent, growing concentrically from the center, or heart, of communion with God, then spreading outward to reach the rest of the world. The outer courts of the Tabernacle and Temple were a place for connecting with the rest of the world. The outer court of the Temple was even named the Court of the Gentiles!

But it's rare in the scriptural record that the people of God ever really understood this. They saw themselves as his chosen people, and were establishing a separatist culture even way back in the earliest days of the storyline. But David got it! He wrote, "All the ends of the earth will remember and turn to the Lord, and all the families of the nations will bow down before him, for dominion belongs to the Lord and He rules over the nations" (Ps 22:27-28). And similarly, "May God be gracious to us and bless us and make his face shine on us—so that your ways may be known on earth, your salvation among all nations" (Ps 67:1-2). The apostle Paul brings us back to the beginning and connects us to the end of the story and the fulfillment of God's purposes:

> Understand, then, that those who have faith are children of Abraham. Scripture foresaw that God would *justify* the Gentiles by faith and announced the gospel in advance to Abraham: "All nations will be blessed through you." So those who rely on faith are blessed along with Abraham, the man of faith... He *redeemed* us in order that the blessing given to Abraham might come to the Gentiles through Christ Jesus, so that by faith we might receive the promise of the Spirit." (Gal 3:7-8, 14; emphasis mine)

Redemption is transliterated from the Hebrew as *pidyon*: "in conventional Hebrew, it refers to a price that must be paid to redeem, to rescue, or to deliver someone... Its root is a legal term that concerns the substitution required for a person to be delivered from bondage... Ancient pictographs communicate a number of important truths, declaring an entrance or a pathway that will require a mighty deed to secure life... Something else found in *pidyon* brings great hope. This *redemption* will bring a new birth or a new beginning for all creation; it has been ordained in heaven, will solve man's enmity with God, and will result in deliverance, followed by rest."[2] (emphasis mine).

Wow. Doesn't that seem like a fitting way to bring all the work of God in the earth to its fullest completion? This *redemption* that ushers in a new beginning for all creation is the picture of creative initiation; to be ordained in heaven is in the place of *intercession*; to solve man's enmity with God reestablishes *relationship* through *reconciliation;* and the resultant deliverance comes through the redeemer's *identification* and *intermediation;* all followed by rest, final *restoration*.

In a way that is just like God—full of grace, forgiveness, restoration and redemption—Korah's descendants (we covered his rebellion and judgment in Chapter 9) knew full well the catastrophic consequences of sin as they wrote about redemption and its price. "No one can redeem the life of another or give to God a ransom for them—the ransom for a life is costly, no payment is ever enough—so that they should live on forever and not see decay" (Ps 49:7-9).

While the sons of Korah know that no one is able to pay the price, they proclaim—in faith— "But God will redeem me from the realm of the dead; He will surely take me to himself" (Ps 49:15). How will He do it? Surely there will be *someone* who will be able to perform the "mighty deed" that will be sufficient to rescue souls from destruction!

...by that will, we have been made holy through the sacrifice of the body of Jesus Christ once for all.

Day after day every priest stands and performs his religious duties; again and again he offers the same sacrifices, which can never take away sins. But when this priest had offered for all time one sacrifice for sins, He sat down at the right hand of God... For by one sacrifice He has made perfect forever those who are being made holy. (Heb 10:10-12, 14)

In a fascinating study of ancient Hebrew word pictures—which are often hidden from our English translations (and even modern Hebrew)—Steve Johnson diagrams the Hebrew origins of "love" and "redeem." God's redeeming love—the love that *initiated* everything and *redeemed* everything—is uniquely highlighted. Love—*ahav* in ancient Hebrew—combines who God is (our Father) and that He is revealed (as through a window): love is "the Father revealed." Redeem—*ga al*—is "God lifted up."[3] This sheds a lot of light on Jesus' teaching to Nicodemus, fulfilling all the prophecies of redemption and all the professions of hope in the Old Testament.

> No one has ever gone into heaven except the one who came from heaven—the Son of Man. Just as Moses lifted up the snake in the wilderness, so the Son of Man must be lifted up, that everyone who believes may have eternal life in him.
>
> For God so loved the world that He gave his one and only Son, that whoever believes in him shall not perish but have eternal life. For God did not send his Son into the world to condemn the world, but to *save* the world through him. (Jn 3:13-17)

Jesus "gave himself as a ransom for all people," (1 Tim 2:6), both fully demonstrating and fully accomplishing God's redeeming love.

Mark recounts a time when Jesus shares this same lesson as He is teaching his disciples about the kingdom of God...about love and humility and sacrifice: "For even the Son of Man did not come to be served, but to serve, and to give his life as a ransom for many" (Mk 10:45). Returning to kingdom language, as it pertains to the restoration of all things and returning to the rule and reign in God's Kingdom, Paul continues in his letter to the Colossians, "For He has rescued us from the dominion of darkness and brought us into the kingdom of the Son He loves, in whom we have *redemption,* the forgiveness of sins" (Col 1:13-14, emphasis mine).

And again, in Paul's opening to the Ephesians, God establishes that his redemptive work was planned—that He had *chosen* us— before the creation of the world!

> For He chose us in him before the creation of the world to be holy and blameless in his sight. In love He predestined us for adoption to sonship through Jesus Christ, in accordance with his pleasure and will— to the praise of his glorious grace, which He has freely given us in the One He loves. In him we have *redemption through his blood, the forgiveness of sins,* in accordance with the riches of God's grace that He lavished on us. With all wisdom and understanding,

> He made known to us the mystery of his will according to his good pleasure, which He purposed in Christ, to be put into effect when the times reach their fulfillment—to bring unity to all things in heaven and on earth under Christ. (Eph 1:4-10, emphasis mine)

This finality of the work of redemption in and through Christ would seem to say there's nothing that we as his Church can do as a continuation of this work, following in his steps. But what of the testimony of the Church in the earth as corroborative testimony to the reality of this divine work of God? The psalmist writes, "Let the redeemed of the Lord tell their story—those He redeemed from the hand of the foe, those He gathered from the lands, from east and west, from north and south" (Ps 107:2-3). This psalm doesn't just refer to Israel's redemption from the usual disobedience and subsequent enemy conquests or oppression we continually read about from the prophets, but a myriad of other difficult challenges, including wandering in desert wastelands, hunger and thirst, imprisonment and enslavement, stormy seas, and drought. God redeemed his people from all these things.

And today, his people stand redeemed in the same way. My friend, you have a story to tell! "Let the redeemed of the Lord tell their story!" That's where we follow in his steps! We must tell our story. The story of his redeeming love at work in our lives. As Jesus rose from the grave, defeating death and hell and the bondage to sin, you have been raised up with him and have been redeemed from the pit of Hell and all sorts of brokenness that came from it! Since we've been "rescued from the dominion of darkness," we now have the privilege of living in "the kingdom of the son He loves." Now that's something worth talking about, wouldn't you say? We have this privilege—and responsibility—of living "in accordance with the riches of God's grace that He lavished on us," so that the world would see something different! "Therefore, if anyone is in Christ, the new creation has come. The old has gone, the new is here!" (2 Cor 5:17). You are a new creation living a new life!

As we live our stories of redemption, we are driven into the world with this hope we so desperately want to share with a world that is shackled with hopelessness. Jesus said, "The thief comes only to steal and kill and destroy; I have come that they may have life, and have it to the full" (Jn 10:10). This is where the motivation in the Church to impact the world for good, in Jesus' name, comes from. In determined opposition to the fatalism that is pervasive in so much of the other world religions and philosophies, Christians are ready to roll up their sleeves and fight for people to "have life and have it to the full." Far from waiting for destruction to come, we embrace our mission in the world as agents making a way for redemption. From the writer of Lamentations (likely Jeremiah), we experience this not just from the perspective of God arriving to rescue, but as one who *mediates*! "You came near when I called you, and you said, 'Do not fear.' You, Lord, took up my case; you redeemed my life" (Lam 3:57,58). You might say He came into the middle of our "mud puddles of human need!" So we do the same.

God's intent to redeem all peoples is repeatedly reinforced in Isaiah's prophetic message to God's people. My friend of many years, Neil Boron, relates a poignant story where God used Isaiah 49:6 powerfully in his life to move him into a different season of ministry as he sought to discover where he fit in God's plan to reach the world. That verse speaks to the truth that we are witnesses to God's redemptive work in the world and in people's lives. "It is too small a thing for you to be my servant to restore the tribes of Jacob and bring back those of Israel I have kept. I will also make you a light for the Gentiles, that my salvation may reach to the ends of the earth" (Is 49:6). As true as that is, then and now, Neil says that an accidental "dyslexic" reading of the verse is actually what God used to move him into a brand new and completely unexpected place where he found a whole new fit in God's plan to reach the world— a very important season of pastoral ministry.

First the backdrop: Neil had grown into a position of influence hosting the largest Christian radio talk show in New York State. And he was good at it! I regularly tried to tune in to his broadcasts on weekday afternoons and might even occasionally call in. I was "Gary, from Amherst," and Neil would never reveal that he knew me at all. But program growth and corporate pressure to commit more time and attention to commercial endeavors began to sour him on his ever-expanding career in radio. His passion for seeing people come to Christ through his talk radio ministry was becoming obscured.

When Neil read Isaiah 49:6, he somehow misunderstood a very important phrase...and would continue to do so for several years! In this text, God says, "It is too small a thing for you to be called my servant..." then goes on to reveal that He had much more in store for the Children of Israel: He was going to make his people a light to the entire world. Neil, however, read it as a question: "Is it too small a thing for you to be called my servant...?" and thought it was a challenge to him to pursue a life of humble service instead of the incredible growth he was beginning to enjoy.

He answered the question almost exactly as I did as I sat on the end of that pew with my cast and my crutches, "Yes. I am OK with being your servant." After individually coming to the exact same conclusion, Neil resigned his position as a state-wide talk radio host, and eventually was led to accept a position as Assistant Pastor of his home church. He served in that capacity for almost five years, truly learning how to love and serve people up close and personally. Later he became the Lead Pastor.

Then, wouldn't you know, in just a few years God returned him to that radio broadcasting role again, where he has faithfully served in his calling to see Christian radio change people's lives across New York State every afternoon. But this time he has new perspective, joyfully persevering in God's call. One day, God opened his eyes, and he was able to see what Isaiah 49:6 actually says! It IS too small a thing that he should be confined to ministering to God's people alone (though that call was completely acceptable). He is also being used as a light to the world! Finally, with confidence and assurance, Neil sees clearly where he fits in God's plan to reach the world!

Through her strong sense of identification, Iyabo Obasanjo, the Nigerian president's daughter, had facilitated our partnership in the specialty women's hospital project to treat fistula. You learned part of the story in Chapter 6. She had passionately "taken up the cause" of the estimated one million young women suffering from this devastating injury. As I briefly described earlier, this injury is almost unheard of in the West. It occurs when a young woman—old enough to conceive, but usually too young to safely give birth because her body frame is still small and developing—is unable to deliver her baby naturally and no medical or surgical relief is available. The young woman labors in the bush environment to no avail and the baby does not survive. As it is wedged against the pelvic bones until it withers, the baby may not be delivered stillborn for perhaps several days. In that much time the soft tissues comprising and separating the birth canal, the bladder, and the rectum are compromised—bruised so badly that sections of the tissue die, and eventually heal with holes compromising the integrity of each organ.

The worst is what follows, as the woman is now unable to control the leaking that occurs, and she is unsanitary, vulnerable to infection, and unable to cope in normal culture. She is often ostracized—even rejected and sent off by her husband—to live a marginalized life on the edges of her rural culture. These young women have been known to band together in leper-like colonies across the Sahel region of Africa from the east all the way to the west side of the continent. The doctors we were working with had years of experience with the first established Christian-run hospital effort in Ethiopia and had implemented a program in a new wing of an existing hospital in Jos, Nigeria, and were now on board to help us with Iyabo's vision to recreate that success in a new hospital completely dedicated to this.

After my initial scouting trip with Iyabo and the surgeons, I returned with a team of engineers, architects, and surveyors to develop the design. This was the same time that future EMI leader Chad Gamble was joining me to train as a leader. The team was unique: in addition to Chad and myself as leaders, we had my architectural intern Ryan Koeniger, two experienced engineers, and five engineering students from Calvin College. It is very unusual to have this many students and interns, and it meant that we senior members of the team would spend more time than usual mentoring these young team members.

Our activities took us back and forth on the difficult red-dust roads of West Africa, from the rural site of the new hospital to the existing hospital in the city of Jos. That hospital had already added a wing for fistula surgery in honor of Dr. Arrowsmith who had pioneered it here. These daily visits and interactions gave us many opportunities to talk to people, see them as they lived and worked, and learn their stories. We witnessed how groups of women—most of whom had made a long, arduous journey on foot after hearing of the possibility of getting help—would camp out in areas around the hospital, waiting for their turn to be admitted. Their lives were literally hanging in the balance, waiting for a surgery that could redeem them.

These groups were not unlike the communities they had developed in other regions of Africa, outcast from their own villages but banded together to support one another—and survive. Even the design of the hospital respected this culture and this need. The new hospital would support and promote this sisterhood among the waiting patients by having small village-like huts designed and clustered together for the women to live together, perhaps for weeks or months at a time. This was all a part of the Christian witness of the hospital, promoting a love for these women and giving dignity to them with a designated and honored place to stay. They called it a "Fellowship of Caring," encouraging and allowing these women to live in a community where they could have their needs met and the women themselves could become a part of meeting the others' needs, some of whom could not walk because their injuries were so severe. The sense of community is unmistakably like the first century church in the book of Acts. I spent a day with the doctors and the chaplain in the clinic with their young patients and toured the hospital wing. From the crowded hallways lined with little wooden benches for the young women to squeeze onto, to the individual patient rooms, we felt like we were intruding on hallowed ground. We did not want to invade their privacy. In the rooms, the one patient recovering from surgery typically was in a bed, while two or three others were using mats on the floors. Their faces are precious, eyes full of brightness and smiles returning to their faces perhaps for the first time in a long time as a result of the hope offered them. Again, only in love and compassion and gentle humor—and extraordinary faith—could these doctors do what they have done. They have perfected surgeries virtually unknown to most American surgeons and have delivered women from misery into a future and a hope.

One thing was very clear. From the hospital staff, medical and otherwise, to the patients themselves, everyone loved Dr. Steve Arrowsmith. He was an honored guest. A hero. And the thing that was constantly uttered from the mouths of patients was how grateful they were to be getting a new start on life. The humor that I had witnessed from the surgeons in my first trip (Chapter 6) peppered their stories of how they have loved literally hundreds of young, abandoned, outcast women into the Kingdom.

Here is where perhaps you will see how the redemptive story unfolds. In studies done by the chaplaincy of the Ethiopia hospital where fistula surgeries had been done for many years, there was nearly a 98% conversion rate among these women—and these are Muslims! Tell me, where else can you find such an astounding success rate of Gospel witness? And what made the difference? Here is the big idea I don't want you to miss. As we live out our redemption stories and get into the middle of the "mud puddles of human need" of other people's stories, they see Jesus. These missionary surgeons have literally restored their lives to them, redeeming all that was lost in their physical existence. In so doing, they become living stories of redemption themselves, and that opens their hearts to the Living Redeemer of their souls!

I can hardly even write these words without shivers and tears! A 10-year anniversary celebration had been planned to honor Dr. Arrowsmith, and women began arriving every day, camping out around the grounds of the hospital (not unusual in hospitals around the developing world). But what was unusual is that each day they could be heard worshipping with traditional African songs and drums and dancing in the halls of the fistula ward. What a stark contrast to the hopelessness that they had come from—and what a beautiful testimony to the Lord's redeeming nature!

On one of our return trips from the remote rural site for the new hospital, Iyabo wanted to take us to a small community pottery-making collective that we passed on our repeated trips out to the new land. The team was exhausted, but I didn't want to deny her intense burden and identification with women's struggles for security as it extended to this small village. As we pulled off the main road, we could see perhaps as many as a dozen little stations in the baking heat of the sun where each woman was selling some of her wares—pots, bowls, and vases—the very personal work of her own life and hands. Off to the side of that open clearing was a long path that appeared to lead to their mud and thatch homes.

Iyabo knows these women, so there was a little more interaction with them than an average passer-by tourist looking to buy and sell. As she explained that this was the main source of income for their village, she took us all to that side path and around behind the sales displays where we could watch the process of a woman making a tall jug in a clearing under some trees. No spinning pottery wheel here. It was a simple stand-like table, on which the piece being created sat. It was the woman herself who did the spinning! With skill and precision, her hands moved quickly up and down and around the inside and outside as she kept moving in a fast concentric circle around the stand. It was impressive and looked quite taxing. We were easily drawn into the concerns of this group of women—another sisterhood that had formed for survival and support. Not wanting to create a sense of competition among them, I encouraged the team to go to all the stations and be sure and buy something from every woman.

And what of the work of God in the hearts of those young men on our team? I have mentored many young men who have interned with EMI. Since that trip and for many years now, I will ask each one this question, often in our first lunch or coffee meeting: where have you—a young, well educated, affluent, usually white (but that is changing!), male—ever learned or lived weakness, humility, vulnerability, or fear? I watched those young men over the course of our time there develop the most tender hearts toward those girls we were there to serve. The girls' injuries—and surgeries—involved all sorts of private and awkward things, unmentionable in polite conversation among young men. But I saw a sweet, tender side in these guys I doubt they had ever shown to one another under normal circumstances. Their regular routines of teasing, joking, and otherwise uniquely "spurring one another on toward love and good deeds" gave way to sharing the emotional and spiritual impact in their lives that the ministry and the young women were making. I often shed tears (that's not hard for me, I cry at a good Hallmark commercial), and some of them did too. They are married with families of their own now, but I dare say, their wives and kids have that EMI ministry experience—and God for providing it—to thank for something new that grew in the hearts of these young men toward anyone who is vulnerable or weak or dependent. "To the weak I became weak,...so that by all possible means I might save some" (I Cor 9:22).

I can remember as a young newly married couple right out of college, my wife and I saw *The Killing Fields* in a movie theatre. I could hardly bear it. Long before I would ever have dreamed I'd set foot in West Africa among human bones in the fields, this was my first truly visceral experience of brutal, horrifying, murderous death. Thirty-five years later, that story of a journalist trapped in Cambodia during the bloody "Year Zero" cleansing campaign by the Marxist Dictator Pol Pot all came flooding back to me as I "toured" the former school—now a genocide museum and memorial in the capital of Phnom Penh—and walked from caged classroom to caged classroom that were left as they had been when taken over by the Khmer Rouge and used as interrogation and torture chambers. Two million people lost their lives. It was 1975 and I was just a kid. I knew nothing of the gruesome story unfolding on the other side of the world. But this day I was now standing in an actual "killing field" on the edge of the city not far from the museum where a 30-foot high concrete and glass memorial has been built containing thousands of skulls and other bones, all recovered from this one field, exhumed from hand-dug mass graves. Skulls were smashed in by hammers because bullets were expensive. In a social engineering effort to level the field for all its people, the genocide was carried out on the upper and educated classes. Citizens were forced out of the cities and into the fields, forced to construct a communist society around agrarian subsistence.

Today, Cambodia is rebuilding with the hope of a new generation. It is quite literally a nation redeemed from the pit. Setan Lee was our earliest Cambodian EMI partner as we came to invest in his vision to rescue women from sex trafficking. As a teenager escaping the Khmer Rouge, Setan met an evangelist in the fields who shared the Gospel with him and led him to Christ. He testifies that God gave him the gift of tongues of English which he never studied or learned. He escaped and met his future wife in the process. They emigrated to the United States, but have since established this rescue work in which they have invested their lives. As EMI entered the story, they were rescuing women by buying them in the open trade, the women never knowing at the time their lives were being redeemed with a price. But then they were brought home to the beautiful new Women's Development Center, designed by EMI. Here they would hear about the one who redeemed their lives and souls from the pit, and receive love and hope, education and healthcare that they might have life, and have it to the full!

In Thailand, Cambodia's neighbor, around the dimming embers of an evening campfire, she began to tell us her story. I love Americans, she said. I'm so thankful for them. I confess, my first thought was, what in the world for? We were captivated by Tutu, the wife of the couple we were there to serve. Two generations ago, American missionaries made the difficult trek high into the mountains. Most of her village is Christian today. She knows what a debt she owes to those who so long ago paid the price, that she might know Christ and be released from the endless search for peace through Buddhism and mysticism in the high tribal villages of Thailand.

Growing up in an impoverished Karen (pronounced /Kah dhin/) village, she prayed for God's intervening hand in her life. She received a scholarship from Compassion International to go to school, married Luke (an itinerant evangelist to the hill tribe villages his whole life), learned English, and went to Bible school. For years she's had a passion in her heart for the orphaned hill tribe girls who are so often forced into prostitution in a country that might count the sex trade as part of their GNP and yet discounts the resultant devastation to human lives. Today they have an orphanage with 20 girls, from 4 to 16 years old. They'll be able to house and disciple many more as they grow. Our team, among other things, created a new master plan for this site where this orphanage building has been constructed in order to accommodate future growth.

The campfire we were sitting around only an hour before had these same 20 girls singing and dancing for us as we all listened to praise choruses in different languages. I've said this before in different settings, but it was just about the most powerful picture of redemption we could ask for—in the flesh, lived out before us in these young girls' lives. A life redeemed. I had to ask myself this question: "Do I live a life worthy of such love and thankfulness, expressed by this tiny woman toward an entire country and people that she doesn't know?"

Luke, her husband, has spent his life trekking into hill tribe villages to share the gospel with strangers. Over a lifetime he has won thousands to Christ. A few days of getting to know Luke, and I learned first-hand the company he's been keeping for 30 years for the sake of Christ, "becoming all things to all men so that by all possible means he might save some." Our team was there to develop a village church design that could be reproduced cheaply and easily over and over in the mountain villages. Luke took us to numerous villages so that we could see village life first-hand and meet some of the people and get to know his world. In the words of my intern, Todd Murphy:

> Watching Luke as he walked and talked in these villages was a highlight of the trip. His ability to speak to the people in their own language (Luke speaks English, Thai, Lahu, Lisu, and at least two other languages, maybe more), his easy-going nature, and his obvious love for these people were all evidence of a man of God uniquely qualified for his calling.

Luke knew where he fit in God's plan to reach the world.

On one of our trips, we visited a village to scout out a potential church site. As we were walking around the village, we encountered the man I mentioned in Chapter 9 - a small, noticeably drunk man who walked up to one of the EMI team members and placed his arm around him (that would be Zac, my 16-year-old son!) like they had known each other for years. And Zac, being Zac, just put his arm naturally around this little man. We all laughed and didn't think much of it (even after he did this to three or four more people). Apparently he wanted to have us over for tea...we all laughed again and figured that by the time we left he wouldn't remember us. But as we were walking toward our truck the man walked up to us again and asked us to tea.

Luke invited our team of ten into this man's bamboo hut for tea. As it turned out, this man was the village's witch doctor and second only to the headman in authority within the village. (Earlier when we arrived, we stopped in at the "head man's" hut-like home, as is the expected and required protocol. Luke chatted with his wife, who was sick, and we prayed for her).

We then made our way to the witch doctor's small house. With the billows of smoke rising and swirling around the low ceiling from the freshly restarted fire and the temperature rising from the dozen people gathered, we sat anxiously waiting for our tea to cool.

But Luke was talking and laughing with our drunk friend in the tribal dialect, Lahu (one of the seven languages he speaks).

He told me later that this is one of the ways he evangelizes in villages. In this village he had already made friends with the headman (a liter of Coke never hurts when making friends—we brought several with us as gifts) and now needed to make friends with the witch doctor. He does this so that they don't feel threatened by him or the Gospel he brings. If he is friendly with the headman and witch doctor everyone else will respect him, and he can then share the Gospel throughout the village.

Luke has been working like this in villages for over 25 years. In the past he would walk two or three days to villages, but now he drives his truck nearly every week over bumpy dirt roads to a hill tribe village in order to share the Gospel or check on those who have become Christians—a modern day apostle Paul. When he arrives, he sits, he laughs, he drinks lots of tea, and he shares the life-transforming news of Christ in a way that his culture understands.

This is why we do what we do at EMI: we know where we fit in God's plan to reach the world in this context. I would never be granted access to these tribal people's lives—not without years of work earning their trust—but Luke has. Identification with this people and culture is his door for bringing the Gospel. I can barely get a glimpse of his culture, and his culture certainly doesn't understand me. But even as an outsider, I *can* serve Luke and this incredible vision that God has given him. This was powerfully demonstrated time and time again while we were there.

Luke asked me to preach for a Sunday morning service at his local church there in Chiang Mai. It was interpreted first in Lisu and then reinterpreted in Thai. By the time I'd finished a sentence, I nearly lost my train of thought! I wondered if I got anything across as I shared from the Scriptures of identification, restoration, intermediation, and redemption. What I know they will remember is a little skit that I've used several times and involved all our team members in different ways to represent serving others as the Body of Christ. No words are really necessary, so it works great in cross-cultural settings!

The team experienced a final demonstration of the desperate need for redemption as we visited different villages to scout out potential church sites. One of these villages was the Karen Longneck village. We detoured to see a particular section of the Karen tribe that sees having a long neck as a sign of beauty, so when the girls are young they begin to wrap wire coils around their necks. Over the years, more coils are added, and their necks get longer (actually the collar bones and muscles around the neck are compressed, but it looks like the neck is lengthened). This village has become an international tourist attraction because of this unique practice. Consequently, the villagers have become prisoners in their own homes. They are no longer allowed to leave freely for fear that they might not return, and the tourist dollars generated by their presence will dry up. The government has likewise condemned any attempts to reach out to them.

Leaving this village, I, along with everyone on the EMI team, had a feeling that could be most closely described as anger and sorrow and regret. No one could quite explain it right away, but as the day wore on we began to piece together what it was that we were all feeling. It is that feeling you get when you know something is extremely wrong and that at some deep level human dignity is being challenged and destroyed. It was one of those experiences that everyone should have, but no one should be allowed to leave without realizing the gravity of the situation. I think one of the things that was more frustrating than the exploitation by the villagers who ran this business was the exploitation by the tourists. I saw more than one tourist ask a villager to perform some act so that they could get just the right picture. Something inside of me wanted to scream "Do you know what you are doing?" but that was quickly tempered by the realization that I, too, had paid to see the "show." Today, when I remember that village visit, I'm reminded of the sadness that I felt. What hope is there for redeeming a people so exploited? And how do we—in the name of multiculturalism and diversity—propagate such a horror of human existence? Pray with me, interceding on behalf of people everywhere, that God's redeeming love would transform hearts and lives through Luke and Tutu's intermediation. By the way, did you notice their names—Luke and Tutu? Unusual names for Thai wouldn't you say? Their names are actually Boonroat and Wilaiponrn Preamjaisanchat, but they mercifully go by Luke and Tutu Bee for those of us who don't even know where to begin with a name like Preamjaisanchat.

PART III

YOUR HEART

CHAPTER 12

INFERENCE

"...but I found no one."

"I looked for someone among them who would build up the wall and stand before me in the gap on behalf of the land so I would not have to destroy it, **but I found no one**.*"*
Ezekiel 22:30

So we come to the end of the verse and fittingly the end of this book. God quite abruptly ends the string of Gospel-induced thoughts in this power-packed, single-sentence, prophetic verse that is full of purpose and hopefulness with a sharp conclusion—an inference—which is a deduction based on analysis and reasoning. Shockingly, but apparently based on factual evidence, there is no one willing to step up in faith to be God's partner in all this inspiring, hopeful work and call to restore and redeem Israel—"but I found no one."

How can this be?

We've seen how God has done all of it himself—all the work outlined in Ezekiel 22:30—revealing his heart, nature, and character along the way through the story line of Scripture. We've seen him leading the way, demonstrating how and why He has done it all, leaving us a clear and present example for his people to follow. And we've even received him to ourselves as He chose his people from "among the least of these."

There must've been someone prepared for it. There must've been someone ready and capable. There must've been someone chosen. All of that is God's part in the dance, extending the invitation—as He *always* does. That's who He is and what He does—He prepares, equips, and positions us with *initiation, relationship, and identification.* Then He extends his hand to us to come join him in the dance to *restore, intercede, reconcile, intermediate, and redeem.* What was missing was someone faithful to respond.

Again, how could this be?

Throughout the book, I have shared a conviction based on evidence that, for me, has only grown firmer over the years: that all around the world we still see God moving in all these ways, and He is still leading us with open hands to this divinely designed and orchestrated dance. He has chosen us and called us and, like a teacher instructing young ignorant pupils, graciously and patiently demonstrates how and why it must be this way. But I have also grown more convinced that although God has invited all of us to the dance, far too few have responded.

So, for the last time, how could this be?

By choosing to use the word inference, I mean to ask you quite boldly, what is the implication, extrapolation, or interpretation for you today? How do you fit in God's plan to reach the world? How do we bring this study into all that God has for us to do to its climactic end in your life? And now that we have seen *God's* heart so clearly, where is *your* heart in the matter?

Before we continue with the application for ourselves, let's once again review. Ezekiel 22 summarizes the faithlessness of the nation. After He looks for someone who would be faithful to stand with him for the nation's sake in verse 30 but finds no one, God speaks through Ezekiel the resulting punishment that Israel's faithlessness and disobedience have earned: *"So I will pour out my wrath on them and consume them with my fiery anger, bringing down on their own heads all they have done,* declares the Sovereign Lord" (Ez 22:31, emphasis mine). How could it be—despite warnings and invitations and pleadings that God repeatedly spoke through the prophets—that there was no one who would, in righteousness, intercede on behalf of the city to see restoration come through God's mercy? Certainly, it was apparent that if God had found that *one* who would be willing to "stand in the gap," the outcome might have looked very different.

That's where I believe we find ourselves today. We stand at the edge of a chasm-like gap between the direction the world is heading, and the kingdom of God being established in the earth to restore and reconcile and redeem the hearts of men and women the world over. To accomplish the task of standing in the gap today, it will take an army of "laborers" sent into the harvest fields—around the world or around the block. And the Church is just that army! God has his people in strategic places—called the local Church—ready to mobilize in literally thousands of different ways. Glenn Packiam closes *Lucky* with these challenging questions that would mobilize God's people this way. "What can God do with people who recognize the blessing that has come to them and understand the calling to carry it to the world? What if we believed that the kingdom of God has come *to* us so that it can come *through* us?"[1]

So, what's stopping us?

We can infer, perhaps, the most commonly held beliefs holding us back from stepping up and standing in the gap are that it is just too big, too difficult to do, or too hard to define—and leaving it big and undefined makes it easier for us to turn a blind eye. The subtle cousin of this line of reasoning is the thought that keeps creeping into our minds (and I wonder just where that could come from?): "What difference can I really make?"

Embracing the cries of the world may indeed seem insurmountable, but for my part, as I get up every morning with Isaiah 61 or Luke 4 on my lips, I am not dissuaded.

> The Spirit of the Sovereign Lord is on me,
>   because the Lord has anointed me
>   to proclaim good news to the poor.
> He has sent me to bind up the brokenhearted,
>   to proclaim freedom for the captives
>   and release from darkness for the prisoners,
> to proclaim the year of the Lord's favor
>   and the day of vengeance of our God,
> to comfort all who mourn,

and provide for those who grieve.... (Is 61:1-3)

Sure, the task is bigger than me, but that's why I've joined my voice to the other authors who have gone before me in asking you to ask God the question, "How do I fit in Your plan to reach the world?" and act on what He says to you!

To encourage us and help us step into each of the unique gaps that God has called us to fill, I love this parable and have heard it told in slightly different ways more than a few times. It is about just one boy—and a million starfish.

> I walked along the beach early one morning after a violent storm had hit the coast the night before. Horrified, I saw that many thousands of starfish had been washed up on the beach by the winds and the waves. I realized that all of them would die, stranded on the shore, cut off from the life-giving ocean. I stood frozen in my sadness and despair, paralyzed by the fact that there was nothing I could do.
>
> But then there in the distance, I saw a boy running among them, repeatedly bending down and then standing up. Curious, I walked toward him. I saw that he was picking up starfish, one at a time, and throwing them back into the sea.
>
> "What are you doing?" I yelled.
>
> "Saving the starfish," he replied.
>
> "But don't you see, boy, there are tens of thousands of them?" I asked, incredulous. "Nothing you can do will make a difference. You can't possibly save them all."
>
> The boy just kept at his task, undaunted, saying, "That may be true, but *this* one won't die, and *this* one won't die, and *this* one..."

By the character and nature of a child, we find a simple trusting faith that is akin to the faith we must have in God if we are to enter into his Kingdom. I get so much inspiration from this story because it is impossible to lose sight of each individual when you are up close and personal to them, just as the boy saw each individual starfish he was saving. That's exactly what happened in my life after my first short-term trip so many years ago. What have you seen in the stories I retold here, chapter by chapter?

> Did you see just a beach littered with bodies, or did you see each unique starfish—a part of God's creation—lying there, with a better life just waiting to be lived? The truth in this familiar story is important: we must never see poverty or justice as "issues: that need solutions; rather we must see the human beings at the heart of those issues as people who need and deserve our love and respect. I believe we really can alter the world, but we can only do it one person at a time. And when enough people choose to do this, even a crisis on a global scale can change.[2]

What we're talking about here can only be described as a movement. My Bible study and stories reveal the masterplan (the Master's plan) that God has for the world, with a timeline for ultimate restoration tied to all the nations of the earth receiving the Gospel of the kingdom (Mt 24:14).

> "Sometimes, I would like to ask God why He allows poverty, suffering, and injustice when He could do something about it."
>
> "Well, why don't you ask him?"
>
> "Because I'm afraid He would ask me the same question."
>
> Anonymous[1]

So how do we hope to see enough people choosing to embrace the task? Charlie Marquis puts his finger on it in his book *Mudrunner*.

> I believe Paul shares the secret as he writes to Timothy: "...the things you have heard me say in the presence of many witnesses entrust to reliable people who will also be qualified to teach others" (2 Tim 2:2). Did you catch it?

Not one, or two, or three, but four spiritual generations are included in this verse! From Paul to Timothy to "reliable people" to "others." Kingdom movement—not by addition but by multiplication! Paul provides the framework for sparking a movement through spiritual multiplication.[3]

In this way, the seemingly impossible task that looks and feels too big, suddenly seems possible.

But from the absence of anyone to respond to God's invitation we might infer another obstacle in our way to a multiplying movement—our own unbelief. Again, I shared with you my own lack of faith at the start of this cataclysmic change that came into my life. That's my confession. God knew that and did not disqualify me. You've heard the saying, "God does not call the equipped, He equips the called?" Well, that surely was me. There was nothing about my city-boy life from Western New York that prepared me for an overnight jungle riverboat ride down the Amazon amidst alligators and piranha, believe me!

But his plan to equip me came in a crucible. The faith that I have today was forged in the fire of a shattered leg, where my earliest faith lesson became immediately obvious. After several weeks in the prone position of an injured man, I could see I was going to go into debt to the tune of about $2000 a month for each month that I was not working my consulting business. You see, we were the classic "house-poor" young American family. I had invested in two properties so far and was pouring every penny I could earn into them and financing even more as I went (back then, you could get 12-24 month no-interest credit cards and I was moving balances annually to never pay interest!)

Six months later, rehabbing a permanently weakened leg, I was down $12,000. I ranted to God. This doesn't exactly help things. I was counting on a nest-egg from the sale of one of the houses to help my family rebuild as we moved across the country and cut our lifestyle in half. But now that nest egg was going to be reduced by this debt. What was God's answer? Shortly after that, I learned that the tanking housing market in the Buffalo area was going to strip me of any nest egg at all! I would barely get out of my little depression-era house what I had put into it, to say nothing of the thousands of hours of my time in eight years renovating it. That can't be right, can it, Lord?

In my quiet time with the Lord, and writing in *My Life of Faith* journal, I distinctly heard from God in my spirit, "Gary, I'm going to get you out of Buffalo by the skin of your teeth so that you will finally learn to trust Me." Really? God uses idioms like that? I'm quite sure that's *not* what I wanted to hear, so I'm also quite sure that it was the Spirit of God speaking to me!

I continued to faithfully do all that was required of me to make it all happen, trusting that God would take care of me and my family, even when it looked bleak during those months. In spite of a very weak leg (I was still on crutches when the cast came off because of how weak it was), I got back to work at the University, began some new consulting projects, and was back up on ladders and roofs finishing construction projects on the house. We raised the support we needed and put the house on the market. In the last couple of months before moving, I got an incredible consulting contract I never saw coming. Head Start—the government-funded early childhood educational program—hired me to survey their sites throughout the city to assess and design solutions for ADA (Americans with Disabilities Act) violations. I had done a lot of this kind of work at the University, so I knew exactly what it would require and gave them a per-site price for the work. You guessed it. Twelve sites at $1000 per site—replacing the $12,000 we'd lost while I couldn't work.

Months later, we had moved to Colorado and began serving with EMI. I had to finish the last of several assessments remotely, and mail them back with invoices. Before the end of that year, we were starting over debt-free for the first time in our married lives, living on half of what I had earned the year before, and incredibly blessed. In God's divine plan, He called me out and taught me how to live differently—it's the heart of the saying, "Live simply, so that others may simply live." We have cautioned our new staff that it's very hard to live as a missionary with debt (aside from a home mortgage), and in all these years, I never have again.

I have continued to learn faith by the things God has called me to do that are bigger than me, always trusting that his ways are higher, his thoughts wiser, his power stronger, his love purer than mine. To remind myself to lay it all down, I have often confessed that God is God, and I am not. As obvious and prosaic as that sounds, there's a real release that comes from that self-evident confession—I am *not* responsible for solving every problem or meeting every need. I *am* responsible to follow closely after God, to walk with him, to rely on him, to love him, and to obey him. Now *that* I can do, as God gives me the faith, courage, and strength.

Psalm 139 is proof of this. Take a moment and refresh your memory. For 18 verses, David extols the power and majesty of God, his glorious omniscience and omnipresence, and his divine *initiating* creative role in each of our lives as we are formed and live. Sounds like he's ready to get on board with whatever God is doing, right? Then, suddenly, for four verses, he lapses into the mode we all do when we take our eyes off God and try to justify ourselves or make our own way in the dark. I might understand this coming from the average Israelite who hardly knew God but through priests and prophets, but David? The man after God's own heart? To be fair, he is simply speaking out the same thoughts as all of Job's friends as they were firmly entrenched in the retribution principle very commonly found in the culture of the day: If we obey God we should be rewarded; disobey and we will suffer punishment. Finally, David comes back to the famous prayer that I have prayed many times when I find myself in the same position—"Search me, God, and know my heart; test me and know my anxious thoughts. See if there is any offensive way in me, and lead me in the way everlasting" (Ps 139:23, 24).

I have led countless teams in a group devotional focused on this psalm at the start of EMI short-term trips. After thorough discussion and thoughtful application, when it appears we are ready to bring it to a close, I will ask this question: "Why do you suppose it's so important to me—and EMI—that we study this psalm at the start of our mission and service?" Sometimes they come pretty close to what I'm looking for, but I am still waiting for the day that someone will put down their Bible, stand up on their chair, and declare, "If my God is this big, there is NOTHING I cannot do!" But a declaration of such faith and power is not possible until we've come to the end of ourselves and begin to live in faith at a level that is simply not the norm in Western life. Living the "American Dream" didn't give me much opportunity to exercise faith. How about you? Where have you trained your heart in faith? I have found myself in places where my faith has grown disproportionately and exponentially because I had no other recourse if God *didn't* show up and do what only He can do!

I've had to do some things, go some places, and say some things that were pretty scary. In my past life, I could never have imagined I could. In this present life, "I can do all this through him who gives me strength" (Phil 4:13). And what's more,

> ...whatever were gains to me I now consider loss for the sake of Christ. What is more, I consider everything a loss because of the surpassing worth of knowing Christ Jesus my Lord, for whose sake I have lost all things. I consider them garbage, that I may gain Christ and be found in him, not having a righteousness of my own that comes from the law, but that which is through faith in Christ—the righteousness that comes from God on the basis of faith. I want to know Christ—yes, to know the power of his resurrection and participation in his sufferings, becoming like him in his death, and so, somehow, attaining to the resurrection from the dead." (Phil 3:7-11)

This is the central message of our faith in Christ. In following him, we lose ourselves. We abandon our own agendas, and we take on his mission for our lives and for the world. We die to ourselves in order that we may serve the world and *follow in his steps.*

Do nothing out of selfish ambition or vain conceit. Rather, in humility value others above yourselves, not looking to your own interests but each of you to the interests of the others.

In your relationships with one another, have the same mindset as Christ Jesus:

> Who, being in very nature God,
>   did not consider equality with God something to
>   be used to his own advantage;
> rather, He made himself nothing
>   by taking the very nature of a servant,
>   being made in human likeness.
> And being found in appearance as a man,
>   He humbled himself by becoming obedient to
>   death—
>   even death on a cross! (Phil 2:3-11)

Even as I profess this whole section of Paul's letter to the church at Philippi as my personal testimony, I am still driven every day by the overwhelming burden that something is wrong in the world, and I am at the heart of it, complicit with it, and swept away by its current. I would never deny the upswing in social concern in evangelicals in the last few decades. There's perhaps no better illustration of the trend for social justice than the exploding short-term missions movement, much of which has focused on ministering to the poor both at home and abroad.

But materialism, self-centeredness, and complacency continue to plague us all. It took me seven years and five moves to rebuild my life for my family. In my mid-30's, we were starting over at zero: no debt, but no assets, either. We bought and sold, gutted and remodeled, moving from house to house until we had enough room for our homeschooling family of 5. Today, we have a house in Colorado Springs, two cars in the driveway, and my wife and I have even begun to talk about a retirement plan—albeit not until into my 70's. I'm still convicted when I read Francis Chan's words in *Crazy Love: Overwhelmed by a Relentless God*:

> Lukewarm people feel secure because they attend church, made a profession of faith at age twelve, were baptized, come from a Christian family, or live in America. Jesus said, "Not everyone who calls me, 'Lord, Lord,' will enter the kingdom of heaven, but only He who does the will of my father who is in heaven." (Mt 7:21)
>
> Lukewarm people *do not live by faith*; their lives are structured so they never have to. They don't have to trust God if something happens—they have their savings account. They don't need God to help them—they have their retirement plan in place. They don't genuinely seek out what life God would have them live—they live life figured and mapped out. They don't depend on God on a daily basis—their refrigerators are full, and for the most part, they are in good health. The truth is, their lives wouldn't look much different if they suddenly stopped believing in God.[4]

One more inference I must make—God found no one to stand in the gap because we are ignorant. There. I said it. Sounds harsh, but it's the plain truth. We are unaware, and happy to remain so. We do not get up every morning with the awareness that the world is terribly broken, and we have the Spirit of the Sovereign Lord upon us to proclaim good news to the poor. Like the example in 1994 of our entire country being mesmerized by OJ Simpson while ignoring the Rwandan genocide, we are captivated by so many superficial or unimportant things that distract us from the eternally significant things. And people's lives—and souls—hang in the balance, just as the people of God and the city of Jerusalem hung in the balance when God went looking.

There are crises here at home that we don't know how to deal with, from immigration and the hordes of desperate people amassing at our southern border, to homeless camps growing in most American cities daily, to gun violence in nearly every public square of life. But most of us remain on the sidelines, content with lawmakers battling it out from their right and left perspectives, never coming to real solutions, but effectively absolving us of any responsibility to get involved. And people's lives are the cost. Perhaps there were some who were hearing God's invitation through Ezekiel to stand in the gap on behalf of the land, but in ignorance or misplaced confidence, they took a sidelined seat and expected the city elders to respond!

After spending nearly three decades within the community of evangelical relief and development workers, I can see clearly we do *not* have it all figured out, we haven't even scratched the surface of knowing what we do not know (our own ignorance), and when Western Christians *do* attempt to alleviate poverty in the name of Christ and preaching the good news of the kingdom, the methods used often do considerable harm to both those we are trying to serve and ourselves. Our methods have often wasted human, spiritual, and financial resources and can actually exacerbate the very problems we are trying to solve!

Until we recognize our own ignorance, we will never live in the anointing of the call we all share with Christ—namely to preach good news to the poor, to bind up the broken hearted, to proclaim freedom for the prisoners and recovery of sight for the blind, and to set the oppressed free! Steve Corbett and Brian Fikkert write, in *When Helping Hurts; How to Alleviate Poverty without Hurting the Poor...and Yourself*, "Until we embrace our mutual brokenness, our work with low-income people is likely to do more harm than good. I sometimes unintentionally reduce poor people to objects that I use to fulfill my own need to accomplish something."[5]

I had already been a mission worker for well over a decade when they wrote their book and I read that for the first time. But it resonated so strongly because that seemed to be a decade for us at EMI where we confronted our ignorance head on, and these two men might have been taking a page out of our own journals! EMI has since made their book one of the fundamental resources we recommend to our staff, volunteers, and partners. When we acknowledge our own brokenness—that we need Jesus as much as anyone we're hoping to serve or introduce to him—we can then receive the same reconciliation and restoration within ourselves that we long for the whole world to know. We admit—as we often did at EMI in that decade—"We don't know what we don't know," but we know the One Who Knows! And at that point, we are ready to receive new *revelation.*

CHAPTER 13

REVELATION
Will you be found?

"I looked for someone among them who would build up the wall and stand before me in the gap on behalf of the land so I would not have to destroy it, but I found no one."
Ezekiel 22:30

How do you fit in God's plan to reach the world? Can you see where you fit? To answer the question, we will end where we began. In *The Purpose Driven Life*, Rick Warren writes these thoughts, and they seem particularly appropriate as we face the challenge today: Will you be found? Will you be that one? Will you be one to stand in the gap? Will you be one to stand with those who are putting themselves in gaps all around the world?

> Dr. Hugh Moorehead, a philosophy professor at Northeastern Illinois University, once wrote 250 of the best-known philosophers, scientists, writers, and intellectuals in the world, asking them, "What is the meaning of life?" He then published their responses in a book. Some offered their best guesses, some admitted they just made up a purpose for life, and others were honest enough to say they were clueless. In fact, a number of famous intellectuals asked Professor Moorhead to write back and tell them if he discovered the meaning of life!
>
> Fortunately, there is an alternative to speculation about the meaning of life. It's *revelation*. We can turn to what God has revealed about life in his word. The easiest way to

discover the purpose of an invention is to ask the creator of it. The same is true for discovering your life's purpose. Ask God.

God has not left us in the dark to wonder and guess. He has clearly revealed his purposes for our lives through the Bible. It is our Owner's Manual, explaining why we are alive, how life works, what to avoid, and what to expect in the future. It explains what no self-help or philosophy book could know. The Bible says, *"God's wisdom... goes deep into the interior of his purposes... It's not the latest message, but more like the oldest—what God determined as the way to bring out his best in us."*

God is not just the starting point of your life; He is the *source* of it. To discover your purpose in life you must turn to God's word, not the world's wisdom. You must build your life on eternal truths, not pop psychology, success-motivation, or inspirational stories. The Bible says, *"It's in Christ that we find out who we are and what we are living for. Long before we first heard of Christ and got our hopes up, He had his eye on us, had designs on us for glorious living, part of the overall purpose He is working out in everything and everyone."*[1]

I have witnessed this kind of revelation coming to the hearts of men and women that I have led overseas to serve with our EMI teams time and time again. As we witness the groaning and the struggle of people up close and personally, our hearts are gripped by the injustice, the poverty, the oppression. Drawn into their pain, we daily debrief as we study God's word in group devotionals and worship together with the local church. We come away changed forever, but perhaps no one more so than Ryan Nice, the brilliant young electrical engineer to whom I introduced you in Chapter 6. Here, in my closing thoughts with you, I want to leave you with the most powerful *revelation* I have ever had the privilege of witnessing in a young man's life.

As you enter into it with me, I know you will see something new and I pray (again!), as the apostle Paul did for the church in Ephesus,

> ...that the God of our Lord Jesus Christ, the glorious Father, may *give you the Spirit of wisdom and revelation*, so that you may know him better. I pray that *the eyes of your heart may be enlightened* in order that you may know the *hope to which He has called you*, the *riches of his glorious inheritance* in his holy people, and his *incomparably great power* for us who believe.... (Eph 1:17-19, emphasis mine)

When our team returned from Sierra Leone, I wrote the brief note for that next month that would accompany all thank you letters to EMI's donors and partners:

> I have just returned from the west coast of Africa again, the third time in nine months. One of my team members (Ryan) wrote an impassioned letter to his friends saying, *"There is not enough time to mince words. Everything looks different now. I feel different about everything. I am failing to come up with any way to explain what I saw and what God showed me and why it is important."*
> I know well the undercurrent of emotions he's feeling; pity and hope, compassion and anger; peace and rage. I am convinced the only reason I live is to bring you this report: that the world is convulsing in need, and we must be the ones to meet that need, in his name. This time we were serving a ministry rescuing orphans in true James 1:27 fashion—orphans who carry the scars of losing their parents in the horrific civil war in Sierra Leone. Thank you for your gift and your partnership that allows us to bring the message of peace to this generation.

Ryan, a 20-something electrical engineer from Pennsylvania, joined me and my team for the first time. I have tried faithfully over more than two and a half decades to paint the pictures of sights and smells and laughter and tears—to strip away the protective layers that insulate my heart in order to bare before my partners and readers the raw emotions that surface when you put yourself in the very center of people in desperate need, but I don't know if I've ever communicated so profoundly yet so succinctly the depths that this man has. Think about it... *Everything looks different now. I feel different about everything. I am failing to come up with any way to explain what I saw and what God showed me and why it is important."*

Why does everything look different now? Why can't he make sense of it? He goes on...

> East and south of what we call home are people. Many, many, many people. Pressed together, living under the weight of crippling poverty, etching out an existence from dirt, and trash, under rusting tin roofs and amongst burned out cars and streams of water reeking with sewage. You drive in a white beat-up van, hired for three dollars US for the whole day, no windows, just holes cut in the sheet metal, and look out into the vast ocean of faces, with those deep, dark, African eyes, that seem to my western mind to hold such peace and such rage and tragedy at the same time. There are the faithless eyes that stare back at you lifelessly and hungry, and you know that inside they have died long ago. There are the faithful, and they laugh, and hope, and pray, and speak of God's love, God's compassion, even in the face of such opposition—they have drawn gloriously close to God in a storm of adversity, and God has strengthened them in mighty and miraculous ways.
>
> Then there is the point of the whole trip. The point of this whole thing. The children. The sweet, innocent children, who are now fed and clothed and loved by their caretakers. Some still remember losing their parents, or

being abandoned, or worse, some bear physical wounds and disabilities that will not leave them while they are on earth without a miracle. All of them have huddled together in a small haven of peace, and treat each other like brother and sister, from the strongest to the weakest. They never leave, for outside is a deathly struggle against an impossible environment where few will last beyond 40 years, and no escape is possible.

He knows something's wrong—very, very wrong, but can't make sense of it. Again, Fikkert and Colbert speak to this:

> North American Christians are simply not doing enough. We are the richest people ever to walk the face of the earth. Period. Yet, most of us live as though there is nothing terribly wrong in the world. We attend our kid's soccer games, pursue our careers, take beach vacations, remodel our homes, save and invest for college and retirement, and tweet, and Facebook, and Instagram our way into a self-indulgent happiness—while 40 percent of the world's inhabitants struggle just to eat every day. And in our own backyards, the homeless, those residing in ghettos, and a wave of immigrants live in a world outside the economic and social mainstream of North America. We do not necessarily need to feel guilty about our wealth. But we do need to get up every morning with a deep sense that something is terribly wrong with the world and yearn and strive to do something about it. There is simply not enough yearning and striving going on.[2]

Let's return to our friend Ryan:

And now I'm back. It takes 40 hours of traveling on a helicopter, buses, trains, and seemingly countless jets to get back to my life as I know it. I drive my Honda to work, where people ask how the trip went, and then complain about their pay, or taxes or the state of their lives, all in the same statement. And the thought is over, never to resurface in their consciousness. They walk away and I swear I come this close to screaming out loud at the top of my lungs because I know something is wrong, but I cannot describe it or make it stop.

...This [what we saw in Africa] is the world. This is how most people live. I am the one in the dream. I am the one in the artificial routine of consuming and selfishness and a tunnel vision that is ever being pressed in. The fight will not always be as noble as defending children in a foreign land. Now is where it counts. Right now, right here I have to step outside of what only relates to me. I have to move out from under what the world expects of me as it says, "This is your life. This is all you'll ever be. And this is all that will ever matter to you." I have to bring everything under the light of God's truth, to lay everything down in submission—knowing full well that I cannot do one thing on my own. My strength must come from Him. This time we have, this is all we have to offer, and with horror I look around today and right now it seems like everyone, including myself, the church, the Body of Christ on earth, has fallen into a slumber of betrayal.

We are indeed the ones living a dream, while most of the rest of the world only knows a nightmare. That is our "slumber of betrayal." When will it end? Where does it stop? And how? It stopped in Sierra Leone when a young American student in a business degree program came face to face with the needs of orphaned children in West Africa and couldn't look away. He founded an orphanage and partnered with two African men—Henry Abu and his brother Joseph (who rescued children from the rebels during the war carrying them on his back across a river). It stopped for an architect, after living 30 some years of the American Dream, when a missionary challenged me to evaluate why I must stay here...and that was it for me: "I can't stay." Some of my closet friends thought perhaps I had lost my mind. And it stopped here, when a young, upwardly mobile, career-aspiring engineer with a promising future says, "I had fallen into a slumber of betrayal. I feel different about everything now."

It stops wherever you do. Stop and ponder that. Like Oswald Chambers so powerfully wrote, "The first thing God will do with us is to force through the channels of a single heart, the interests of the whole world." Like Ryan, I have thought of and witnessed many times the "slumber of betrayal" in the Church. But where we stop, the nightmare stops. I cannot live my privileged life without the crushing realization that others depend on us to bring the message of restoration, rescue, and reconciliation to them. How we *choose* to live really does have a direct bearing on how others *must* live.

In Sierra Leone, each day brought more of this new revelation, not just to Ryan, but the whole team. We drove into the heart of a small African village on the edge of Freetown (in that horrible little cargo van, with round holes cut into the sheet metal walls and steel welded-frame benches to sit on that made us ache so badly that we dreaded each time we had to drive somewhere). The city and village are a study in developing world contrasts, each bound to the other in a grave partnership, both subjecting their inhabitants to eking out an existence below any poverty level you might know or see domestically. I'm confronted regularly by comments from Americans such as, "what about the poor of our country?" ... one EMI trip and they'd never ask again.

Now Freetown, like Nairobi or Delhi, Port-au-Prince or Kathmandu, is strangled by a mix of old and crumbling infrastructure left from colonialism or war; terrible overcrowding from people forced into the city from rural areas hoping to find work; rampant unemployment; and thousands of people sitting and staring at us or walking along roads; crowding against us everywhere. Having turned off the once-paved main road (now scarred with deeply rutted holes and ditches), we headed down a dirt road bordered by dense forest. We arrived at a small clearing between mud homes, thatch-roofed lean-tos, and shelters open to the elements. Immediately a crowd of barely clothed, barefooted children gathered. A few adults remained on the periphery at a safe enough distance away to communicate distrust, resentment, or perhaps even their own pain. Our American host—the typical tall white-man missionary—hopped out of the van, followed by the rest of us, and stood out starkly among the small African children pressing in around him, like a tree swarmed by bees on their hunt for a new home.

We were there to begin the process of identifying the newest orphans that would be brought to live at the orphan home. It can be quite lengthy, involving weeks and months of time, from the initial visit to discover the hidden orphans to the final transferring of guardianship. Interviews are conducted with the villagers and the stories are told...this one's parents died in a raid, that one's mother was raped and murdered by soldiers, the father disappeared in the middle of the night, this one watched as her parents were... The stories only get worse: tales of one of the most heinous civil wars in history, marked by young rebels who, in response to the government's slogan 'The future—it's in your hands," brutally slashed off the limbs of civilians with machetes—from babies in their cribs to the mothers rushing from the fields in desperation to save them. These orphans—like most around the world—live as outcasts among kin, with no one to be their advocate when the meager rations are doled out. They are malnourished, lice-infested, uneducated, forgotten, and neglected in the worst of ways.

There we were, in the middle of the crowd watching the future about to change for a few little children as drastically as any rags-to-riches, Cinderella fairy tale story. Could they possibly imagine the new life they are being brought into? Are their village friends envious of them? (It would be years before I met the young woman outside the shop in Kenya who shared that exact testimony). The redemptive drama being played out before us was an amazing revelation of what it must be like to God and to the on-lookers, as we who have been redeemed and reconciled to God participate in his ministry of reconciliation in the world. (2 Cor 5:18). How God must take such delight as each of us turn to him, for the first time, as He invites us into his family. The question I asked my team later that day, as we debriefed and shared our impressions, was this: What will you do with this revelation you have received? Will we live our lives in such a way that the world will see and become envious for oh so great a redemption?"

Hopefully by this point, you are convinced—if you weren't already—to press into God with the very personal question for yourself, "How do I fit in Your plan to reach the world, Lord?" God has provided fundamental and sure ways to receive revelation—His written Word, which attests to his character, nature, and will; His Spirit within us, giving understanding, peace, strength, confidence, boldness, and faith; and our brothers and sisters in Christ, who can provide prayer support, wisdom, and counsel.

Before the trip to hear Jackie Pullinger's message at Asbury Seminary—the weekend road trip that changed the course of my entire life—I thought I was checking all the right spiritual boxes: faithful reading and study of God's Word, a regular pattern of worship and prayer, and involvement in ministry. But the practice of spiritual disciplines could not replace the fire of God that came into my life with that one burning question—"Why must you stay?"

I've been vulnerable and transparent about my long list of reasons; but in the end, it felt like my life—with all its success, blessings, and ministry happening in various places—had turned into either a corpse or a ghost, to use E. Stanley Jones's personified metaphor. I never saw it happening, but neither does the frog in a slow boiling pot of water—until it's too late. That story is intended to caution us to be aware of gradual changes that lead to undesirable—perhaps disastrous—consequences. That's where my life was headed. *New revelation*—my own *kairos* moment, a burning bush, my Damascus Road epiphany—is what it took to move the bubble I had so carefully levelled out for my life.

Is it a risk? Of course it is. But nothing worth gaining comes without risk. I know I used to live according to a risk-averse kind of theology, where I never needed to put God to the test. I planned, strategized, executed, and stayed within the confines of a carefully crafted plan for my life—the American Dream version of my Christianity, a walk with God that was bounded by very defined parameters. It was also heavily financed! And though very carefully planned, it was also burdensome. I had bought one double rental property that I funneled into buying another property—the one we lived in while I was gutting and remodeling it from top to bottom, and though everything was costing just about all I could earn in both my jobs, I was thinking about the next one to add to the portfolio. It was costly to extricate myself from that whole life, but once we did, my wife and I were able to cut our monthly budget in half, raise support in about six months, move across the country, and start serving God in a whole new way—a much smaller life, but debt-free, and available to reach a hurting world in Jesus' name. Simplicity, faith, assurance—they have all become the signposts of life for us, and our walk with God.

I was once in Cairo doing a feasibility study for a new hospital with a consortium of doctors from the US and Egypt. We held a prayer meeting in an apartment very high up in a high-rise apartment building packed into and overlooking the dense urban fabric of the city, not 30 feet away from the next high-rise. During an extended time in prayer, I was pacing—as I often do in prayer — and found myself out on the balcony of this apartment and suddenly got a sense of just how high and precarious it was near the railing's edge. Instantly, I felt a clear message from the Lord, "Gary, do not fear death." I walked away from the edge thinking, "Well, now what was *that* all about?!" Am I walking into something I have no clue about, Lord? If so, then that's exactly where I want to be—walking in the dark with Jesus calling me (Is 50:10).

Few of us will be called to surrender our lives as Jim Elliot did, but all of us should be ready to settle that issue and daily take up our crosses and follow him, *in his steps*. In fact, that is the harder call, to be sure. To live as Jesus to a world in desperate need will continually challenge us for the rest of our lives. But Jesus said, "Truly I tell you…no one who has left home or brothers or sisters or mother or father or children or fields for me and the gospel will fail to receive a hundred times as much in this present age...and in the age to come eternal life" (Mk 10:29).

All of the authors I have referred to along the way have closed their books with a challenge to look for something to do with your life that would fit your gifting and passions, open you up to the things of God and his heart for the world and the poor, and draw you out of your life full of Western wealth, privilege, and self-centeredness, and provide you a plan going forward to make a change. Here is mine. We can—and really, we *must:*

- Give more money away: look for the ways to invest in what you're most burdened about or connected to (like the design professionals who support EMI).
- Sell or donate more stuff and downsize to live more simply. The implications in this are far reaching.
- Sponsor at-risk children overseas (check out The Gem Foundation, Compassion International, or World Vision).
- Begin to pray and intercede for the world—at all times, in every place and for everyone: join a prayer group or set up reminders to pray at many times of the day.
- Share your faith more boldly: read more on this topic or attend training such as a *Plan A* conference by Forge.
- Become more personally involved in missions at home and abroad. Start something in your church that's about mission, such as: promoting and attending a *Perspectives on the World Christian Movement* class (perspectives.org); serving in or starting a soup kitchen or food pantry; volunteering on a short-term mission; supporting a local charity; joining an advocacy group (again, start with your local church and its missions efforts).
- Learn more: I urge you to read all the books I've cited to learn more—more of the need, more of God's heart!

All good things. All necessary things! I know the world would be profoundly impacted if we all begin making these kinds of changes.

However, more than a list of things to do, I want to leave you with this: *If you must stay*, then know that you are *called* to it. Make the list for yourself of *why* you *must* stay. And if, when you are done you can honestly say that you are indeed a "living epistle" to the world where you are, then continue to live and grow there, where God has firmly planted you. Make your local church a beach head for God's missional work in your community and around the world —that his kingdom may come, and his will would be done, on earth as it is in heaven. That is the heart of God, and it's inclined toward "all the peoples of the earth!"

But if like me, you finish your list and are left with disappointment, disillusionment, or even self-incrimination, knowing that you are only firmly rooted because the American Dream has entangled itself around the foundations of your life, then join me in faith and take a step today. Tell God, your friends and family, "I can't stay!"—shout it from the rooftops if you need to take a stand. And then begin walking into a new future with God to see your life become an offering to the world. But be ready to walk in the darkness a bit—and at times, repeatedly! Be ready for the questions, for they will surely come. And if they're not being asked, you will ask them yourself. It took me two years—two years!—to figure out what God had for me. So don't be in a hurry, just find that new determination to *not* stay just because it's what you've always done and it's what everybody else seems to be doing. Incline your heart today towards God's heart, knowing fully how his heart for the world cannot help but become your heart—the *missionary heart*—that will not stop beating until your last breath when God welcomes you into his eternal presence.

Thirty-five years ago, our friend Marsha Matanick, missionary to Malaysia whom we were visiting at Asbury Seminary that glorious Thanksgiving weekend, taught us a simple, heart-touching chorus. I've never heard it anywhere since, but it has stayed with me all these years:

Will you be poured out like wine upon the altar for Me?
Will you be broken like bread to feed the hungry?
Will you be so one with Me that you would do just as I will?
Will you be light, and life, and love, my Word fulfilled?

As we embrace the missionary heart, *if you must stay*, the first thing God will do is to force through the channels of a single heart the interests of the whole world. We can sing our response back to God:

Yes, I'll be poured out like wine upon the altar for You.
Yes, I'll be broken like bread to feed the hungry.
Yes, I'll be so one with You that I would do just as You will.
Yes, I'll be light, and life, and love, Your Word fulfilled.[3]

It will kill you. But who wants that old life anyway?

ENDNOTES

Introduction

[1] Ron Sider, Rich Christians In an Age of Hunger (Copyright 1997, First FCS Edition, Family Christian Stores, 2001 with Word Publishing), xix.
[2] Gabe Lyons, The Next Christians (Multnomah Books, 2010), 51, 230
[3] Richard Stearns, The Hole in Our Gospel (W Publishing, an imprint of Thomas Nelson, 2009), xxi
[4] Rick Warren, The Purpose Driven Life (Zondervan, 2002), 15
[5] Dwight Robertson, You are God's Plan A (Forge, 2022), 8
[6] David Platt, Radical (Multnomah Books, 2010), 3
[7] David Platt, Radical, 16
[8] Ibid., 18
[9] Gabe Lyons, The Next Christians, 4
[10] Ron Sider, Rich Christians in an Age of Hunger, 1
[11] Ibid., xi
[12] Eugene Cho, Overrated (David C. Cook, 2014), 17
[13] Charlie Marquis, Mudrunner (Forge, 2021), xvv
[14] Glenn Packiam, Lucky (David C Cook, 2011), 56, 62
[15] Charles Sheldon, In his Steps (Whitaker House, 1979), 14
[16] David Platt, Radical, 77
[17] Ibid., 19

Chapter 1: If You Must Stay

[1] Jackie Pullinger, Asbury Seminary recorded sermon (Oct 3, 1993)
[2] Simon Sinek, How Great Leaders Inspire Action—Start With Why, Ted Talks, 2010
[3] C. S. Lewis, The Problem of Pain (MacMillan Publishing Company, 1962), 93

Chapter 2: The Principles of Positioning

[1] David Platt, Radical, 161
[2] Dwight Robertson, You are God's Plan A, 117
[3] Paul Johansson, New Covenant Tabernacle recorded sermon (Jan 1997)
[4] Bob Sorge, In his Face (Oasis house, 1994), 37
[5] C. S. Lewis, The Problem of Pain, 93
[6] Rick Warren, The Purpose Driven Life, 235-236

[7] Dwight Robertson, You are God's Plan A, 19
[8] Rick Warren, The Purpose Driven Life, 227, 281
[9] Don Richardson, Eternity in Their Hearts (Regal, A Division of Gospel Light Ventura, 1984), 31

Chapter 3: The Missionary Heart

[1] Jackie Pullinger, Asbury Seminary recorded sermon (Oct 3, 1993)
[2] Gabe Lyons, The Next Christians, 31
[3] Donald Miller, Blue Like Jazz (Thomas Nelson, 2003), 182
[4] Ibid., 21,22
[5] Oswald Chambers, "Missionary Predestinations," My Utmost for His Highest (Barbour and Company, Inc., 1935, 1963), 195
[6] Bob Sorge, In his Face, 51
[7] Ibid., 52
[8] Oswald Chambers, My Utmost for his Highest,195
[9] Ibid.,195
[10] Ibid.,195
[11] Don Richardson, Eternity in Their Hearts, 154
[12] Brother Yun, The Heavenly Man (Monarch Books, 2002), 113
[13] Oswald Chambers, My Utmost for His Highest,195

Chapter 4: Initiation: "I looked"

[1] Lawrence J. Crabb, Jr., Understanding People (Zondervan, Grand Rapids, 1987), 91-92
[2] Lawrence J. Crabb, Jr., Understanding People, 96
[3] Gabe Lyons, The Next Christians, 97
[4] Ibid., 52
[5] Jackie Pullinger, Asbury Seminary recorded sermon (Oct 3, 1993)

Chapter 5: Initiation: "I looked"

[1] Glenn Packiam, Secondhand Jesus (David C. Cook, 2009), 43
[2] Bob Sorge, Secrets of the Secret Place (Oasis House, 2001), 196
[3] Ibid.,196
[4] Ann Morton Voskamp, Waymaker (W Publishing Group, Thomas Nelson, 2022), 28 Abraham Joshua Heschel, God in Search of Man: A Philosophy of Judaism (New York: Farrat, Strauss & Giroux, 1955), 425-26
[5] C. S. Lewis, Mere Christianity (1952, repr., New York Harper One, 2001), 177, 199
[6] C. S. Lewis, Mere Christianity, 17

[7] Ann Morton Voskamp, Waymaker, 31
[8] Ibid., 33
[9] Dwight Robertson, You Are God's Plan A, 16-17
[10] Ibid., 29
[11] Ibid., 33
[12] Gabe Lyons, The Next Christians, 37
[13] J. Mack & Leeann Stiles, Mack and Leann's Guide to Short-term Mission (InterVarsity press, 2000), 135
[14] Jackie Pullinger, Asbury Seminary recorded sermon (Oct 3, 1993)

Chapter 6: Identification: "...among them..."

[1] Gabe Lyons, The Next Christians, 31
[2] Ibid., 33
[3] Steve Corbett and Brian Fikkert, When Helping Hurts (Moody Publishers, 2009) 171

Chapter 7: Restoration: "...who would build up the wall..."

[1] Stanley A. Ellisen, "Everyone's Question," Perspectives on the World Christian Movement, Fourth Edition (William Carey Library, 2009), 17
[2] David Long, A Call to Manhood in a Fatherless Society (Huntington House Publishers, 1994), 116
[3] Ibid., 121
[4] Tim Keller, The Reason for God: Belief in an Age of Skepticism (Riverhead Books, 2008), 233
[5] Gabe Lyons, The Next Christians, 50-52
[6] Ibid., 53
[7] Ibid., 55
[8] John Rucyahana, The Bishop of Rwanda (Thomas Nelson, 2007), xviii
[9] Ibid., 7
[10] Ibid., 30
[11] Gabe Lyons, The Next Christians, 60

Chapter 8: Intercession: "... and stand before me..."

[1] Don Richardson, Eternity in Their Hearts, 155
[2] Dietrich Bonhoeffer, Life Together (Harper One, 1954), 36
[3] John Piper, Desiring God (Multnomah, 1996), 199

Chapter 9: Reconciliation: "...in the gap ..."

[1] Dinesh D'Souza, What's So Great About Christianity? (Regnery Publishing Inc., 2007), 284
[2] Ibid., 287
[3] David Long, A Call to Manhood in a Fatherless Society, 124
[4] Ibid., 127
[5] "Candid 1988 Mother Teresa Interview Reveals Her Thoughts on Reason for Her Success", National Catholic Register (ncregister.com), Edward Desmond, September 6, 2016. Originally published by Time Magazine, Dec. 4, 1989
[6] Michael Hart, The 100: A Ranking of the Most Influential Persons in History (Citadel Press, Carol Publishing Group, 1993), 17
[7] Michael Hart, The 100, 20-21, *emphasis original*
[8] www.goodreads.com/author/quotes/6649.Stephen_Colbert
[9] Jayson Georges, The 3-D Gospel (Time Press, 2017) 10
[10] Jayson Georges, The 3-D Gospel, 12
[11] John Rucyahana, The Bishop of Rwanda (Thomas Nelson, 2007) xvi
[12] Ibid., 222
[13] Ibid., 221

Chapter 10: Intermediation: "...on behalf of the land ..."

[1] Jackie Pullinger, Asbury Seminary recorded sermon (Oct 3, 1993)
[2] E. Stanley Jones, "Running toward the Unshakeable Kingdom," (Good News magazine, Mar 21, 1970)
[3] Jackie Pullinger, Asbury Seminary recorded sermon (Oct 3, 1993)
[4] Helen Keller, The Story of My Life (Doubleday, Page & Co, 1903, reprint Thornton, CO 2021), 145

Chapter 11: Redemption: "...so I would not have to destroy it..."

[1] Ann Voskamp, Waymaker, 28
[2] The Living Word Discovery (Rock Island Books, 2019), www.youtube.com/watch?v=94xCB8QtUJ4
[3] Steve Johnson, Embrace The Question (2022), www.youtube.com/watch?v=ZBiarnn1rCM

Chapter 12: Inference: "...but I found no one..."

[1] Glenn Packiam, Lucky, 181

[2] Richard Stearns, The Hole in Our Gospel, 145
[3] Charlie Marquis, Mudrunner (Forge, 2021) 71
[4] Francis Chan, Crazy Love (David C Cook, 2008) 78
[5] Corbett & Fikkert, When Helping Hurts, 64-65

Chapter 13: Revelation: Will you be found?

[1] Rick Warren, The Purpose Driven Life, 20
[2] Corbett & Fikkert, When Helping Hurts, 28
[3] Poured Out Like Wine | hymnstudiesblog (wordpress.com 1977) Special Sacred Selections, an arrangement by editor Ellis J. Crum https://hymnstudiesblog.wordpress.com/2021/05/16/poured-out-like-wine/#:~:text=Let%20us%20be%20poured%20out%20like%20wine%20upon,light%20and%20life%20and%20love%20His%20Word%20fulfilled.

Made in United States
Troutdale, OR
09/15/2023